INTRODUCING THE

# QUR'AN

"Kaltner wonderfully captures the Qur'an's profound beauty, complex theology, intricate ritual practices, and intimate ordering of social relations for a contemporary audience by shrewdly exploring such diverse themes as creation, love, gender, and *jihād*. Within these presentations, he touches upon common human questions, beliefs, and desires. *Introducing the Qur'an* offers a timely, knowledgeable, and accessible view into a scripture whose message and meaning so often eludes a Western audience, as our current political discourse has sadly shown."

### KATHRYN KUENY
Associate Professor of Theology
Fordham University

"Accessible, timely, informative—a valuable introduction to the Qur'an."

### JOAN E. COOK
Professorial Lecturer
Georgetown University, Washington, D.C.

# INTRODUCING THE
# QUR'AN

## FOR TODAY'S READER

John Kaltner

FORTRESS PRESS
Minneapolis

INTRODUCING THE QUR'AN
For Today's Reader

Unless otherwise noted, biblical quotations are taken from the New Revised Standard Bible, copyright © 1989 by the Division of Christian Education of the National Council of Churches of Christ in the USA. Used by permission. All rights reserved.

All Qur'an translations are by John Kaltner.

Cover image: The Art Archive/Gianni Dagli Orti
Cover design: Laurie Ingram
Book design: James Korsmo

*Library of Congress Cataloging-in-Publication Data*
Kaltner, John, 1954-
  Introducing the Qur'an : for today's reader / John Kaltner.
    p. cm.
  Includes bibliographical references and index.
  ISBN 978-0-8006-9666-5 (alk. paper)
1. Koran—Introductions. I. Title.
  BP130.K35 2011
  297.1'2261—dc22
                        2010045032
The paper used in this publication meets the minimum requirements of American National Standard for Information Sciences—Permanence of Paper for Printed Library Materials, ANSI Z329.48-1984.

Manufactured in the U.S.A.

16    15    14    13    12    11    10    1 2 3 4 5 6 7 8 9 10

*In memory of*
*Virginia Ballou McGehee*

# Contents

GALLERY

A s the sacred text of Islam, the Qur'an is one of the most influential books in history. Since it first appeared in the seventh century C.E., Muslims have turned to it for spiritual, moral, and practical guidance on how to live their lives. It has been translated into many languages, and it has been the focus of countless books, articles, essays, websites, and blog postings. The attitudes toward the Qur'an in these writings have varied widely, running the gamut from celebrating it as the word of God to denigrating it as a manual for breeding terrorists. Unfortunately, though they present a distorted or incomplete reading of the Qur'an, many of the latter characterizations of the text are often widely disseminated and popular among non-Muslims. Despite its influence and widespread presence, and on account of such common misperceptions, the Qur'an remains a largely unknown and mysterious book to non-Muslims. A survey conducted by the Pew Research Center in 2009 found that almost one-half of Americans were unable to identify the Qur'an as the Islamic equivalent to the Bible. In addition, only about 40 percent of us could both identify the Qur'an and knew that Allah is the term Muslims use to refer to God. If so many Americans are incapable of naming Islam's scripture, it stands to reason that many more, likely the vast majority of us, have no idea what is written on its pages. And yet, you would be hard-pressed to find an American who doesn't have an opinion about the Qur'an.

That is a troubling and dangerous situation. How can we be so ill-informed about the book that is at the heart of one of the world's great religions? And how can that ignorance be overcome? This book attempts to respond to the second question by introducing the reader to what the Qur'an has to say about a number of themes. It does not offer a comprehensive treatment of the Qur'an's contents but presents a summary of its teachings on selected topics that were chosen because of their importance for Muslims and their relevance for the modern world. After an introduction that explains what the Qur'an is, how it is studied, and how it is experienced by Muslims, the next seven chapters treat the following themes in order: the natural environment, the family, gender and sexuality, Muslim/non-Muslim relations, *jihād*, violence and war, and death and the afterlife. Other topics undoubtedly could be added to this list, but these have been selected because they provide an overview of the Qur'an's perspective on human existence and what it means to be a Muslim. In addition, some of these topics are among the most hotly debated and controversial issues being discussed around the world today.

Some features have been included in the book to make it more user-friendly and to facilitate its use in the classroom or in small-group settings. Each chapter begins with an outline of its contents that orients the reader to what lies ahead. Textboxes that call attention to key concepts or comment on things mentioned in the main text are interspersed throughout each chapter, and in a few places, maps and timelines provide visual aids to matters under discussion. A number of photos are provided throughout the book and in a gallery that contains full-color images, including many of the Qur'an.

Each chapter concludes with a listing of the key terms found within it. Most of these terms are Arabic words that have been transliterated into English, and a glossary containing all of them with their definitions is found at the end of the book. A set of suggested readings for further study and a list of questions to initiate discussion and conversation also appear at the end of each chapter. The book's companion website (www .fortresspress.com/kaltner) provides a number of additional resources, including instructional materials that will prove useful to both instructors and students. It also contains the glossary of Arabic terms with audio samples of how they are pronounced.

The issues treated in this volume will be addressed and debated by many in the years ahead. Muslims will be vocal and valued participants in that conversation, and many of their views will be informed by what their sacred text teaches. Non-Muslims must therefore make every effort to become familiar with the Qur'an if they wish to be effective dialogue partners in the quest to make the world a better place. If this book is able to facilitate that process in any way, it will have served its purpose.

# Acknowledgments

I wish to recognize a number of people who played important roles in the preparation and writing of this book. Michael West, editor in chief of Fortress Press, offered encouragement and support from the inception of the project through to its completion. It has been an immense pleasure to work with Fortress senior acquisitions editor Ross Miller, an extremely thorough editor whose suggestions and insights were invaluable. Closer to home, I would like to thank Debra Bartelli for her feedback, advice, and patience as the manuscript was being written. I am indebted to Kenan Padgett and the staff of the interlibrary loan office at Rhodes College for their assistance and prompt replies to my many requests for resources.

I first began to formulate my ideas for this book during the spring semester of 2009, when I taught a course at Rhodes titled "The Qur'an and Contemporary Issues." I extend special thanks to the students in that course for their engagement with the material and the many stimulating conversations we had both inside and outside the classroom. Two students in that group deserve special recognition. Lars Nelson and Bradley Arnold served as my student research assistants during the two years the book was conceived and written, and words cannot express my gratitude for their commitment and many hours of hard work. Finally, this book is dedicated to the memory of Virginia Ballou McGehee, a woman of passion who was deeply committed to improving relations between Muslims and non-Muslims.

# Introduction

| | | The revelations of the Qur'an | | |
|---|---|---|---|---|
| | | The beginning 610 of the revelations of the Qur'an | 622 The *hijra*, or migration, from Mecca to Medina | |
| | 570 Muhammad's birth | | 632 Muhammad's death | |
| C.E. | 575 | 600 | 625 | 650 |

The Qur'an has spoken to countless Muslims throughout history, but its original audience was composed of only one person—the Prophet Muhammad. He was born in the year 570 C.E. in Mecca, a city in the western portion of what is now Saudi Arabia. Sometime around the year 610, Muhammad had an experience that profoundly influenced the future course of human history. It was the first of what he and his followers would come to understand as a series of revelations from God, identified by the Arabic word *allāh*. The revelations continued intermittently throughout the rest of Muhammad's life and ceased only with his death in 632. They are

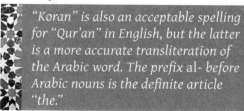

*"Koran" is also an acceptable spelling for "Qur'an" in English, but the latter is a more accurate transliteration of the Arabic word. The prefix al- before Arabic nouns is the definite article "the."*

1

preserved in the book known as *al-qur'ān*, an Arabic term meaning "the recitation."

The Qur'an addresses many issues and topics, and some of those that are of most interest to modern readers will be discussed in this book. But if the basic message of the Qur'an could be boiled down to one word, it would be the one that came to be used to describe the faith of those who consider it to be the word of God—submission (*al-islām* in Arabic). The Qur'an urges people to submit themselves to the will of the one God, and anyone who does so is called a *muslim*.

*The Arabic word* allāh *literally means "the deity."*

FIGURE 1 *Mt. Hira, where the Qur'an was first revealed to the Prophet Muhammad.*

That monotheistic message was not well received by many of Muhammad's contemporaries in Mecca, which had been a prominent pilgrimage destination for Arabs since long before Muhammad's birth. The city was home to the Ka`ba, a shrine where numerous gods were worshiped, and so Muhammad's call to reject polytheism challenged the dominant form of religious expression and threatened the positive economic effect that pilgrims visiting the Ka`ba had on the city. Tensions between the fledgling Muslim community and members of the Meccan establishment ensued, and the two factions coexisted uneasily until the year 622, when Muhammad and a small group of followers accepted an invitation to journey to Yathrib, a city located about 250 miles to the north.

Muhammad had been asked to come to Yathrib to serve as an arbiter who would help resolve problems among the city's citizens, among whom was a sizable Jewish population. He spent the last ten years of his life there, and it was in Yathrib that the Muslim community began to flourish. Muhammad became so closely identified with the place that it was renamed "the city of the prophet" (*madīnat al-nabī*), now known as Medina (sometimes spelled Madina).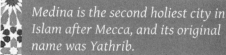

*Medina is the second holiest city in Islam after Mecca, and its original name was Yathrib.*

Muhammad returned to Mecca on several occasions after he left the city, and he was finally able to convince the majority of its inhabitants to embrace Islam prior to his death in Medina in 632.

The migration from Mecca to Medina, known in Arabic as the *hijra*, was a turning point in the early history of Islam that is considered to be the founding event of the Muslim community. Its significance was commemorated by making the *hijra* the starting point of the Islamic calendar which, as a lunar-based system, is organized by the phases of the moon. The Qur'an emerged within and responded to this historical context, and the chapters that follow will discuss and explain some of the events and developments of that context in greater detail. The remainder of this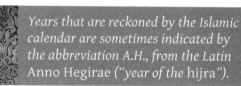

*Years that are reckoned by the Islamic calendar are sometimes indicated by the abbreviation A.H., from the Latin Anno Hegirae ("year of the hijra").*

chapter introduces the Qur'an through a consideration of three topics—what it is, how it is studied, and its presence in Muslim life.

## Describing the Qur'an

This section provides a general overview of the Qur'an with particular attention devoted to two areas. The first is the contents of the text and includes a discussion of such issues as the Qur'an's arrangement, distinct elements, literary features, and canonization. The second area is the nature of the Qur'an as understood by Muslims. Belief in the Qur'an as the word of God has raised important questions throughout history—about its origin, uniqueness, and character—that have had a significant effect on how Muslims view their sacred text.

### The Contents of the Qur'an

The Qur'an is composed of 114 chapters, which contain about 6,300 verses, making it approximately the same length as the New Testament.

FIGURE 2 *The Ka`ba in the Great Mosque of Mecca.*

The Arabic term for a chapter is *sūra,* and the word for a verse is *āya,* which often has the meaning "sign." Each chapter has a name, and it is common for Muslims to refer to chapters by their names, although it is not unusual for them to identify a chapter by its number. The titles are normally taken from some word found in or associated with the chapter. It might be a personal name, an unusual term, or a theme present in the chapter. Examples of chapter titles in the Qur'an are "The Cow" (chapter 2), "Women" (4), "The Table" (5), "Abraham" (14), "Mary" (19), "The Spider" (29), "Divorce" (65), and "The Disaster" (101).

> *Like the Bible, it is common practice to cite a Qur'an passage by identifying the number of its chapter and verse(s).*

ARRANGEMENT

The organizing principle of the Qur'an is chapter length, with the longest ones coming first and the shortest found at the end. This is more of a general pattern than a hard-and-fast rule, as seen in the fact that the shortest chapter in the Qur'an is number 108, not 114. The only chapter that clearly violates this principle is the first one, known as *al-fātiḥa* ("The Opening"). It contains only 7 verses but precedes the longest chapter in the Qur'an, which has 286 verses. The opening chapter is generally held to be an introduction to the entire text of the Qur'an.

### BASMALA

Every chapter in the Qur'an but one begins with the same phrase—"in the name of God, the merciful One, the compassionate One." This formula is sometimes referred to as the *basmala*, based on the Arabic words that translate "in the name of God." Only in the case of *al-fātiḥa* is the *basmala* considered to be the first verse of the chapter. Everywhere else it functions as a superscription or introduction to the chapter. The *basmala* is missing only in chapter 9, and two main reasons have been proposed for its absence there. It might be that chapters 8 and 9 were originally one unit that was separated at a certain point. Another explanation holds that chapter 9 is unsuitable to begin with the *basmala* because one of its main themes is the punishment that God will exact on idolaters and others who do not obey the divine will. The expression is also found in 27:30, where it is the introduction to a letter that King Solomon sends to the Queen of Sheba.

### THE MYSTERY LETTERS

A curious aspect of the Qur'an that has generated much discussion and fascination among scholars and non-scholars alike is the presence of letters from the Arabic language at the beginnings of twenty-nine chapters. In a few cases these are single letters, but most of the time they consist of groups of two or more. Muslim tradition has referred to this phenomenon as "the opening letters" or "the cut-off letters," and various explanations have been put forward to account for them.

Among other theories, it has been suggested that they are abbreviations for the names of God or names of Qur'an chapters, division markers between chapters, symbols of numerical values, or secret messages that are shortened words and phrases. None of these proposals has been met with widespread acceptance, and Muslims often adopt the position that the meaning of these letters is a secret known to God alone.

*Examples of the mystery letters include n, y-s, a-l-m, and a-l-m-r. The twenty-nine chapters that begin with them are 2, 3, 7, 10, 11, 12, 13, 14, 15, 19, 20, 26, 27, 28, 29, 30, 31, 32, 36, 38, 40, 41, 42, 43, 44, 45, 46, 50, and 68.*

### BIBLICAL FIGURES

The references already made to Abraham, Mary, Solomon, and the Queen of Sheba point to the fact that biblical figures are frequently cited on the pages of the Qur'an. This is so because the text frequently states that the God of the Qur'an is the God of the Bible. Seven are mentioned often by name—Adam, Noah, Moses, Abraham, Joseph (who was sold into Egypt by his brothers), Mary, and Jesus—but a number of others are referred to on occasion, either by name or anonymously. Many parts of the Qur'an therefore have an air of familiarity for the Bible reader, as events in the lives of key biblical characters are recounted and discussed.

But their presence in the Islamic text also raises issues and questions that can have the opposite effect on one accustomed to the parallel Bible traditions. The Qur'an never presents the stories in exactly the same way as their biblical counterparts, and sometimes the differences are quite profound. In general, the Qur'an tends to present these figures and the traditions associated with them in conformance with the beliefs and practices of Islam. In other words, they reflect and cohere to the literary ambiance of the Qur'an as an Islamic text.

The example of Noah demonstrates this well. Throughout the four chapters of Genesis in which he appears, Noah speaks only one time, and that only after the flood has subsided and he has returned to dry land. The Noah of the Qur'an is effusive by comparison, as he engages in much conversation and debate. The reason for this difference is simple—the Qur'an considers Noah to be a prophet, and a prophet's primary job is to speak God's message. So the qur'anic Noah constantly implores his people to be faithful and warns them of the consequences if they fail to do so. Bible readers must keep in mind the reasons behind such shifts in character and story line, and should not wrongly assume that the Qur'an's presentation of material familiar to them is due to animosity or disrespect toward them or their religion.

Those who are unfamiliar with the Qur'an often find it to be a confusing and difficult book to read when they first open it. This is particularly the case for Bible readers, who usually expect it to follow the style and structure of their own text. Unlike the biblical literature, which unfolds in chronological order in many places, the Qur'an appears to be random and haphazard in its arrangement because it often shifts modes and topics. A story about Abraham might lead to a discussion of how to relate to non-Muslims, followed by an explanation of regulations involving inheritance that segues into a narrative about Moses.

This has led some, especially non-Muslims, to conclude that the Qur'an lacks coherence and organization. But this opinion has been challenged recently, as more scholars are identifying structures and patterns that had escaped notice earlier. This is especially the case in the analysis of individual chapters, many of which are now recognized to be carefully organized units that likely emerged within and in response to the framework of the socioreligious context of the early Muslim community. Consequently, non-Muslims should be careful to avoid using the Bible or other sacred texts as a yardstick by which to measure and evaluate the Qur'an.

MECCAN/MEDINAN PASSAGES

As noted above, it is impossible to fully understand the Qur'an without some knowledge of the events of the Prophet Muhammad's life. His migration from Mecca to Medina, known as the *hijra*, is of paramount importance when discussing the contents of the Qur'an (see Map, p. 8). Already in the first Islamic century, scholars were making a distinction between material in the Qur'an coming from the period prior to the *hijra* and that from the time after it.

Scholarship into the present day has continued to adopt this approach, although with some modifications, the most notable being the division of the pre-*hijra* material into several subperiods. Although not all scholars agree with this classification, the most common breakdown is into four discrete periods, each with its own literary characteristics and thematic concerns—early Meccan, middle Meccan, late Meccan, and Medinan. Although these categories will not be of great significance throughout this book, the differences between the Meccan and Medinan material, which will be treated more fully below, should be kept in mind.

> *The most commonly accepted way of categorizing the material in the Qur'an uses a four-part chronological division: early Meccan, middle Meccan, late Meccan, and Medinan.*

LITERARY FEATURES

It is sometimes claimed that the Qur'an should be categorized as poetry, but that is not correct. It is written in a distinct style of prose that has characteristics often associated with poetry. The most distinguishing feature of the text is its rhyme. Some studies have concluded that almost 90 percent of the Qur'an is written in rhymed prose, but it does not always take the form of having the same letter or sound at the end of each verse. The final syllable or word of most verses echoes that of surrounding verses, but this effect is realized through either using the identical sound or relying on assonance that approximates another sound without being the same.

The most common way rhyme is achieved in the Qur'an is through the use of the word endings -ūn/-ūm/-īn/-īm. Some of these endings indicate the plural form of an Arabic noun or adjective, and sometimes they

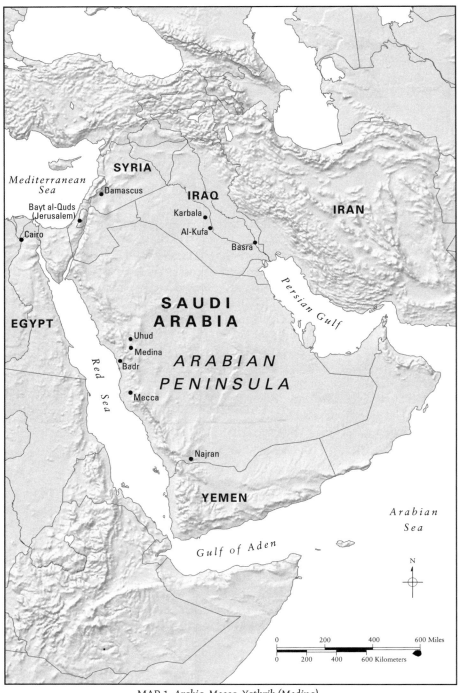

MAP 1 *Arabia, Mecca, Yathrib (Medina).*

are found throughout an entire chapter. A good example of this is seen in chapter 23, where every one of its 118 verses ends with one of these sounds. A shorter example is found in the first chapter (*al-fātiḥa*), which alternates the sounds -*īn* and -*īm* in its final syllables.

> *bismi allāh al-raḥmān al-raḥīm*
> *al-ḥamdu lil-llāḥ rab al-ʿālamīn*
> *al-raḥmān al-raḥīm*
> *māliki yawm al-dīn*
> *iyyāka naʿabudu wa iyyāka nastaʿīn*
> *ihdinā ṣirāt al-mustaqīm*
> *ṣirāt al-ladhīna anʿamta ʿalayhim ghayri al-maghḍūbi ʿalayhim wa la ḍāllīn*

In this opening chapter of the Qur'an, the two sounds -*īn* and -*īm* are similar and therefore in assonance, but they are not identical. In addition, the final line indicates that the sections that rhyme are not always of similar length. Elsewhere, rhymed endings are found in lines that are of more or less the same length throughout. This combination of rhyme and assonance is the main literary feature of the Qur'an.

> *"In the name of God, the merciful One, the compassionate One! Praise be to God, Lord of all creation, the merciful One, the compassionate One, king of judgment day. We worship You; we ask You for help. Guide us along the straight path, the path of those You have favored, those who incur no anger and do not go astray."*

It is so central to the text that sometimes grammatical norms are violated and stylistic conventions are bypassed in order to maintain the rhyme or assonance. It is important to keep in mind that this is an aspect of the text impossible to convey in translation. Consequently, those who read it in English or another language are unable to experience this defining trait, and that is one of the reasons why Muslims say that a translation of the Qur'an is not really the Qur'an but merely an interpretation of it.

Scholars have often noted parallels between the Qur'an's rhyming system and a pre-Islamic literary form called *sajʿ*. This is especially the case regarding passages from the early Meccan period. There is some disagreement over whether *sajʿ* is best categorized as prose or poetry. It is characterized by brief phrases and sentences that often rhyme and are similar in their rhythm and meter. These qualities typify many of the earliest sections of the Qur'an but are not present in the later Meccan and Medinan periods.

As will be seen in later chapters of this book, the Qur'an employs a wide variety of literary devices and figures of speech, including metaphors, parables, and rich imagery. One such stylistic technique that has generated much discussion among exegetes and commentators is its use of anthropomorphic language to speak of God. Anthropomorphisms like the hand, eye, and throne of God are mentioned throughout the text to describe various divine attributes like authority, power, and omniscience. "Your Lord is God who created the heavens and earth in six days and then set Himself upon the throne, overseeing everything" (10:3a; cf. 3:73; 7:54; 13:2; 23:88; 32:4; 48:10). This language is somewhat at odds with Islam's view of God as utterly transcendent and beyond human comprehension, but its presence in the Qur'an is usually explained as a way of speaking about the deity in human terms that are immediately understandable to people.

In a related but different vein, the Qur'an's use of plural first-person pronouns like "we," "us," and "our" in divine speech might strike the reader as odd given Islam's monotheism and emphasis on the unity of God. An example is seen in 97:1, where God explains how the Qur'an was revealed. "We sent it down on the Night of Glory." Commentators throughout history have agreed that such language does not in any way violate the oneness of God that is central to Muslim belief. Most prefer to see it as a stylistic device meant to exalt the deity, and they compare it to the use of the "royal we" or "divine we" found in other cultures and contexts.

An example of the "divine we" from the Bible is seen in Genesis 1:26a. "Let us make humankind in our image, according to our likeness."

THE WRITTEN TEXT

What began as a message that circulated orally was eventually written down and went through a process of formation that eventually resulted in the book known as "the Qur'an." The term that refers to the written form of the Qur'an is *mushaf*, which can describe anything from an ancient manuscript to a modern copy of the text. Many very old manuscripts of the Qur'an exist, but none can be dated with certainty to the time of the Prophet Muhammad. Nonetheless, Islamic sources state that during his lifetime some of his followers had begun to record portions of the Qur'an on surfaces like the skins and bones of animals.

According to the traditional account, soon after Muhammad's death in 632 his successor, the caliph Abu Bakr, ordered that the Qur'an be collected while those most familiar with the revelations were still alive. Muhammad's scribe, a man named Zayd bin Thabit, was charged with coordinating this task. Upon Abu Bakr's death his successor `Umar received the leaves on which Zayd had recorded the Qur'an, and when `Umar died they were passed on to his daughter Hafsa, who had been married to Muhammad. During the reign of the third caliph, `Uthman, who ruled 644–656 C.E., controversies erupted among various groups that were all claiming to have the correct version of the Qur'an in their possession. This led `Uthman, in consultation with scholars and experts, to determine which version was authentic and to order the destruction of all others. This became the accepted text and the basis for all subsequent editions of the Qur'an.

*Certain elements of Arabic personal names indicate family relationships. Among the most common are "Abu," meaning "father," and "Ibn" and "Bin," which both mean "son."*

Some scholars, primarily non-Muslims, have questioned the reliability of this traditional account. But there is evidence to suggest that an official written version of the Qur'an was already in existence late in the first Islamic century, which means `Uthman's reign is a plausible period in which to locate the origin of the text of the Qur'an that has come down to us.

Although the precise details of its origin will likely remain unknown, the canonized text of the Qur'an was the basis for thousands of manuscripts produced throughout the centuries, many of which are preserved today in museums and libraries around the world. Occasionally these manuscripts disagree with the received text, and these discrepancies raise interesting and important questions about the history and transmission of the Qur'an. In addition to manuscripts written in Arabic, there are many others written in languages from other parts of the Islamic world like Persian, Urdu, and Turkish.

A common way to date and identify a manuscript is by its script. Someone who is trained in the history of scripts can immediately recognize characteristics like the shape and slant of individual letters that place it within a given time frame and/or location. Among the most commonly used scripts in the Arab world, from earliest to latest, are Ḥijāzī, Kūfic, Naskhī, and Maghribī.

In the Arabic language some consonants can function as long vowels, but short vowels are not indicated by letters. The three vowels in Arabic (*a*, *i*, and *u*) are marked by a set of signs and strokes placed above and below consonants, one for each vowel. Arabic also has several diacritical points and markers to help distinguish among similar looking letters and to indicate phenomena like doubled consonants or the lack of a vowel. This system was not used in Qur'an manuscripts until the tenth century C.E. Since the earliest manuscripts contain none of these features, reading these texts is often a very difficult undertaking. By the ninth century C.E., a system for indicating vowels by the use of red dots had been developed that facilitated reading.

> Markers commonly used in Arabic script:
> the vowel a
> the vowel i
> the vowel u
> lack of a vowel
> doubled consonant

The chapter titles are another component of the Qur'an not found in the oldest manuscripts, not appearing until the second Islamic century. Prior to that time, chapters were separated from one another either by an ornamental design or a blank space. Later manuscripts typically include chapter titles and elaborate designs, along with an indication of whether the chapter is Meccan or Medinan and the number of verses it contains.

## The Nature of the Qur'an

Muslim belief holds that the Qur'an is a mediated message that was revealed to the Prophet Muhammad through the angel Gabriel. The role Gabriel played in the process is mentioned in 2:97-98, and it is further developed in extraqur'anic sources and traditions. The first revelation Muhammad received is generally held to be chapter 96, whose first word "Recite!" (iqra') comes from the same Arabic root as qur'ān. "Recite! In the name of your Lord who created. He created humanity from a clinging form. Recite! Your Lord is the noble One, Who taught by means of the pen. Who taught humanity what it did not know" (96:1-5).

The Qur'an refers to itself frequently, and those self-references are often found in passages that explain its nature and source. In many of these texts the divine origin of the Qur'an is reiterated, and words from the Arabic root n-z-l, meaning "to send down," are commonly used to describe the act of revelation (26:192; 39:1; 41:2; 46:2; 69:43). Its view of revelation therefore has an element of top-down physicality to it, as God communicates the message from heaven

> Arabic is built on a root system, with most words derived from a three-letter root. Each root has one or more primary meanings associated with it. For example, the root k-t-b primarily conveys meanings related to writing, as seen in the word for book (kitāb).

to Muhammad on earth through the agency of Gabriel. The gradual, piecemeal unfolding of the revelation over time is described in 17:106: "It is a recitation that We have divided in parts, so you can recite it to people in stages. We have sent it down as a revelation [*nazzalnāhu tanzīlan*]."

The Qur'an is silent about the effects the experience of receiving revelations had on Muhammad. The matter is treated in nonscriptural sources that refer to various consequences of the revelatory state. Among the most commonly mentioned are that revelation was accompanied by the ringing of a bell and that Muhammad experienced physical symptoms, including a trancelike state, loss of consciousness, fatigue, perspiration, a change in skin complexion, and general physical discomfort.

An important element of the Qur'an's self-understanding is that it contains the same message that was given to previous prophets and messengers. Muhammad is the last of a chain of prophetic figures going back to Adam, and for this reason he is called the "seal of the prophets" (33:40). Similarly, the Qur'an is the last of a series of books that communicate God's will for humanity. Among its predecessors are the Torah and Gospel, given to Moses and Jesus, whose followers tampered with and distorted the revelations they received. This necessitated the sending down of the Qur'an, which accurately preserves God's message and validates the previous revelations. "This Qur'an could not have been brought forth by anyone other than God. It is a confirmation of what came down before it and an explanation of the book. There is no doubt that it is from the Lord of the worlds" (10:37; cf. 2:89; 3:81; 4:47; 5:48; 35:31; 46:12).

A HEAVENLY PROTOTYPE

The Qur'an says it was revealed on the "Night of Power," and Islamic tradition has designated the twenty-seventh of the month of Ramadan as the date on which Muhammad began to receive revelations (97:1). Copies of the Qur'an have existed since the earliest decades of Islam, but Muslims believe the urtext, or origin, of all those written copies resides  *"Truly, We sent it down on the Night of Power." (Qur'an 97:1).* with God in heaven. This idea derives from a number of related passages that have been interpreted collectively as describing a heavenly book that contains a comprehensive record of the revelation God has sent down to humanity.

One set of texts refers to the *umm al-kitāb*, literally "mother of the book," which is generally considered to be a way of designating the source of all the scriptures. "God erases and confirms whatever He wishes, and the *umm al-kitāb* is with Him" (13:39; cf. 4:7; 43:4). According to the most common way of understanding this verse, it describes a heavenly archetype of the Qur'an and other revelations that is with God.

An allusion to this otherworldly copy of the text is often seen in 85:21-2, a somewhat ambiguous passage that could simply be a reference to a written copy of the Qur'an. "Truly, this is a glorious Qur'an on a preserved tablet." Because it is not explicitly stated, those who see this as a comment about the *umm al-kitāb* argue from inference that it refers to the prototype found in heaven. A third text that factors into this discussion is 56:77-78, with its reference to a book that is "hidden" or "protected" (*maknūn*). "It is a noble Qur'an, in a hidden book."

Taken together, these references to a hidden, preserved book that is the "mother" of the Qur'an form the basis for the belief in its heavenly origin and ongoing existence with God. According to a tradition found in other Islamic sources, on the "Night of Power" the whole Qur'an was sent down from the *umm al-kitāb* to the lowest portion of heaven just above the earth, and from there Gabriel communicated portions of it to Muhammad during the last twenty-two years of his life. The notion of a heavenly book has been a factor in the debate over whether or not the Qur'an is created, a topic that will be discussed below.

INIMITABILITY

An important belief held by Muslims about the Qur'an is that it is sui generis and incapable of being imitated. A set of passages often referred to as the "challenge verses" have been influential in the development of this idea. These texts are directed toward the enemies of Muhammad who criticized and mocked the Qur'an as being nothing more than human speech, akin to the poetry of the pre-Islamic period. The passages respond to this claim by challenging these opponents to duplicate the Qur'an by coming up with a text like it. "If they say, 'He has invented it,' say (Muhammad), 'Then bring about ten invented *sūras* like it and call on whoever you can besides God, if you are speaking the truth'" (11:13; cf. 2:23; 10:38; 17:88; 52:33-34).

*Unlike English, Arabic uses different forms for the second person singular and plural. To avoid confusion, translations in this book will often indicate when the addressee is Muhammad and not a group of people.*

The Arabic term used to describe the inimitability of the Qur'an is *i'jāz*, which derives from the same root as the word for a miracle (*mu'jiza*). According to this doctrine, the language of the Qur'an is unsurpassable and impossible for any human being to replicate. During the third and fourth centuries of the Islamic era (ninth/tenth centuries c.e.), there was much debate within the Muslim community regarding key elements of the faith, including the nature of the Qur'an. One of the main groups involved in these discussions was the Ash`arites, a prominent theological movement that was very influential in shaping the future direction of Islamic theology and piety. By the latter part of the tenth century c.e., they had successfully lobbied on behalf of the inimitability of the Qur'an, and it has continued to be part of mainstream Muslim belief into the present day.

CREATED OR UNCREATED?

Another debate that was raging during the same time as the one about the inimitability of the Qur'an centered on whether the Qur'an was created or uncreated. This dispute emerged in part as a result of the idea mentioned above that there is a heavenly copy of the Qur'an that resides with God. Some argued that this means the Qur'an has existed with God from eternity and is therefore uncreated, while others countered that it is not coeternal with God but a created entity that is dependent upon the divine will for its existence.

The group most commonly associated with the idea of a created Qur'an was the Mu`tazilites, who were often pitted against the Ash`arites on matters of faith and doctrine. This issue was no different, as the Ash`arites argued in favor of the view that the Qur'an is uncreated.

> One of the main differences between the Ash`arites and the Mu`tazilites concerned the role of reason. While the former group maintained that revelation was the starting point and reason must cohere to it, the Mu`tazilites held that reason must inform and influence belief.

The Mu`tazilites countered that to hold such a position would be a form of dualism because it suggests that the Qur'an shares the eternal nature, which is reserved only for God. The debate intensified when the caliph al-Ma'mūn, in the first half of the ninth century c.e., ruled that all judges had to publicly state their belief in a created Qur'an.

The controversies surrounding the inimitability and created/uncreated nature of the Qur'an are examples of the theological disputes Muslims were engaging in during the early centuries of Islam over issues related to God and divine revelation. Eventually, the Ash`arite position in favor of the Qur'an being uncreated became the dominant one, and that has been the majority view within Islam ever since. But there continue to be Muslim voices that speak in favor of a created Qur'an and call for a reopening of the discussion.

## Studying the Qur'an

Because of the important role Islamic tradition ascribes to the third caliph, `Uthman, in establishing the canonized Arabic version of the Qur'an, it is often referred to as "the `Uthmanic text." Although there are a number of variant readings of the Qur'an that show differences in matters like the use of vowels, most modern copies of the text are the same and are based on the Royal Egyptian edition that was published in 1924 under the auspices of al-Azhar University. In addition to the text of the Qur'an itself, a number of additional books and other materials are frequently consulted that assist scholars in their analytical work.

### Tools

Over the centuries, many study tools and resources have been developed to facilitate the task of studying and interpreting the Qur'an. These aids are similar to those found in related disciplines like biblical studies, and include lexicons, concordances, grammars, commentaries, and general introductions. Three that are unique to study of the Qur'an are connected to the events of Muhammad's life—the *sīra*, the *ḥadīth*, and the *asbāb al-nuzūl*. These resources are valuable because they often help to contextualize the content of the Qur'an by connecting passages to specific moments during the Prophet's lifetime. In this book, references will sometimes be made to "extraqur'anic sources," and these three are among the most important in that category.

#### THE *SĪRA*

The term *sīra* refers to a genre of literature whose main aim is the presentation of a biographical account of Muhammad's life. Very often, such works also include information about God's relationship with humanity prior to Muhammad's time and stories about the companions of the Prophet and the early caliphs who ruled after his death. They are a combination of narratives, poetry, lists, writings, and speeches meant to provide background on events of importance to the Muslim community.

Many *sīra* works have been written throughout history on into the present day, but the most important is that of Ibn Ishaq, who died in 767 c.e. His was a three-volume compilation that began with the creation of the world, traced the lives of the prophets, and concluded with a description of Muhammad's life and times. Ibn Ishaq's complete work has not survived, but it is known to us through citations in other sources and through the work of his editors, especially Ibn Hisham (d. 830), who limited its scope to Muhammad and events associated with him. Another well-known scholar whose writings preserve portions of Ibn Ishaq's *sīra* is al-Ṭabarī (d. 923), a prominent exegete and historian who will be discussed in more detail later in this chapter. As their dates of death indicate, all of these individuals lived long after Muhammad's time and were not eyewitnesses to any of the events they report.

The *sīra* literature commonly links Qur'an passages to events in Muhammad's life and in this way establishes a context for many passages whose historical circumstances would remain a mystery if one were to rely solely on the text of the Qur'an. Usually the text in question is no more than a verse or two, and its connection with the Prophet's life is typically made in one of two ways. In some cases, the *sīra* describes the starting point as the revelation of a particular verse, which then causes Muhammad to act or speak in a certain way. More commonly, things occur in the opposite order as an event occurs and then a verse is revealed in response to it. The latter type is sometimes referred to as an "occasion of revelation," a type of writing that will be discussed below. The frequent references in the *sīra* to the historical contexts related to particular Qur'an passages have been a valuable aid in efforts to establish the chronological order of the text.

In addition to the way it historicizes verses, the *sīra* literature is also useful for study of the Qur'an because it sometimes explains or comments upon particular aspects of the text. It does this in different ways, including by clarifying the meanings of problematic passages or words, identifying unnamed people in the text, and providing additional information that gives important background to a particular story. An example of this is seen in the reference in 18:83 to an enigmatic figure referred to as "the two-horned one" (*dhū al-qarnayn*), who is identified by Ibn Isham as Alexander the Great.

### THE ḤADĪTH

The early Muslim community turned to the Prophet Muhammad as a model when looking for guidance on how to behave and live. Upon his death, his family members, companions, and others who knew him personally shared their memories of what he did and said while he was still alive. These stories eventually began to circulate among members of the wider community and became very influential in shaping ideas about proper Muslim behavior.

The word *ḥadīth*, an Arabic term meaning "report" or "account," can refer either to one of these prophetic traditions individually or to the entire group of them. Each is composed of two parts, a chain and a body. The chain (*isnād*) is a list of names that traces the history of transmission of the report. The standard formula is "A heard from B who heard from C . . . ," always ending with Muhammad himself. The body (*matn*) is the tradition itself, which recounts something the Prophet did or said.

Many thousands of these traditions were in circulation in the centuries following Muhammad's death, and by the ninth century c.e., some individuals had begun to study and collect the *hadīth* material. Several collections are considered to be authoritative, with the two most important being those of al-Bukhari and Muslim, who both died around the year 870. Each contains thousands of *hadīth* that cover topics as diverse as prayer, revelation, business contracts, and menstruation.

A science of *hadīth* criticism was developed that analyzes the traditions to determine their reliability and how accurately they reflect Muhammad's words and deeds. The chain of transmitters is particularly important in this regard. If a chain is composed of trustworthy individuals and it has no chronological gaps, it is more likely to be deemed authentic. Each *hadīth* is placed in one of several categories, like "sound," "acceptable," and "weak," based on careful study.

The role of the *hadīth* in Islam has been a point of debate, particularly in recent years. Because the authenticity of a tradition is determined by its chain of transmitters, a spurious *hadīth* can be legitimated simply by attaching to it a chain that is known to be reliable. The possibility of such abuses has led many scholars, especially non-Muslims, to question the value of the *hadīth* to provide useful data about the Prophet Muhammad's life and times. Some Muslim scholars also view them cautiously, with some rejecting them completely because of questions about their reliability. Nonetheless, the prophetic traditions continue to play a vital role in the faith lives of many Muslims into the present day.

Each of the *hadīth* collections has sections that treat various aspects of the Qur'an. For example, in al-Bukhari's collection there are portions on prostrating during recitation of the Qur'an (which contains 12 *hadīth*), prophetic commentary on the Qur'an (501 *hadīth*), virtues of the Qur'an (80 *hadīth*), and holding fast to the Qur'an (95 *hadīth*). In addition, there are other traditions that treat such topics as what Muhammad experienced while receiving revelations, how the Qur'an was collected, how the Qur'an should be recited, and the proper way to interpret particular passages in the Qur'an. For example, one *hadīth* relates a tradition that explains Muhammad's practice when it came to performing an extra prostration while reciting certain sections of the Qur'an. "Whenever the Prophet recited the *sūra* that contained the prostration of recitation, he used to prostrate. Then, we would also prostrate, but some of us could not find a place to do so."

Like the *sīra* literature, the *ḥadīth* material also provides information on the historical context of particular verses and passages that can be of assistance in determining the chronological sequence of the Qur'an. The collections contain sometimes lengthy descriptions of events and circumstances that were the cause or result of a revelation to Muhammad. For example, 24:11-17 makes reference to a lie that was told about someone and admonishes members of the community for not exposing it as a falsehood. The details of the episode remain unreported in the Qur'an, but the *ḥadīth* connect it to an incident involving Muhammad's wife 'Ā'isha, who was wrongly accused of marital infidelity. Similarly, 17:1 is generally understood to contain a veiled reference to Muhammad's miraculous night journey from Mecca to Jerusalem on the back of a winged beast. This episode in the Prophet's life, which has been widely celebrated throughout history, is not mentioned explicitly in the text but is described in detail in the *ḥadīth*.

> *The two parts of a* ḥadīth: *(1) the* isnād, *or chain of transmitters, which can cover generations of Muslims; (2) the* matn, *or body, which recounts something the Prophet Muhammad did, said, or observed.*

### THE *ASBĀB AL-NUZŪL*

Another genre of writing that shares features with the *sīra* and the *ḥadīth* is the "occasions of revelation" (*asbāb al-nuzūl*) material. These are reports that identify the cause, place, and time of a given portion of the text of the Qur'an. They follow a more or less set formula that contains all or most of the following components: (1) an event or set of circumstances; (2) a place; (3) one or more individuals; (4) a reference to time; (5) a statement that the elements listed above led to a divine revelation; (6) the Qur'an passage that was revealed.

One of the first and most well-known examples of this genre is "The Book of the Occasions of Revelation of the Qur'an," by al-Waḥīdī (d. 1075). In this work, al-Waḥīdī compiles background information on the historical context of passages in more than eighty chapters of the Qur'an. To collect these reports, he likely drew from oral traditions, legal scholarship, exegetical works, and sources like the *sīra* and the *ḥadīth*.

## Chronology

This discussion of the *sīra*, *ḥadīth*, and *asbāb al-nuzūl* has highlighted the importance of chronology in study of the Qur'an. As noted above, the most basic chronological analysis of the text has centered on the distinction between the Meccan and Medinan material. The first to attempt to identify chapters in this fashion was Ibn 'Abbas (d. 688), who is considered

FIGURE 3 *Muhammad (surrounded by a flame) and his followers build a mosque in Medina.*

to be one of the founding figures of study of the Qur'an. His designation of each chapter as either Meccan or Medinan was broadly accepted and is still found in most copies of the text.

In the standard division, 24 of the Qur'an's 114 chapters are from the Medinan period. In general, the Meccan chapters are briefer and are characterized by calls to convert to monotheism and warnings of the punishment that awaits those who fail to do so. This material attempts to persuade its audience by appealing to proofs found in the natural world, and it also refers to the lives and messages of the earlier prophets, like Moses, to validate Muhammad's prophetic identity. The Medinan chapters, by contrast, are longer and tend to focus more on issues related to the establishment and social organization of the expanding Muslim community. Because the Medinan chapters tend to be longer and are therefore found first in the book's canonical ordering, one can get a better sense of the chronological development of the Qur'an by reading it backward, beginning with chapter 114.

The subdivision of the Meccan chapters into three periods (early, middle, and late) was a further refinement that was introduced by Western non-Muslim scholars. This began to take shape in the mid-nineteenth century, when methods related to historical-critical study of the Bible were emerging. In fact, a number of key figures in European Qur'an scholarship during this time were also well-respected Bible scholars. Drawing upon advances in biblical scholarship, they sought to develop a more detailed understanding of how the Qur'an's chronological development reflected the changing contexts and circumstances of Muhammad's prophetic career.

Since the nineteenth century, various proposals have been put forward that attempt to lay out the chronological order and sequence of the Qur'an's contents. While no single one has gained universal acceptance, the one suggested by the German scholar Theodor Nöldeke (d. 1930) has been widely recognized as a plausible reconstruction of the development of the text. Another scholar whose work is frequently discussed is Richard Bell (d. 1952), a Scotsman who rejected the traditional division into Meccan and Medinan chapters and proposed an alternative system that dated smaller sections and individual verses. Bell's scholarship has been criticized for being idiosyncratic and incoherent, but many believe he has raised important questions about the complex nature of the Qur'an's formation and transmission.

There is a similar lack of agreement among scholars about when the text of the Qur'an was written down. John Burton (b. 1929), also from Scotland, dates it very early by arguing that the Prophet Muhammad himself helped to establish the final form of the Qur'an's consonantal text. At the other end of the spectrum, the American John Wansbrough (d. 2002), who taught in London, contended that the Qur'an was the product of Jewish, Christian, and other sources that did not reach its final form until two centuries after Muhammad. The work of these four, as well as that of other prominent Western scholars, has been more influential among their fellow non-Muslims than among Muslims.

### ABROGATION

An important feature of the Qur'an that is understood through appeal to chronology is the fact that it appears to contradict itself in places. This is especially the case regarding certain legal matters and practices. Some passages conflict with other ones by prescribing different laws or guidelines for the same set of circumstances. This situation has important theological implications for the Muslim community because the presence of contradictory material in divine revelation could suggest that God's will is subject to change or is imperfect.

To address this and similar concerns, a theory of abrogation was developed to explain how the ruling of one verse is able to replace that of another. This is determined on the basis of chronological order—later verses negate and abrogate earlier ones. The designation given to this field of study of the Qur'an is *al-nāsikh wal-mansūkh* ("the abrogating and the abrogated"), which is the title of the work written by al-Qāsim ibn Sallām (d. 838) that first addressed the topic. Abrogation rests on the notion that the Qur'an's message is sometimes modified or expressed in a different way in order to fit the changing circumstances to which it is addressed. In other words, it recognizes that divine revelation is always directed to a particular context and situation.

A good example of how abrogation works can be seen in the Qur'an's legislation regarding drinking wine. There are three references to the consumption of wine in the text, and each one says something different. In 4:43 believers are told they should not pray if they are intoxicated, but the verse does not explicitly forbid them from drinking wine. But then in 2:219a, the pros and cons of consuming wine and gambling are mentioned, and the verse comes down in favor of avoiding both activities. "They ask you (Muhammad) about wine and games of chance. Say, 'There is both great sin and benefit for people in them, but their sin is greater than their benefit.'"

That recommendation to abstain is an outright ban in 5:90-91, which forbids Muslims from drinking wine and engaging in other questionable practices. "Oh believers, wine, games of chance, idolatry, and divining with arrows are vile things that are Satan's works. Avoid them so you may prosper. Satan wants to instill enmity and hatred among you with wine and games of chance, and so prevent you from remembering God and praying. Will you not cease these activities?"

The Qur'an's inconsistency in what it teaches about wine is resolved through appeal to abrogation. The third text is held to be among the last ones revealed to Muhammad, and so it is taken as the Qur'an's final and definitive statement on the matter. The other two passages give evidence of the fact that prior to that point alcohol consumption was permitted but frowned upon until it was eventually prohibited by later revelation.

As important as abrogation is for interpretation of the Qur'an, the term appears relatively few times in the text. The Arabic root from which it is derived is *n-s-kh*, which means "to abrogate, annul." Words from that root are found four times in the Qur'an, with the most important being 2:106, which describes God's decision to substitute certain verses with others. "Whatever revelation we abrogate [*nansakh*] or cause to be forgotten We replace with something better or similar to it. Do you (Muhammad) not know that God has power over everything?" More than any other, this passage led to the development of the concept of abrogation.

Another verse that is sometimes cited in support of abrogation is 16:101: "If We substitute one revelation in place of another—and God knows best what He sends down—they say, 'You are inventing it,' but most of them do not know." Here the Arabic root *nasakha* is not used, but the reference to God replacing one revelation with another is very much in line with the way the process of abrogation is commonly understood.

### Interpretation

Study of the Qur'an began in the earliest years of Islam. Over time, various subdisciplines of qur'anic study emerged that were referred to as "the sciences of the Qur'an" (*'ulūm al-qur'ān*), including lexicography, grammar, rhetoric, and exegesis. The two terms most commonly used to describe exegetical study of the Qur'an are *tafsīr* and *ta'wīl*. The word *tafsīr* comes from an Arabic root that means, "to interpret, explain," and it can refer both to exegetical study of the Qur'an in general and to a specific work or commentary that is the result of such study.

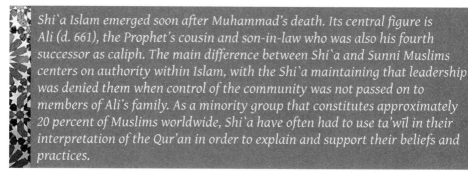

*Shi`a Islam emerged soon after Muhammad's death. Its central figure is Ali (d. 661), the Prophet's cousin and son-in-law who was also his fourth successor as caliph. The main difference between Shi`a and Sunni Muslims centers on authority within Islam, with the Shi`a maintaining that leadership was denied them when control of the community was not passed on to members of Ali's family. As a minority group that constitutes approximately 20 percent of Muslims worldwide, Shi`a have often had to use ta'wīl in their interpretation of the Qur'an in order to explain and support their beliefs and practices.*

The Arabic word *ta'wīl* stems from a root that conveys the sense of returning or going back to the beginning of something. In the Qur'an, it often describes the ability to interpret a dream or a story and sometimes refers to a mysterious interpretation that goes below the surface level. For this reason, a distinction is sometimes made between *tafsīr* as describing the interpretation of a text that has only one meaning and *ta'wīl* as a type of interpretation that chooses one among several possible meanings of a text. This section presents a brief overview of important figures and developments in the history of interpretation of the Qur'an, with greater attention paid to recent scholars whose work has been marked by innovative approaches to the text.

MUSLIM SCHOLARSHIP

Islamic tradition teaches that the Prophet Muhammad and his companions engaged in interpretation of the Qur'an during their lifetimes, but written exegetical works did not begin to appear until the second century of the Muslim era. The initial efforts did not attempt detailed analysis of passages, and they tended to rely on paraphrase and to discuss the contents of the Qur'an in relation to the tales and legends that were circulating in Arabia from Jewish and other sources.

Among the first sciences of the Qur'an to emerge were grammar and philology, and scholars skilled in these disciplines often tried to make sense of rare or problematic words and phrases present in the text. In this early period, little attempt was made to present a verse-by-verse analysis of the Qur'an. Such a method was introduced with the work of al-Ṭabarī (d. 923), mentioned above, whose magnum opus was titled "The Compilation of Clarity Regarding the Interpretation of the Verses of the Qur'an." It drew upon the results of previous scholarship and included discussion of the prophetic traditions found in the ḥadīth in its analysis of the text of the Qur'an. It is a massive work that pays attention to grammar, philology, rhetoric, and meaning, and it remains an invaluable tool. Among other medieval exegetes whose commentaries have been influential are al-Zamakhsharī (d. 1144), Fakhr al-Dīn al-Rāzī (d. 1210), Nāṣir al-Dīn al-Bayḍāwī (d. 1315), Ibn Kathīr (d. 1373), and Jalāl al-Dīn al-Suyūṭī (d. 1505).

The successors to these prominent figures in the Muslim exegetical tradition frequently cite them, and sometimes later commentaries have been nothing but a compilation of the views and opinions of early and medieval scholarship. Nonetheless, some scholars and the methods they have employed have taken study of the Qur'an in interesting new directions that have introduced fresh ways of thinking about the text and its interpretive possibilities.

Sometimes these innovative approaches have arisen in response to sociopolitical contexts that have raised questions about the role Islam and the Qur'an should play in society. A significant factor in this regard has been the strong presence, some would say dominance, of Western non-Muslim culture throughout the world, including in Muslim-majority areas. Western influence in the form of colonialism, science and technology, and media has occasionally had an impact on views regarding how the Qur'an should be read and interpreted.

Some have argued that analysis of the Qur'an needs to be informed by the rationalism and scientific worldview that developed in Europe in the eighteenth and nineteenth centuries. Two leading figures in this movement were the Indian Sayyid Ahmad Khan (d. 1838) and Muhammad

Abduh (d. 1905) of Egypt. Working in two different contexts, these two reformers shared the opinion that the modern Muslim world must somehow embrace the findings of science and adapt to contemporary cultural norms and attitudes, or run the risk of becoming irrelevant.

This is seen in the principle Khan called "the criterion of conformity to nature." He argued that there can be no contradiction between the work of God as found in creation and the word of God as revealed in the Qur'an. He believed the truth of any religion, including Islam, can be found in how well it conforms to nature. Consequently, when there is a disagreement between what the Qur'an teaches and what creation teaches through the senses and reason, one should accept the latter as correct and reject the former. This led Khan to deny any references in the Qur'an to miraculous events because they are in conflict with the laws of nature. He also questioned the historical accuracy of the ḥadīth, and so he rejected use of the prophetic traditions in interpretation of the Qur'an.

Muhammad Abduh thought Qur'an scholars needed to be addressing the great social problems of their day rather than debating the fine points and minutiae of grammar and philology. From his prominent position as rector of al-Azhar University and chief judge of Egypt, he and his student Rashīd Riḍā (d. 1935) opposed colonialism while arguing for the compatibility of Islam and science.

He made a distinction between the essential core of Islam and its general principles, a distinction that influenced how he read the Qur'an. Abduh believed that only its essential core is timeless and unchanging, and so only those parts of the Qur'an that constitute that core are relevant for all times and places. The general principles are adaptable and temporary because they were meant only for the context of seventh-century Arabia. Abduh said this distinction must be kept in mind when interpreting the Qur'an, and it formed the basis for his reform efforts in Egypt that addressed issues like women's education and the negative effects of polygamy.

The reformist views of Khan, Abduh, and others like them were controversial at times and not accepted by all. Nonetheless, they called attention to the social implications of the Qur'an's message and raised important questions about the text's role in the world. In this way, they began to develop a methodological framework for future generations of modernists who continue to argue that the effects of study of the Qur'an should be felt in the town square and not just in the scholar's library.

A development in study of the Qur'an that has a parallel in biblical studies is the adoption of tools and methods from the field of literary theory to analyze the sacred text. This approach is most closely associated with Amīn al-Khūlī (d. 1967), who taught at the Egyptian University (now the University of Cairo). He and his students have approached the Qur'an with the same questions one would ask of any other piece of literature in their exploration of various narratological, structural, and semiotic dimensions of the text. Literary study of the Qur'an has not been received as warmly or practiced as widely as literary study of the Bible. The legitimacy of the method has sometimes been questioned by those in positions of authority, and some who have employed it have been reprimanded by the guardians of tradition and orthodoxy. Literary study of the Qur'an is still undertaken, but those who engage in it tend to do so cautiously.

Fazlur Rahman (d. 1988) was a prominent Pakistani intellectual who taught for many years at the University of Chicago. Much of his scholarship addressed the Qur'an, and he believed that a basic theme of the text concerns how humans are to behave. In order to determine what the Qur'an has to say on this topic, Rahman attempted to outline its ethical system. He felt it was necessary to do this because legal scholars throughout history have consistently denied the historical context of the revelation of the Qur'an, leading to an archaic and ossified system of law that does not reflect the essence of its message.

To address this problem, Rahman argued for the importance of historical criticism of the Qur'an that would take seriously its originating context. At the heart of the method, he proposed what he called a "double movement" for interpreting the Qur'an. The first movement required a return to the original revelation of the passage being studied in order to establish its context during Muhammad's lifetime. According to Rahman, the specific content of the passage should not then simply be applied to the modern day, as is often done. Instead, the interpreter must identify the general principle that underlies it, like equality, justice, or improving the status of women. In the second movement, that general principle is then applied to the modern context in a way that is appropriate given the norms and standards of society. In this way, it is the essence of the Qur'an's teaching, rather than the specific form it took in seventh-century Arabia, that is being passed on to future generations. The distinction Rahman makes here, what he refers to as the "ideal" and the "contingent" messages of the Qur'an, is not unlike the one Muhammad Abduh makes between the essential core and general principles of Islam.

The Tunisian scholar Mohammed Talbi (b. 1921) is another modernist who has proposed a new way of reading the Qur'an. Like the others mentioned above, he believes that recognizing the difference between the text's historical context and our own is the key to proper interpretation. He suggests that the "analogical reading" of the Qur'an that has come to dominate be replaced by an "intentional reading." An analogical reading views the present by way of the past and insists that the modern world must conform to and replicate how things were done in the past. Talbi criticizes this approach and says all it does is force onto later times outmoded ways of thinking and acting that were acceptable in the seventh century.

An intentional reading, on the other hand, is based on a text's orientation. It is a dynamic approach that does not stop at the literal words of the text but tries to discern its general tendency and then acts accordingly. Talbi uses the example of slavery to illustrate how an intentional reading works. Nowhere does the Qur'an explicitly prohibit slavery, but in a number of places it insists that slaves be treated humanely or encourages that they be given their freedom. According to Talbi, the text's intent is to abolish slavery, but the context of seventh-century Arabia was not yet ready for such a move. But prohibiting slavery was acceptable and appropriate for later generations, who then fully realized the Qur'an's orientation by outlawing the practice. Talbi believes that an interpretation that pays attention to the Qur'an's intent and inclination in this manner enables the community to evolve as it acts in accord with God's will. It is no longer simply perpetuating the way things were done in the past but tapping into the Qur'an's capacity to creatively respond to new circumstances and changing contexts.

This is just a representative sampling of some of the innovative and interesting work being undertaken by Muslim scholars that gives a sense of possible future directions in study of the Qur'an. To it might be added the many contributions of feminist scholars who are exploring issues related to gender in the text. Scholars like

> The three principles of reformist interpretation of the Quran: (1) It is a mistake to continue to try to replicate the past; (2) There is a distinction in the Qur'an between its unchanging core and the changing principles it articulates; and (3) The Qur'an must be read contextually.

Asma Barlas (Pakistan, b. 1950), Riffat Hassan (Pakistan, b. 1943), Fatima Mernissi (Morocco, b. 1940), and Amina Wadud-Muhsin (United States, b. 1952) are among the leading figures in this growing field, and some of their work will be discussed in the chapter on gender and sexuality.

NON-MUSLIM SCHOLARSHIP

Christians and other non-Muslims have studied and commented on the Qur'an ever since their initial contact with it in the first century of the Muslim era. Most of the early writings were polemical in nature and were characterized by attempts to denigrate Islam and its sacred text or to show the Qur'an's dependence on the Bible and other Judeo-Christian sources. Their work shows little, if any, familiarity with Muslim exegesis of the Qur'an, and it would not qualify as scholarship by modern standards.

Critical study of the Qur'an in the West began in the nineteenth century and was centered in the German-speaking world. Theodor Nöldeke was mentioned above as a scholar whose work has had a major influence on reconstruction of the chronological development of the Qur'an. He built upon and refined the scholarship of Gustav Weil (d. 1889), who was the first to propose the three-part division of the Meccan material that has become widely accepted. Much of the scholarship since then has been undertaken in response to the work of Weil and Nöldeke, to either develop it further or to offer alternatives to it. An example of the latter type is seen in Richard Bell (d. 1952), also mentioned earlier, who proposed a radically different understanding of the Qur'an that rearranged its chapters and the material within them.

> Among the most prominent Christians to discuss the Qur'an prior to the rise of critical scholarship were John of Damascus (eighth century), Peter the Venerable (twelfth century), and Nicholas of Cusa (fifteenth century). Of the three, Nicholas of Cusa had the most positive view of Islam and the Qur'an.

In addition to its chronological ordering, another area of interest in nineteenth-century non-Muslim study of the Qur'an was its linguistic features, especially philology and lexicography. This was commonly done through an examination of the meanings of individual words and phrases, both in the Qur'an and within the wider context of Arab literature and poetry. Similarly, key concepts and themes of the text were explored with particular attention given to their precise meanings and points of origin.

This interest in linguistic issues continued into the twentieth century, which also saw the rise of new areas of inquiry, including foreign (non-Arabic) words in the Qur'an, the variant readings of the text that are reflected in manuscripts and other sources, and the relationships between the other monotheistic faiths and the Qur'an. The latter area has been of particular interest. While some scholars continued to be motivated by a desire to demonstrate the Qur'an's derivation from or dependence upon the Bible and other Jewish/Christian sources, others have tried to come to a better understanding of how and why the traditions and beliefs shared by the monotheistic religions are expressed in diverse ways in various historical and literary contexts.

Non-Muslims were not the first to pay attention to these issues. The history of Islamic exegesis demonstrates that Muslim scholars have frequently commented on topics like the foreign vocabulary and alternative readings of the Qur'an and its relationship to Judaism and Christianity. In recent times, non-Muslims scholars have begun to pay more attention to Muslim exegesis, and they have drawn upon sources like the *tafsīr* and *asbāb al-nuzūl* to inform their own study. This has given a broader perspective to their work and has helped to ground it in the rich heritage of Muslim scholarship on the Qur'an.

At the same time, new methods continue to be developed and employed by both Muslims and non-Muslims that put study of the Qur'an in conversation with work being done in other disciplines. Insights and approaches from fields like literature, anthropology, archaeology, and sociology have been adopted that allow scholars to study the text of the Qur'an in innovative and creative ways. Many of these efforts have led to a deeper understanding of the contents of the Qur'an and an appreciation of its role throughout history.

Although it is an obvious point, it is worth noting that non-Muslim scholars of the Qur'an have a different relationship to the text than their Muslim colleagues do. Because they are not members of the community that believe it to be the word of God, they approach and study the Qur'an from a perspective that is not informed by faith. As a result, non-Muslims sometimes ask questions or reach conclusions that many Muslims would not. At times, some Muslims might find non-Muslim scholarship to be flawed or disturbing. Those who view it in theological terms might even label it sinful.

That is an inevitable outcome when dealing with matters of faith about which not all people agree. But non-Muslims (and Muslims) can avoid many of the pitfalls that might result if they adopt an attitude of respect and tolerance. These qualities typify much of the work being done on the Qur'an by non-Muslims, but not all of it. Some authors adopt an inflammatory and hostile tone that belittles Islam and disparages its sacred text. They are driven by agendas and biases that dominate their work so much that it cannot be considered scholarship. Unfortunately, works of this sort are often pitched to a popular audience and are written for mass consumption, and their wide dissemination only ends up reinforcing stereotypes and misperceptions about the Qur'an and Islam.

## Experiencing the Qur'an

Just as Jews and Christians relate to and interact with the Bible in various ways and on many levels, the same can be said about Muslims and the

Qur'an. It is a book, but its role in their lives extends far beyond that of mere words on a page. It instructs them on matters of morality and faith, but the Qur'an is more than just a source from which a theoretical set of ethics is derived. It also has a cultural identity and tangible presence that leaves its mark in many ways, both obvious and subtle. Throughout their lives, Muslims encounter their text in assorted contexts and settings that shape their overall view and understanding of it. In this section, some of the ways Muslims experience the Qur'an are identified and briefly discussed.

## Mosque and School

The Qur'an has always played a central role in the spiritual formation and education of Muslims. The Prophet Muhammad instructed his followers via sermons he preached in the mosque attached to his home in Medina, thereby establishing a practice that continues to this day. During the noon prayer service each Friday, a sermon is delivered prior to the formal prayer ritual. The address is called a *khuṭba,* and the one who gives it is the *khaṭīb,* who is often the *imām* responsible for leading the community in prayer.

A typical sermon is made up of two parts. The first includes statements of praise of God, a request for blessings on Muhammad, the Muslim creed, and at least one verse from the Qur'an. This part of the sermon is usually theological in nature and is meant to encourage or admonish the congregation on matters of faith. The second part normally has a more

FIGURE 4 *Boys reciting the Qur'an in a madrasa in Kashmir.*

FIGURE 5 *Courtyard of the Ben Youssef madrasa in Marrakesh, Morocco. (Photo by Debra Bartelli.)*

political or practical tone and discusses some issue or current event that directly affects the Islamic community. The sermon normally concludes with a call for peace, blessings on the Prophet and his companions, and a prayer for all Muslims.

In addition to those of the Friday noon prayer service, formal sermons are also given on other occasions. One is delivered on each of the two major feast days of the Islamic calendar, the "Feast of Fast-Breaking" (`īd al-fiṭr`) and the "Feast of Sacrifice" (`īd al-'aḍḥā`), and a sermon is also often given when the community gathers to address some major concern like a drought or other natural disaster. In addition, sermonlike addresses are sometimes delivered outside the structure of formal Friday prayer, and these are referred to as "lessons" or "instructions." On all of these occasions, the Qur'an is read and commented on with the purpose of enriching the faith lives of those present.

Study of the Qur'an originally took place within the context of the mosque, either in groups or in a one-on-one format through a master-student relationship, and this educational system lasted more than a millennium. Variations on these models have endured in places, but in many countries public and private schools are now the primary means by which young people are taught about Islam and the Qur'an. In many of these institutions, students learn classical Arabic through the text of the Qur'an. Most universities in the Muslim world offer opportunities for advanced training in the sciences of the Qur'an, and there are also numerous programs associated with mosques, institutes, and schools that provide less formal study of the text.

Many non-Muslims associate Qur'an study with the *madrasa*. A word that means "place of study," the *madrasa* traces its roots to the eleventh century and originally described an educational institution that was associated with a mosque. They developed into centers of learning that provided male students an education in various disciplines related to study of Islam. The university system was established throughout much of the Islamic world during the nineteenth and twentieth centuries, and this development led to a decline in the influence and importance of the *madrasa*. Nonetheless, they continue to exist in some areas, and the less expensive costs associated with them tend to attract students from lower socioeconomic groups and rural communities.

*The main feasts of the Muslim year are associated with two of the Five Pillars of Islam. The Feast of Fast-Breaking (ʿīd al-fiṭr) takes place at the end of Ramadan, the ninth month of the Muslim calendar, during which Muslims fast from dawn to dusk. The feast lasts for several days, and it is an opportunity for people to share meals, exchange gifts, and engage in communal prayer. The Feast of Sacrifice (ʿīd al-'aḍhā) is associated with the pilgrimage to Mecca that takes place every year during the twelfth month. The last activity for the pilgrims entails sacrificing an animal and sharing it in a meal. As they do so, all Muslims around the world also participate in this ritual and celebrate the feast with their families and friends.*

### Ritual

Recitation of the Qur'an is an essential component of the obligatory prayers of Islam. During each of the five prescribed prayer times, the opening chapter of the Qur'an (*al-fātiḥa*) is recited as well as other sections of one's own choosing. Beyond the use of the Qur'an in this formalized setting, Muslims also engage the text in a variety of other ways that might be considered ritualistic. Included among these is reading/reciting the Qur'an in the home or somewhere else outside the mosque as an act of personal or communal devotion. In order to facilitate this practice, the text of the Qur'an is divided into thirty parts so it can be read in its entirety over the course of a month.

Other rituals include kissing the Qur'an, requesting a blessing (*baraka*) or protection from the Qur'an, and weeping as the Qur'an is read. This latter practice is mentioned specifically in the text. "Say (Muhammad), 'Whether you believe it or not, those who were previously given knowledge fall down prostrate on their faces when it is recited to them, and they say, "Praise be to our Lord! His promise has been fulfilled." They fall down on their faces weeping, and it builds up their humility'" (17:107-9).

Muslims are encouraged to recite certain verses or chapters at particular times. According to tradition, the Prophet Muhammad regularly recited the last three chapters of the Qur'an on various occasions, including when he went to sleep at night and when he was sick. As often occurs with such prophetic practices, this was subsequently adopted by many later Muslims.

Some rituals involving the Qur'an have generated controversy and debate over their legitimacy. This is the case with the practice of kissing the cover of the book and then holding it in one's right hand over one's head in order to receive a blessing, which some consider to be an improper use of the text that lacks support in prophetic traditions.

It is not a requirement in Islam that one seal an oath by placing the right hand on a copy of the Qur'an, but this is sometimes done. Some jurists maintain that such an act is not permissible because one should swear only by God, while others are of the opinion that swearing by the Qur'an is virtually the same thing because it contains God's words. Another practice commonly found in Muslim communities is recitation of the Qur'an upon the death of a person, and chapter 36 is commonly read on such occasions. While legal scholars disagree on the permissibility of reciting the text over the body of the deceased, family and friends often gather after the burial—which takes place the same day as the death according to Islamic custom—to listen to recitation of the Qur'an by someone trained in that skill.

## Popular Practices

Throughout history, Muslims have sometimes used the Qur'an in efforts to achieve certain effects like healing, blessing, protection, and pregnancy. This talismanic use of the text is based on belief in the power of the Qur'an and its ability to transform lives. Many of these expressions of popular religiosity have endured into the present day, but they were more common in earlier periods, when they reflected the religious mindset and worldview of a larger percentage of the populace.

Some examples of these practices have already been mentioned, like seeking a blessing (*baraka*) by holding the Qur'an over one's head or

FIGURE 6  *Mosque lamp from the fourteenth century inscribed with verses from the Qur'an.*

saying the *basmala* prior to engaging in everyday activities. Books and manuals from the medieval and modern eras discuss many other activities that express belief in the transformative power of the Qur'an. In some cases, the text must be spoken aloud in order to realize the desired effect. Particular passages are to be recited to address specific problems like bodily ailments, marital infidelity, and childlessness. Other texts are effective in combating the evil eye, insomnia, or loneliness. One ritual entails reciting the Qur'an over food, which is then eaten to ensure the physical and spiritual health of a person. A similar practice calls for reciting the Qur'an over water so that a sick person might bathe in it and be healed.

At other times, the mere physical presence of the Qur'an is all that is required. A copy of the text is often prominently displayed in a home, automobile, or place of business as a way of seeking success or protection. Plaques, posters, trays, and other objects that contain passages from the Qur'an decorate many homes and offices for the same reason. Some believe that to eat or drink from a cup or plate that has a text from the Qur'an written on it will bring good fortune to an individual.

Similar beliefs exist regarding what a person wears. Pendants containing a small copy of the Qur'an, as well as amulets, necklaces, and other jewelry inscribed with verses from it, are sometimes worn to guarantee personal safety. Articles of clothing, especially shirts and tunics, have been decorated with text from the Qur'an in order to secure the good health and protection of the one who wears it. The latter were often worn as a type of spiritual armor by soldiers in battle and others who put themselves in harm's way.

Through these and similar practices, Muslims, like members of other faiths, attempt to bridge the gap between the human and the divine. God's word is brought into the realm of the everyday, and it is called upon to assist and accompany people as they negotiate the demands and challenges of human existence. In this way, the message remains transcendent, but its effects on the here and now are acknowledged.

## Recitation

The Qur'an is meant to be heard, not simply read. Sources indicate that within the first few decades after Muhammad's death, a system of recitation of the Qur'an was developed that drew upon the conventions of Arab music and melody current at the time. The term that refers to the rules and guidelines that govern recitation of the Qur'an is *tajwīd*, which establishes such things as the vocalization (use of vowels) of the text, which words and syllables should be stressed, and where pauses are permitted. Textbooks and manuals that present the details on *tajwīd* have been available since the fourth Islamic century. The set of rules they contain traces the roots of *tajwīd* to the time of Muhammad and standardizes how the text is recited.

There are different ways of reciting the text of the Qur'an, depending on which of seven accepted readings one adopts. The differences among them are not considerable and for the most part are limited to matters like variations in the choice and length of vowels in certain passages. The precise number of acceptable alternate readings is sometimes debated, but the number seven is found in a frequently cited *ḥadīth* in which Muhammad tells his followers that they are free to use whatever reading is easiest for them.

It takes many years of training and practice to become skilled in the art of Qur'an recitation. Its best practitioners are well-known throughout the Muslim world, and festivals and competitions are regularly held in which reciters, known as *qurrā'*, display their talents. Some go on to achieve the exalted status of the *ḥāfiz*, one who has memorized the entire text of the Qur'an.

## Textual Adornment

Virtually all modern copies of the Qur'an contain only text, but manuscripts from earlier periods are often visually stunning works of art. This is especially the case after the tenth century C.E., when paper began to replace parchment as the primary medium for manuscripts. The practice of adding ornamentation to copies of the Qur'an is similar to what occurred with the Bible, but with an important difference. Biblical manuscripts, especially within the Christian community, are often illustrated with pictures that represent individuals, locations, or scenes described in the text. Such depictions are never found in Qur'an manuscripts, which adhere to Islam's prohibition against drawing the human form and other types of representational art. Qur'an manuscripts were illuminated, rather than illustrated, with the most common style being the use of geometric designs and patterns throughout the text.

The reasons for the use of illumination are both aesthetic and practical. In addition to enhancing the physical attractiveness of the manuscript, some forms of ornamentation also improve its readability by indicating where a verse, chapter, or section of the Qur'an begins and ends. Because many manuscripts lack verse numbers, a gold symbol, usually a pyramid of dots or a rosette, became the usual way to indicate where a verse ends. Manuscripts also commonly use markers to set off groups of five or ten verses—usually a teardrop-shaped mark for five and a circle for ten—placed both in the text and in the page margin. This system is very helpful for locating a particular passage in longer chapters. Many copies of the Qur'an are divided into seven or thirty parts to facilitate the reading of the text over the course of a week or a month, and these divisions are also indicated by decorative symbols in the manuscripts.

Chapter divisions are marked in a number of different ways in the manuscripts. Sometimes breaks between chapters are indicated by a blank space, but usually some kind of geometric design or decoration is found. This block of illumination often also contains information on some of the details of the chapter, like its name, whether it is Meccan or Medinan, and how many verses it contains. These chapter divisions can be quite ornate and adorned with decorations.

Other features of Qur'an manuscripts serve primarily artistic purposes. In later periods, the text on each page is sometimes enclosed in a frame of ornamental decoration composed of lines and geometric patterns. Elaborately designed frontispieces and back pages are often included that attest to the creativity and imagination of those who designed and executed the manuscripts. Bindings of leather or wood sometimes protect the manuscript, and these covers are usually decorated with carving, stamping, or metalwork.

Depending on the dimensions of the material on which it is written, the amount of illumination it contains, and the size of its script, a single copy of the Qur'an might be contained in one manuscript or it might be a multivolume work. The libraries and museums of the world contain examples in many different shapes and lengths. The high quality of the artwork and attention to detail found in many of them highlight what a time-consuming and expensive process producing a Qur'an manuscript must have been. Those involved in the effort were undoubtedly motivated by a desire to create a work of high artistic quality, but the theological significance of the outcome also must have been apparent to them. In addition to being artists, they were charged with the task of giving visual expression to the word of God.

## Art and Architecture

It was noted above that Islam does not allow representational art, particularly depictions of the human form. The Qur'an does not say anything specific about the topic, but the prohibition is probably an extension of core Islamic teachings like its condemnation of idolatry, a practice

FIGURE 7   *The Ka'ba covered by the kiswa*
*containing verses from the Qur'an.*

the Qur'an criticizes (5:90; 6:74; 7:138; 14:35-36), and the belief that only God can create life. In this light, a person who produces representational art therefore runs the risk of either making something that might lead to sin or trying to engage in an activity that is reserved only for God.

*The kiswa is a black cloth covering placed over the cube-shaped Ka'ba, which is at the center of the Sacred Mosque in Mecca. Each year it is replaced by a new one that is elaborately decorated with verses from the Qur'an.*

The proscription against such representations led to the use of script as a frequent element of Islamic art. Not surprisingly, the text of the Qur'an is often used for such purposes, especially when the object or building it adorns has a religious function. The use of the Qur'an for artistic purposes goes back to the first century of the Islamic era, and some of the most impressive examples of it that have survived are found on mosques and monumental buildings.

The Dome of the Rock in Jerusalem is one of the most famous buildings in the world associated with Islam, and it provides an excellent example of use of the Qur'an in architecture.

*The prohibition against representational art applies primarily to the Qur'an and decoration found in mosques. Artwork depicting the human form, including that of the Prophet Muhammad, is sometimes found in other contexts.*

It was built in the late seventh century C.E., and many Qur'an passages are contained in the more than seven hundred feet of inscriptions that run along the base of its dome. The *basmala* is repeated seven times, and the largest section contains several texts that summarize the Qur'an's teachings about who Jesus was and what constitutes true faith (3:18-19; 4:171-72; 19:33-36).

An interesting aspect of these Qur'an citations is that they do not agree perfectly with the official version that is the basis for translations into English and other languages. These discrepancies have been explained in various ways. Some suggest that the Qur'an passages on the Dome of the Rock may have been communicated orally rather than taken from a written copy of the text. Others believe that the variation might reflect the existence of multiple versions of the Qur'an that were circulating at the same time.

Certain Qur'an passages appear with great frequency in Islamic art and architecture. Because it makes a direct reference to mosques, 9:18 is commonly found in houses of worship. "The ones who frequent God's places of worship are those who believe in God and the Last Day, maintain prayer, pay alms, and fear only God. These may hope to be among those

FIGURE 8  *The Dome of the Rock, with Arabic text inscribed around the base of the dome.*

who are rightly guided." The lengthy "Light Verse" of 24:35, so designated because it compares God to light, is often found in a mosque around the border of its *miḥrāb*, a niche in the wall that indicates the direction toward Mecca for prayer. Another section of the Qur'an often used for decorative purposes is chapter 112, which provides a brief summary of Muslim belief about the nature of God. "Say, 'He is God the One, God the eternal. He has begotten no one, nor was He begotten. He has no equal.'"

FIGURE 9  *The* miḥrāb *of the Great Mosque in Cordoba, Spain.*

## Technology

Technological advances have enabled the Qur'an to have a presence in society that was unimaginable in prior times. The text, in whole or in part, is now available in a variety of forms and media that have transformed the way people are exposed to and interact with the Qur'an. The first experience of technology's impact occurred in the nineteenth century, when publishers began to mass produce the Qur'an by means of the printing press. This development was not without its controversies, particularly in the early stages, when copies were often of inferior quality and marred by errors. But the advantages of mass production and distribution were immediate and undeniable—the sacred text was now available to all at a fraction of the price it would have cost to produce a manuscript.

This allowed the public to have a completely different relationship with the Qur'an than it had in the past. Direct access to the text was no longer the exclusive privilege of the scholar and those wealthy enough to afford it. For the first time in history, anyone was able to own a copy of the Qur'an, and those who were literate, regardless of their level of formal training, could read the text and study its contents. Large-scale publication of the Qur'an had a profound impact on Muslims outside the Arabic-speaking world, as translations into the vernacular were now much more accessible and affordable. This "democratization" of the Qur'an has enabled it to play a larger role in the everyday lives of Muslims everywhere.

The effects of the printing revolution have been obvious and permanent. The Qur'an is present throughout the world in virtually every language and is one of the most widely distributed books in history. But the Qur'an is also now available through other means beyond the traditional book format. Radio and television have been vehicles for communicating the text for a long time through the broadcast of Qur'an recitation and other forms of religious programming, with some stations devoted exclusively to that purpose. Countless tapes, CDs, and DVDs that contain recordings of the Qur'an are sold every year, and Qur'an ringtones for one's cell phone are now available.

FIGURE 10 *A digital version of the Qur'an.*

There has been a virtual explosion of the Qur'an's presence on the Internet in recent times. Audio and written forms of the text are available on thousands of websites, in both Arabic and translation. Besides their being searchable, these sites incorporate commentary from ancient and modern scholars into the text so that the user is given a sense of how the Qur'an has been studied and interpreted. Some websites provide information on the Qur'an, while others contain images, video, and audio related to it. This is to say nothing of the thousands of conversations and exchanges about the Qur'an taking place in cyberspace on any given day among people all over the world via the Internet and email.

Whenever the tools of an emerging technology—be it the printing press, television, or the Internet—have come in contact with the Qur'an, the encounter has presented new challenges and opportunities for the Muslim community. In each case, the boundaries of the text are expanded and redefined as people begin to experience it in ways they had not in the past. Inevitably, some respond cautiously and warily to the changed circumstances, while others welcome them. This is, of course, a situation that is not unique to Islam. Like all faiths, it will continue to wrestle with the practical, theological, and ethical implications of technological progress for its adherents, traditions, and texts.

## key TERMS

*allāh; al-qur'ān; al-islām; muslim; Ka`ba; hijra; sūra; āya; al-fātiḥa; basmala; muṣḥaf; Night of Power; umm al-kitāb; i`jāz; sīra; ḥadīth; asbāb al-nuzūl; abrogation; tafsīr; ta'wīl; khuṭba; madrasa; tajwīd; miḥrāb*

## further READING

M. A. S. Abdel Haleem, trans., *The Qur'an: A New Translation* (Oxford: Oxford University Press, 2005).

Farid Esack, *The Qur'an: A User's Guide* (Oxford: Oneworld, 2005).

Daniel A. Madigan, *The Qur'an's Self Image: Writing and Authority in Islam's Scripture* (Princeton: Princeton University Press, 2001).

Ingrid Mattson, *The Story of the Qur'an: Its History and Place in Muslim Life* (Oxford: Blackwell, 2008).

Fazlur Rahman, *Major Themes of the Qur'an*, 2nd ed. (Oxford: Oxford University Press, 2006).

Michael Sells, *Approaching the Qur'an: The Early Revelations* (Ashland: White Cloud, 1999).

Suha Taji-Farouki, ed., *Modern Muslim Intellectuals and the Qur'an* (Oxford: Oxford University Press, 2004).

# 1
# The Natural Environment

The Qur'an has much to say about the natural world, but it does not espouse an environmental ethos in the modern sense of that term. For example, it doesn't speak of global warming or the dangers posed by limitless consumption and irresponsible exploitation of the Earth's resources. The Arabic word most commonly used today to refer to conservation and preservation of the environment (*ḥimāya*) is not found in the Qur'an, nor is the term that refers to the environment itself (*bī'a*). These are modern concerns that have emerged only in relatively recent times, and so it is not surprising that we find no evidence of them in Islam's sacred text.

Despite the lack of explicit terminology that might resonate with a modern-day conservationist or someone who is concerned about environmental issues, the Qur'an nonetheless contains many passages that such a person could endorse and affirm. This is so because the Qur'an repeatedly stresses a theme that is at the heart of the modern environmental movement—human beings must have a proper relationship with and respect for creation and the world around them. The Qur'an has a unique understanding of the reasons why this is an essential component of human existence, and it is one that many people of other faiths can accept and embrace because it resonates with their own beliefs.

## A Parable

(Q 18:32-43; 36:13-29; 2:17; 7:176; 14:24-26; 29:41; 62:5)

The qur'anic perspective is uniquely articulated in an interesting parable found in 18:32-43 describing two men and the different ways they relate to the natural world. "Tell them a parable about two men. We made for one of them two gardens of grapevines that were surrounded by date palm trees, and We put farmland in between them. Each of the gardens brought forth produce without fail. We made a stream flow through them, and so the man had plenty of fruit. One day he was speaking with his companion and said, 'I have more wealth than you and a stronger backing among people,' and He entered his garden. Then he wronged himself by saying, 'I do not think that this will ever disappear or that the final hour will ever arrive. And even if I were to be brought back to my Lord, I would certainly find something there better than this.' His companion responded, 'Do you not believe in the one who created you out of dust, from a drop of fluid, and formed you into a man? As for me, He is God, my Lord, and I do not associate anything with my Lord. You should have entered your garden and said, "Whatever God wills! All power resides in God." Even though you consider me to be less than you in wealth and children, my Lord might provide me with something better than your garden and send a thunderbolt from the sky on your garden so that it becomes a bare hillside. Or perhaps its water might sink so far into the ground that you will not be able to find it.' And so it happened that his fruit was ruined, and he began to wring his hands over how much it had cost him. As it withered on its trellises he said, 'Woe is me! I should not have associated anything with my Lord!' He had no one to help him but God, and he could not help himself."

*The Arabic word the Qur'an uses for a parable is mathal, but it does not always refer to a comparison between two things, as is normally understood by the English term. Extended narrative parables in the Qur'an like that discussed here include one about a city that rejects the messengers sent to it (36:13-29). Among the elements of creation that are used for parabolic purposes in briefer passages are fire (2:17), a dog (7:176), trees (14:24-26), spider webs (29:41), and donkeys (62:5).*

The parable neatly illustrates and summarizes some of the Qur'an's essential teachings about creation and humanity's place in it. The men personify two different ways of relating to the natural environment. The first man, with the two gardens, is materially prosperous and successful, but he does not understand the reason for his prosperity or its fleeting nature. He boasts to his friend of his superior status while forgetting where his good fortune comes from. In the first few verses of the parable, we are told that God is responsible for all that the man has, but he is oblivious to the source of his success. He wrongly assumes that his gardens will last forever and that he is the supreme authority over them. He goes so far as to say that he does not believe he will ever die, and in the unlikely event that he were to pass away his situation would be even better than it is now. This is someone who sees himself as the center of the universe, unchanging and forever in charge. In the end, everything falls down around him and he is a broken, defeated person.

Not so the second man. He may not enjoy the material prosperity of his friend, but he possesses something of greater value—an awareness of God's role as the source of all that exists—which allows him to have a completely different relationship with the world. He boasts about God, not himself. This man is not in charge but in debt. He recognizes that all he has comes from God and is subject to change.

Both men understand the first one's problem in theological terms—he has set up a partner with God. In other words, he is guilty of the sin of *shirk*, or association, the one offense the Qur'an says will not be forgiven. The parable does not tell us specifically what he has associated with God, but the most logical conclusion is that it is himself. By ignoring God's involvement as the source of his success and setting himself up as the authority, the man has usurped the deity's role.

This is seen most obviously in his claim that his gardens will last forever and that he will not perish. Only God has control over life and death, as the man learns at the end of the parable. But it is also seen in his distorted sense of the relationship he has with the rest of creation. Despite what he thinks, he does not have the authority to control the created world and bend it to his will. Such power is reserved only for God. In the Qur'an, an important dimension of the nature of God is that this is the God of nature. The man in the parable serves as a reminder of what can happen when people forget this.

# A Theocentric Framework

(Q 2:29; 14:32-34; 16:10-17; 43:9-14; 45:12-13)

Certain passages in the Qur'an could be interpreted as placing humanity in a position of superiority vis-à-vis the rest of creation. They appear to suggest that other elements of the created order are here for our pleasure and use, and we are to dominate and control them. "It is He who created for you everything on the earth, and then turned to the sky and fashioned the seven heavens. He knows all things" (2:29). On its own, this verse can give the impression that everything that has been created is for humanity's benefit and enjoyment and we can do with it as we like. But when read in context, it is apparent that this verse is primarily about God, not us. It is preceded by a section that highlights God's power and control over all that exists, particularly humanity. In fact, then, 2:29 is meant to put us in our place as beings that are dependent on God, and it does not privilege us above the rest of creation.

This is usually the point behind the passages in the Qur'an that speak about our unique role as human beings—they are actually theocentric texts meant to underscore God's total authority over the world. This becomes clear in those sections that enumerate and describe the various elements of creation. "God created the heavens and earth, and He sent down water from the sky to bring forth produce to sustain you. He made the ships that sail the sea subservient to you by His command, and he also made the rivers subservient to you. He has made the sun and the moon subservient to you in their predictable paths. He has made the night and day subservient to you, and He has given you something of everything you have asked of Him. You could never keep track of all that God has done for you. Truly, humanity is unjust and ungrateful" (14:32-34; cf. 16:10-17; 43:9-14; 45:12-13). As the last section suggests, any special status humanity enjoys that allows it to benefit from the rest of creation is due solely to the favor and largesse of God. This is part of the theocentric framework that shapes much of the Qur'an's treatment of creation and humanity's place in it.

## God's Traits

(Q 7:180a; 17:110; 20:8; 59:24)

Various traits and qualities have been identified with God throughout the history of Islam. The most well-known collection of these is the list known as the "ninety-nine names of God," each of which describes some component of the divine essence. In the early centuries of the

Islamic era, Muslims debated the merits of assigning these traits to God, but it was eventually decided that it is permissible to invoke God by these names as long as they are properly understood. They do not call into question God's unity by fragmenting it into parts. Rather, the divine names use language and images that allow people to gain some insight, in however imperfect a way, into what must ultimately remain a mystery for them–the nature of God. Some of these qualities have been important in shaping Muslim understanding of the natural environment.

> Several Qur'an passages that describe God as having the most beautiful names were influential in the development of the Muslim belief that the deity has ninety-nine names. "God's are the most beautiful names, so call on Him by them" (7:180a; cf. 17:110; 20:8; 59:24).

### GOD'S UNITY
(Q 2:163; 5:73; 9:31; 18:110; 112; 6:19; 16:51; 17:111; 21:108; 37:4; 41:6)

The first of the divine names was just alluded to—God's unity (tawḥīd). The oneness of God is a theme found frequently in the Qur'an. At the core of the message that the Prophet Muhammad brought to his contemporaries was a call to shun polytheism and embrace worship of the only God. "The One" is one of the ninety-nine names of God, and it has its basis in the Qur'an (2:163; 5:73; 9:31; 18:110).

Among the many passages that speak of God's unity one of the most celebrated is chapter 112, already mentioned as frequently found adorning mosques, monuments, and other works of art. It is a very brief sūra that stresses the oneness of God while containing an implicit critique of Christian belief in the Trinity, which makes Jesus divine. "Say, 'He is God the One, God the eternal. He has begotten no one, nor was He begotten. He has no equal'" (cf. 6:19; 16:51; 17:111; 21:108; 37:4; 41:6).

### GOD AS CREATOR
(Q 6:102; 13:16; 23:14; 39:62; 40:62; 59:24; 10:34; 27:64; 29:19; 85:13; 54:24)

Another set of titles identifies God's role as creator. The first is al-khāliq ("The Creator"), which comes from an Arabic root that is commonly used in the Qur'an to describe God's creative activity. "That is God, your Lord. There is no God but He, the Creator of everything, so worship Him. He has authority over everything" (6:102; cf. 13:16; 23:14; 39:62; 40:62; 59:24).

A second title is "The One who Originates" (al-mubdi'). This term is not found in the Qur'an, but words from its root appear many times in reference to God's work as a creator. For example, 10:34 points out how inferior the gods of unbelievers are because they are incapable of creating. "Say, 'Can any of your partners (associated with God) originate creation, and then repeat it again?' Say, 'It is God who originates creation and then repeats it again. How are you deceived?'" (cf. 27:64; 29:19; 85:13).

A third name for God worth mentioning is *al-muṣawwir*, "The Fashioner," found in 54:24 at the end of a list of more than a dozen titles that describe God. This term comes from an Arabic root that sometimes refers to artistic activity like shaping and sculpting.

*The letters d, s, t, and z are sometimes written with a dot underneath them when transliterating Arabic. This is done to distinguish them from other Arabic letters that have a similar sound but are not identical.*

These two aspects of the divine nature—God's unity and creative capacity—work in tandem to help shape the Qur'an's view of humanity and the rest of the natural world. There is no division within God and no separation between God and what God creates. Everything is dependent upon God for its existence and so, in a certain sense, all of creation is imbued with God's presence. That may explain why, in a well-known *ḥadīth* attributed to him, the Prophet Muhammad said, "The whole earth is a mosque that is a place to worship." It is also why some scholars have said that *tawḥīd*, or unity, is the starting point for an Islamic understanding of the environment. If all is created by God, and God is one, it follows that there is a unity and connectedness within creation.

GOD AS ENVIRONMENT

(Q 3:120; 2:19; 4:108; 8:47; 11:92; 41:54; 85:20; 4:126)

The connectedness of creation is captured well in another title given to God in the Qur'an, albeit one that is not found in the established list of the ninety-nine names. In eight places, God is described as *muḥīṭ*, which is commonly translated as "surrounding" or "encompassing." In most cases, it is used to describe the fate of evildoers who think they can hide from God and not suffer the consequences that await them. They are warned that God will surround them and hold them accountable. "If something good happens to you it upsets them, but they are glad when something bad happens to you. If you persevere and stay aware of God, their scheming will not harm you at all. God surrounds all that they do" (3:120; cf. 2:19; 4:108; 8:47; 11:92; 41:54; 85:20).

The other reference to *muḥīṭ* is different in that it describes how God encompasses all that exists. "All that is in the heavens and on the earth belongs to God. God surrounds everything" (4:126). This text—which envisions God as "The Surrounder" or "The Encircler"—has sometimes been interpreted as a description of God as the environment in which all of creation exists and survives. There is no linguistic or theological reason why such a suggestion should be rejected, and so this verse may be one of the Qur'an's most poignant statements about creation's dependence on its creator.

The theocentric qur'anic view that has been summarized here has significant implications for how humans should understand their place in the world and relate to the rest of the environment. Before addressing that issue, however, it is necessary to consider how the Qur'an presents the origin of the world and what the text has to say about the nonhuman components of creation.

## The Work of Creation

(Q 7:54; 10:3; 11:7; 25:59; 32:4; 50:38; 57:4; 2:255; 41:9-12; 22:47; 46:33; 50:38; 40:68; 2:117; 16:40; 36:82; 3:47; 3:59; 19:35; 3:42-47; 19:16-21)

Like Genesis 1 in the Bible, the Qur'an holds that God created the heavens and the earth in six days (7:54; 10:3; 11:7; 25:59; 32:4; 50:38; 57:4). Most of these texts go on to say that God then took a seat on a throne that extends over all creation (2:255). Unlike the biblical tradition, the Qur'an does not identify what was created on each of the six days, but 41:9-12 makes a distinction between the first four days, when the earth was formed, and the next two days, during which the heavens were created.

*References to God's throne (ʿarsh) are not infrequent in the Qur'an and are often ways of speaking about the deity's authority or dominion. Throughout the history of interpretation they have played a role in debates related to divine transcendence/immanence and the use of anthropomorphisms to describe God.*

According to 22:47, a day for God is like one thousand years for humans, and this has led some commentators to say that we should not adopt a literal interpretation of the six-day period of creation. In another difference from its biblical counterpart, which has God rest on the seventh day, the Qur'an states that the deity was not tired after the work of creation (46:33; 50:38).

Some texts have been cited to argue that God creates from nothing—a doctrine known as *creatio ex nihilo*—but there is actually little support for this in the Qur'an. A number of times, it is stated that God simply has to speak in order to create something. "He brings to life and causes death.

When He decrees something, He says, 'Be,' and it is" (40:68; cf. 2:117; 16:40; 36:82). This expression is most famously seen in the case of the conception of Jesus, which the Qur'an teaches was realized without a human father. When Mary doubts the angel's message that she will bear a child, he responds, "Thus God creates what He wishes. When He has decreed something, He says to it, 'Be,' and it is" (3:47b; cf. 3:59; 19:35).

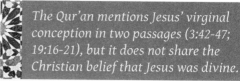

*The Qur'an mentions Jesus' virginal conception in two passages (3:42-47; 19:16-21), but it does not share the Christian belief that Jesus was divine.*

Such passages are not examples of *creatio ex nihilo*, despite what some commentators have claimed. In each case, as in 40:68 above, there is already some "thing" or matter to which God is speaking, and so it is better to think of this as a transformation or reordering rather than calling something into being out of nothing. That is the case with Jesus, since in 3:59 he is compared to Adam, who was created from dust. "Before God, the example of Jesus is like that of Adam. He created him from dust and then said to him, 'Be,' and he was." It is therefore inaccurate to claim that the Qur'an requires that divine creative activity be understood as *ex nihilo*. The opposite is the case—many of the elements of creation mentioned below come from preexisting material or matter.

## The Works of Creation

(Q 39:62a; 40:62; 1:2)

The Qur'an leaves no doubt that everything that exists is the work of God. "God is the creator of everything" (39:62a; cf. 40:62). It does not offer a detailed inventory of creation in a single passage, but throughout the text there are frequent reminders of God's creative activity. The word commonly used in the Qur'an to describe the totality of creation—like the English terms *universe* and *cosmos*—is ʿālamīn. This is the plural form of the word for "world," and it appears almost seventy-five times in the Qur'an. Depending on the context, it can refer either to all of creation or to humanity specifically. It is found in the second verse of the first chapter of the Qur'an, known as *al-fātiḥa* ("The Opening"). "Praise be to God, Lord of the worlds" (1:2).

## The Heavens and the Earth

(Q 46:3; 2:117; 6:101; 12:101; 13:16; 21:56; 35:1; 39:46; 42:11; 64:3; 91:5-6; 21:16-17; 38:27; 40:64; 2:22; 21:30; 41:9-12)

A phrase that conveys this same sense is the merism "the heavens and the earth," usually used in a way that includes everything that exists between the two. There are many references in the Qur'an to God's being the creator of the heavens and the earth (al-samāwāt wa al-arḍ), including one in 46:3 that explicitly mentions the other elements of creation: "We created the heavens and earth and everything between them in truth and for a set time, but the unbelievers disregard the warning given to them" (cf. 2:117; 6:101; 12:101; 13:16; 21:56; 35:1; 39:46; 42:11; 64:3; 91:5-6). The opening words of this verse, not cited here, state that creation was not a random occurrence and that God had a reason for bringing things into existence (cf. 21:16-17; 38:27). In other words, creation is a structured system with meaning and significance. This is one reason why wahdat al-wujūd, or the unity of creation, is an important concept in Islam—in the qur'anic worldview, everything works together to achieve a common purpose.

In the Qur'an's cosmology, the sky is understood to be a type of dome or roof that covers the earth: "God has made the earth a dwelling place for you and the heavens as a canopy. He formed you well, and has provided you with good things. That is God your Lord, so blessed be God, the Lord of the worlds" (40:64; cf. 2:22). This is similar to the biblical understanding of the sky as expressed in Genesis 1.

But according to one text, things were not always this way. Heaven and earth were originally one entity that was split apart by God, resulting in the world as we know it. "Do the unbelievers not know that the heavens and the earth had been joined together and that We split them apart, and that We made every living thing from water? Do they not believe?" (21:30). This text indicates that heaven and earth were created at the same time, but other passages point in the direction of a two-step process, with earth created before heaven. This appears to be the case in 41:9-12, where the earth is created in the first two days and the heavens are brought about in days five and six.

### THE SEVEN HEAVENS

(Q 67:3; 71:15; 2:29; 17:44; 23:17, 86; 78:12; 41:12; 67:5; 15:17; 37:6-10; 65:12)

In a few places, the Qur'an speaks of God creating seven heavens, one above the other (67:3; 71:15). "It is He who created for you everything on the earth, and then turned to the sky and fashioned the seven heavens. He knows all things" (2:29; cf. 17:44; 23:17, 86; 78:12). There is an allusion to the sun and other heavenly bodies in 41:12, which describes the level nearest the earth as illuminated and protected. The nature of this protection is explained in other texts that add the detail that some of the heavenly bodies, probably a reference to meteors, act as weapons that are hurled from the heavens at demons and other enemies of humanity. "We have adorned the lowest heaven with lamps and We have made them for stoning devils. We have prepared for them the punishment of hellfire" (67:5; cf. 15:17; 37:6-10). Heaven is commonly identified as the location of paradise in Islamic thought, a topic to be discussed in a later chapter. The text is somewhat ambiguous, but 65:12 appears to have a curious reference to God also creating seven earths in addition to seven heavens.

### MUHAMMAD'S NIGHT JOURNEY
(Q 17:1; 53:1-18)

The references in the Qur'an to seven heavens relate to a well-known tradition about Muhammad that is not explicitly referred to in the text but is frequently treated in the *ḥadīth* and other Islamic sources. According to the account, one night the Prophet was miraculously transported on a winged beast from Mecca to Jerusalem, from where he ascended through the seven levels of heaven. Along the way, he met important prophetic figures from the past like Moses, Jesus, and Abraham, until he eventually found himself before the throne of God at the highest level. The Dome of the Rock in Jerusalem is built on the site that is venerated as the place from which Muhammad's heavenly journey began.

According to most commentators, this episode in the Prophet's life, known as the ascension (*miʿrāj*), is indirectly referred to in the Qur'an in 17:1. "Glory be to Him who made His servant journey by night from the sacred place of worship to the furthest place of worship, whose precincts We have blessed, in order to show him Our signs. He is the One who hears, the One who sees." The identity of the traveler is not stated,

FIGURE 11 *Image from the seventeenth century of the ascension of the Prophet Muhammad.*

but throughout history Muslim exegesis has considered this to be a reference to Muhammad. The "sacred place of worship" is held to be the sacred space in Mecca near the Ka'ba, while the "furthest place of worship" is considered to be an allusion to Jerusalem. The signs he is shown are the seven heavens and the prophets he meets in them.

Many scholars think that two originally separate sources lie behind this tradition, one having to do with a journey Muhammad made from Mecca to Jerusalem, and another that had him experience a trip through the seven heavens. At a certain point in time, they were joined together, and perhaps 17:1 was influential in bringing about that process despite the fact that it does not mention Muhammad or his ascension.

Also commonly associated with the *mi'rāj* is 53:1-18, which speaks of a vision that Muhammad had and shares with 17:1 a reference to God's signs. "I swear by the star when it sets! Your companion [Muhammad] has not strayed, nor is he deceived, nor does he speak from his own desire. It [the Qur'an] is nothing but a revelation that is revealed. It was taught to him by one with great power and tremendous strength, who was standing on the highest part of the horizon. Then he descended and came near until he was no more than two bow-lengths away and revealed to His servant what He revealed. The heart did not falsify what he saw. Will you argue with him over what he observed? He saw him descend again near the lote tree that serves as a border, near the garden of rest, when the tree was covered in what covers it. He never looked away, nor did he gaze too intently, and he saw some of the greatest signs of his Lord." Here, too, there is nothing in the text that explicitly ties it to Muhammad's ascension, and there has been some debate about this among scholars. Some prefer to divide the passage in two, saying that only the second part of it describes that event while the first part is in reference to the beginning of the Qur'an's revelation to Muhammad.

*The association with Jerusalem in 17:1 is seen in the fact that the name of Al-Aqsa mosque, which is near the Dome of the Rock, is taken from the Arabic word for "furthest" in the verse. There is no reference to a winged beast in 17:1, but Islam has a long-standing tradition that such an animal, named Buraq, was Muhammad's mode of transportation during his night journey.*

The development of the account of Muhammad's night journey and ascension was undoubtedly a long and complex process, and the attempt to link it to the Qur'an says much about Muslim attitudes toward the text and its authority. Like no other source, it has the power to legitimate traditions that have no clear scriptural support and to resolve issues about which there is controversy and debate within the community. In this case, it is interesting to see how that influence can also sometimes work in the opposite direction. The extraqur'anic tradition about the Prophet's journey and what he saw helps to fill in the gaps in the Qur'an regarding what is found in the various levels of heaven.

## Light and Darkness
(Q 10:67; 39:5; 40:61; 6:1; 5:15; 42:52; 64:8; 5:46; 6:91; 14:5; 33:43; 2:257; 57:9; 67:11; 24:35-36)

The Qur'an considers God's creation of light and darkness to be one of the primary reasons why people should reject worship of other gods. "Praise be to God who created the heavens and the earth and made darkness and light; still, those who disbelieve in their Lord turn away" (6:1). It is in the alternation of day and night that people are most aware of the difference between light and dark, and the Qur'an reminds its readers that God is responsible for that daily change. Each portion of the day has its own purpose and reason, and all is part of the divine plan—daytime is for seeing, and nighttime is for resting (10:67; 39:5; 40:61).

In addition to their literal meanings, light and darkness are sometimes used metaphorically in the Qur'an. Light (nūr) can be used in reference to the guidance God provides through the Qur'an (5:15; 42:52; 64:8) or previous scriptures like the Torah and Gospel. "In their footsteps We sent Jesus, son of Mary, to confirm the Torah that had come before him. We gave him the Gospel as a guidance, light, and confirmation of the Torah that had come before him. It is a guide and instruction for the pious" (5:46; cf. 6:91). Light also sometimes describes the proper way to live and behave (14:5; 33:43).

Similarly, darkness (ẓulumāt) can be used to describe the opposite state of unbelief, as seen in 2:257: "God is the protector of believers, and He brings them out of darkness and into light. But the protectors of disbelievers are false gods who take them from light into darkness. They are the inhabitants of the fire who will remain there forever" (cf. 57:9; 67:11).

The Light Verse: "God is the light of heaven and earth. God's light is like a niche in which is a lamp. The lamp is inside a glass like a shining star with oil from a blessed olive tree from neither the east nor the west. The oil practically gives light even when it is not lit—light upon light. God guides to the light whomever He will. God gives such examples for people and knows everything" (24:35).

The most celebrated mention of light in the Qur'an is found in 24:35-36, in a chapter whose title is "The Light," which is also one of God's ninety-nine names. The "light verse," as it is known, is a remarkable composition that celebrates God as the light of creation that draws people to its glow and guidance. Rich in similes and metaphors, it is well-known among Muslims as a passage that offers a unique and memorable meditation on the divine nature. It is also very popular within the mystical tradition of Islam known as Sufism, whose advocates often make use of the image of light and darkness to explore the relationship between the individual and God.

## Sun, Moon, and Stars
(Q 7:54b; 13:2; 31:29; 35:13; 39:5)

Heavenly bodies are mentioned frequently in the Qur'an. As elements of creation, they all come under God's authority and are dependent upon their creator. "The sun, moon, and stars are subservient to His command. Do not creation and authority belong to Him? Blessed be God, Lord of the worlds" (7:54b; cf. 13:2; 31:29; 35:13; 39:5). The important position the sun, moon, and stars hold in the Qur'an's cosmology is seen in the fact that all three are the names of chapters in the text—91, 54, and 53 respectively, although the last one refers to a particular star.

FIGURE 12 *An astrolabe from the thirteenth century.*

### SUN
(Q 6:78-79; 18:17; 36:38; 21:33; 36:40; 75:9; 20:130)

The sun (*al-shams*) is mentioned thirty-three times in the Qur'an, and the text reflects the geocentric view of the universe that was typical of the prescientific world. Common human experience and observation by the naked eye suggested that the sun journeys across the sky throughout the course of the day, and the Qur'an gives evidence of this "fact." When

Abraham rejects worship of the sun, he does so because it is not fixed in the sky. "When he saw the sun rising he said, 'This is my Lord! This is the greatest.' But when it set he said, 'My people, I reject what you associate with God. I turn as an upright person toward Him who fashioned the heavens and the earth. I am not an idolater'" (6:78-79; cf. 18:17; 36:38). In the verses prior to these, Abraham refutes worship of the moon and stars for the same reason. Elsewhere in the Qur'an, it is noted that the sun and moon each has its own orbit (21:33; 36:40), but one of the signs of the end time will be that they will be brought together in a cosmic collision (75:9).

The five daily prayer times in Islam are based on the location of the sun in the sky. Because those locations needed to be determined precisely, Muslims played a central role in the rise and development of astronomy and related sciences. The astrolabe and other aids were invented by Muslims and later passed on to other peoples, who benefited from them for their own purposes. The five

> *The Muslim prayer times: dawn* (fajr), *noon* (zuhr), *afternoon* (`asr), *sunset* (maghrib), *and evening* (`ishā').

prayer times were not fixed until after Muhammad's lifetime, but already in the Qur'an we see that the sun's position should be consulted to guide Muslims regarding when they are to pray: "So be patient with what they are saying. Glorify and praise your Lord before the rising of the sun and its setting. Praise Him throughout the night and at the beginning and end of each day, and perhaps you will find favor" (20:130).

### MOON

(Q 22:18; 41:37; 2:189a; 2:185; 75:8; 54:1; 2:189)

Like the sun and the rest of creation, the moon (*al-qamar*) also submits to God's authority. In a striking image, 22:18 refers to the moon and all things prostrating before God, using the same Arabic root (*sajada*) that is commonly employed to describe what Muslims do during prayer. "Do you (Muhammad) not know that everything in the heavens and earth prostrates [*yasjudu*] before God—the sun, the moon, the stars, the mountains, the trees, and the animals? Many people do as well, but many others deserve the punishment they receive. The one disgraced by God will not be honored by another. God does what He wishes."

Texts like this are a reaction to the tendency among Arabs of the pre-Islamic period, along with most other cultures of antiquity, to divinize nature and associate deities with various parts of the created world. This verse highlights the error of that practice by showing nature in a position of submission and inferiority toward a supreme being greater than itself. Because of its theocentric worldview, which holds there is only one God, the Qur'an criticizes and condemns the divinization of the natural world as an example of *shirk*, or association: "Among his signs are the night, the day, the sun, and the moon. Do not bow down to the sun or the moon. Bow down to God who created them, if it is truly Him that you worship" (41:37).

The Islamic calendar is based on the lunar cycle, with each month beginning when the new moon is first sighted. There are references in the text to the moon's being a source of light, but the Qur'an acknowledges that the moon's primary role is to assist in measuring time. "They ask you (Muhammad) about the crescent moons. Say, 'They mark the times appointed for people and for the pilgrimage'" (2:189a). The month of pilgrimage is the twelfth one in the Islamic calendar, and its name is derived from the annual ritual.

> The only month mentioned by name in the Qur'an is Ramadan, the ninth of the year, in which Muslims fast during daylight hours (2:185).

There is a single reference to a lunar eclipse in the Qur'an, listed among the signs that will indicate the end of the world (75:8). It comes just before the reference to the sun and moon being "brought together" that was mentioned above, a verse that might be describing either a lunar eclipse or a physical joining of the sun and moon, perhaps in a violent collision.

Another cosmological sign is described in chapter 54, titled "The Moon," which begins, "The hour approaches, and the moon is split in two." Commentators disagree over whether this verse is recounting something that has already happened or an event that will accompany the end times. Some believe the verse is referring to the tensions among the Quraysh, the dominant tribe of Mecca, when Muhammad began to preach his monotheistic message. The moon was the symbol of the Quraysh, and its rending in the verse might represent the division that resulted within the tribe when some chose to follow Muhammad and embrace Islam while others refused to do so.

The crescent moon is universally recognized as a symbol of Islam, perhaps its most distinctive icon. But it is found only one time (in its plural form) in the Qur'an, in 2:189, a passage cited above that discusses the moon's role in measuring time. In pre-Islamic poetry, the moon, especially in its crescent form, was frequently mentioned and celebrated. Within the first few decades of Islam, it was used as a symbol of the faith, and its continued association with it is seen in the fact that it appears on the flags of many Muslim countries today, usually with the star.

STARS

(Q 53:49; 15:16; 25:61; 85:1; 6:97; 7:54; 16:12, 22; 22:18; 52:49; 53:1; 55:6)

The Arabs of antiquity had names for the planets and for hundreds of stars, but only one star is identified by name in the Qur'an. In reference to God, it is said in 53:49 that "He is the Lord of al-shi'rā." This is the name for Sirius, the brightest star in the sky and part of the constellation Canis Major. That star was worshiped by many Arabs in the pre-Islamic era, and this verse continues the familiar pattern of challenging such practices by identifying God as the Lord of the star many took to be divine.

No constellation is named specifically in the Qur'an, but the text mentions them in a number of places. Here, too, they are placed in a position of inferiority in relationship to God, their creator, upon whom they are dependent for their existence. "We have set constellations up in the sky and made it beautiful for all to see" (15:16; cf. 25:61; 85:1). The Arabic term for constellations is burūj, which is the name of chapter 85 in the Qur'an. During Muhammad's lifetime, the Arabs were aware of some of the constellations, but it was only after they came in contact with Greek astronomy centuries later that they learned of the existence of all twelve signs of the zodiac, which can be observed with the naked eye.

The most commonly used Arabic word in the Qur'an for "star" is najm (pl. nujūm), which is found thirteen times. As with passages that discuss the sun and moon, the majority of those occurrences are in creation texts that highlight God's role in bringing the stars into existence. "It is He who made the stars, so that they can guide you when the land and the sea are dark. We have made the signs clear for those who know" (6:97; cf. 7:54; 16:12, 22; 22:18; 52:49; 53:1; 55:6). This verse recognizes the utilitarian value of stars in that they can provide light for humans, but once again the key point is found in the first part of the verse, which identifies the divine source that brought the stars into existence.

OATHS

(Q 91:1-8; 53:1; 74:32-4; 84:16-18; 85:1; 86:1; 89:1-4; 92:1-3; 93:1-2; 52:1-6; 51:1-4; 77:1-6; 95:1-2; 95:3; 100:1-5)

A final aspect to consider is how heavenly bodies function in oaths in the Qur'an. An oath is a solemn statement that normally entails invoking God's name or that of some object, person, or place in order to add force to what one is saying. The Qur'an has many such statements, particularly within its earliest chapters, and a number of them invoke the sun, moon, and stars. Calling upon objects other than God for such a purpose might seem strange, especially since the Qur'an consistently affirms God's authority over all creation. But such passages probably reflect the context out of which the text emerged and to which it initially responded. Swearing by the created world was a common practice among Arabs of the pre-Islamic period, and some scholars see the presence of oaths in the Qur'an as an adaptation of contemporary Arab forms of expression.

The opening of chapter 91 contains a remarkable string of seven such oaths in a litany identifying many of the elements of the created world. "By the sun in its brightness, and by the moon as it follows it. By the day as it manifests the sun, and by the night as it hides it. By the sky as it is built, and by the earth as it is spread out. By the soul and its fashioning, as He placed into it its wickedness and its piety!" (91:1-8; cf. 53:1; 74:32-34; 84:16-18; 85:1; 86:1; 89:1-4; 92:1-3; 93:1-2). A similar passage is found in 52:1-6, which contains an eclectic list of things that can be invoked in an oath, including Mount Sinai, the written text, a house (perhaps the Ka`ba, in Mecca), the sky, and the ocean. Among the other things associated with oaths in the Qur'an are the wind (51:1-4; 77:1-6), fig and olive (95:1-2), Mecca (95:3), and horses (100:1-5).

### Water
(Q 4:102; 7:84; 25:40; 26:173; 27:58; 56:68; 6:99; 2:22, 164; 7:57; 8:11; 15:22; 20:53; 22:63; 27:60; 41:39; 78:14; 26:134; 36:34; 39:21; 79:31; 16:15; 13:13; 14:32; 27:61; 10:22; 17:66-67; 31:31; 6:59; 16:14; 35:12; 55:22; 25:53; 27:61; 35:12; 18:109; 31:27; 11:25-49; 11:40; 11:44; 2:49-50; 26:63; 44:24; 7:134-40; 10:90-92; 26:146-59; 25:49; 54:23-32; 91:11-15)

Water is mentioned in a variety of different contexts in the Qur'an. The Arabic word for water is mā', and it is found more than sixty times in the text. In many of those passages, it is used in reference to rain, described as "water from the heavens/sky." The Arabic word commonly used today for rain (maṭar) appears only seven times in the Qur'an, usually in descriptions of punishment from God upon evildoers (4:102; 7:84; 25:40; 26:173[2x]; 27:58[2x]). When rain as "water from the sky" is mentioned, it normally has the positive sense of a sign meant to remind people of God's care for and protection of humanity. "Have you considered the water that you drink? Did you send it down from the clouds, or did We? If We had wished, We could have made it salty. Why are you not thankful?" (56:68).

The Qur'an calls attention to the fact that water is necessary for the survival of all living things, not just human beings. Rainfall is the first of a series of events that ultimately lead to the fruit and other vegetation that are pleasing to the eye and stomach, and God is involved in each step of the process. "It is He who sends down water from the sky, and with it We produce all kinds of vegetation. We bring forth greenery from which we then bring forth piled-up grains. From the palm trees are clusters of dates hanging low. There are gardens of grapes, olives, and pomegranates, similar yet different. Watch as the fruits form and ripen. In this are signs for those who believe" (6:99). The last sentence points out that, in addition to the physical benefits it provides, rain is essential for one's spiritual well-being because it is a reminder of humanity's dependence upon God. This is reinforced throughout the Qur'an because most of the verses that speak of rain identify its divine origin (cf. 2:22, 164; 7:57; 8:11; 15:22; 20:53; 22:63; 27:60; 41:39; 78:14). In the same way, the few texts that refer to springs and similar water sources all consider them to be gifts from God (26:134; 36:34; 39:21; 79:31).

Large bodies of water are prominent in the Qur'an, and passages that mention them often treat some of the same themes. God is the one responsible for rivers, which serve as a form of transportation for those who navigate upon them. "He placed firm mountains on the earth so it does not shake under you, and rivers and paths so that you may make your way" (16:15; cf. 13:13; 14:32; 27:61).

A similar thing is said about the sea (10:22; 17:66-67; 31:31), and some of these texts speak of it as a dangerous place where storms can threaten ship and crew. God's superiority over humanity and nature is manifested in God's ability to see into the ocean's depths and penetrate other mysteries of the natural world. "He has keys to what is hidden—no one knows them but Him. He knows everything on the land and in the sea. A leaf does not fall without His knowledge, and there is no grain in the recesses of the earth, fresh or withered, that is not found in a clear record" (6:59).

Other passages speak of the ocean as a resource whose products humans may take advantage of as long as they do so responsibly by acknowledging God as the one who makes this possible. One text alludes to extracting pearls and other precious objects from the sea. "He subjects the sea to you so that you may eat from it and bring out of it jewelry to wear. You see ships cutting through it so that you may seek His bounty and give thanks" (16:14; cf. 35:12; 55:22). In several places, the Qur'an calls attention to the difference between salt water and fresh water, and acknowledges God as the creator of both and the one who keeps them separate (25:53; 27:61; 35:12).

The Qur'an contains an interesting use of the word "sea" (bahr) to describe the inexhaustibility of God's word. "Say (Muhammad), 'If the ocean were ink for [writing] the words of my Lord, it would be used up before my Lord's words were exhausted'—even if We brought forth another ocean like it" (18:109; cf. 31:27). This verse conveys the ancient understanding of the vastness of the ocean and, indirectly, has a bearing on the topic under discussion. The idea of the ocean being used to do

God's bidding, but not being up to the task, hints at the gulf between creation and creator that is explicitly stated elsewhere in the Qur'an.

Divine authority over creation is clearly seen in those passages that describe God's manipulation of the forces of nature, especially water. Two examples of this are the Qur'an's account of the flood during Noah's time and the scene depicting the Israelites' exodus from Egypt as they fled Pharaoh's troops.

The story of the flood is told in 11:25-49. It is briefer than the three-chapter account in Genesis, and it contains some elements not found in the biblical book, but the general outline of the story is the same in the two texts. They both agree that God has supreme power over nature, and this is seen in the Qur'an in two ways. To initiate the flood, God simply utters a command, and water begins flowing out from the earth (11:40). A literal reading of the Arabic describes an oven or furnace erupting or boiling over, but the intent of this unusual phrase is clear—as soon as God speaks, nature immediately obeys, and water spreads over the earth's surface. Similarly, God directs an order at creation to bring the flood to an end. "It was said, 'Earth, swallow up your water, and sky, hold back [your rain].' Then the water subsided, and the command was fulfilled" (11:44). Both verses contain the word "command," highlighting God's superiority over the created world.

The exodus story, like the flood, is mentioned in several different places in the Qur'an. These texts lack the narrative detail and dramatic tension of the account in the Bible, but they still underscore God's involvement in rescuing the Israelites from their enemies by controlling the forces of nature. "Remember when We rescued you from Pharaoh's people, who subjected you to great hardship, killing your sons and letting your women live. That was a great trial from your

*The entirety of chapter 71, which carries the title "Noah," is taken up with a description of his life and prophetic career. Other passages that treat the exodus story can be seen in 7:134-40 and 10:90-92.*

Lord. And (remember) when We parted the sea for you, rescuing you and drowning Pharaoh's people as you watched" (2:49-50; cf. 26:63; 44:24). Passages like these offer visible demonstrations of the "signs" the Qur'an repeatedly says that water and other elements of creation should be for humanity.

Another passage that speaks of water conveys a message that is very much in line with modern views on the environment and would be heartily endorsed by those who insist humanity must have a proper respect for the rest of creation. It calls for fair distribution of water among all, humans and animals alike.

It is set in the context of a story about the unfaithful people of Thamūd, an ancient Arab tribe. They are punished when they fail to heed the message of their prophet, Ṣāliḥ, and they ignore the obligation to care for an animal placed in their charge. It begins with Ṣāliḥ addressing the people of Thamūd, who have a distorted understanding of the environment and their place within it: "'Do you think you will be left secure in what you have here—with gardens, springs, fields, palm trees heavy with fruit—while skillfully carving your houses from the mountainside? Fear God and obey me. Do not obey the wasteful ones who spread corruption in the land instead of improving it.' They said, 'You are bewitched! You are nothing but a human being like us. Give us a sign, if what you are saying is the truth.' He said, 'This she-camel should have her turn to drink at a specified time and so should you. Do not mistreat her, or you will receive a great punishment.' But they hamstrung her, and then regretted what they had done. The punishment came upon them—there is truly a sign in this, though most of them do not believe. Indeed, only Your Lord alone is the mighty One, the merciful One" (26:146-59; cf. 11:61-8).

*Besides Ṣāliḥ, two additional otherwise-unknown Arabian prophets from the pre-Islamic era are mentioned in the Qur'an. Hūd was sent to the people of ʿĀd (7:65-72; 26:123-40), and Shuʿaib to the people of Madyan (11:84-95; 26:176-91). In all three cases, the prophet's message to embrace monotheism went unheeded and the people were punished. In this way, the texts reflect the common prophetic paradigm in the Qur'an that was experienced by Muhammad.*

## Animals

(Q 16:68-69; 29:41-43; 24:45; 35:27-28; 40:79-80; 6:142; 16:5-8; 23:21-22; 3:14; 2:57, 172; 7:160; 23:51; 16:80; 5:2, 95; 5:96; 16:14; 137:139-48; 21:87-88; 37:139-48; 11:6; 11:56; 36:71-73; 6:37-38; 38:17b-19; 34:10; 24:41; 22:18; 16:48-50; 27:16-28; 3:48-49; 5:110)

Six chapters in the Qur'an have titles associated with animals: The Cow (2); Livestock (6); The Bee (16); The Ant (27); The Spider (29); and The Elephant (105). The titles of chapters 79 and 100 might be references to horses, but their precise meanings are ambiguous. In addition, animals are mentioned fairly frequently in the text, with more than two hundred passages making reference to one or more types of creatures, including birds, fish, reptiles, and insects.

Despite their fairly strong presence in the text, however, the Qur'an does not contain very much detailed information about the animals it mentions. The two most common Arabic words in the text for animals

FIGURE 13 *Depiction of running animals.*

are 'an'ām (sing. *na'am*), which is used thirty-three times to describe cattle or livestock, and *dābba*, which is found eighteen times and can refer to any nonhuman living creature. These are both general terms that include more than one kind of animal, and they and other zoological vocabulary in the Qur'an tend to remain on that level of generality by rarely discussing things like specific forms of animal behavior.

Exceptions to this are seen with two of the six animals mentioned above that serve as chapter titles. Some of the bee's traits and habits are discussed in 16:68-69: "And your Lord instructed the bee, saying, 'Build your hives in mountains, trees, and what people build. Then eat every kind of fruit and humbly follow the ways of your Lord.' From within them comes a drink of different colors that heals people. That is truly a sign for those who think." Following the pattern that has been seen with other elements of the created world, the bee is a sign for humans. It follows God's instructions, and the result is honey, which benefits people. An interesting aspect of this passage is that the verb (*awḥa*) that describes God's speaking

FIGURE 14 *Depiction of rabbits, snakes, and turtles.*

to the bee is used elsewhere in the Qur'an in reference to the revelation God gives to humanity. In more than seventy occurrences of the verb in the Qur'an, this is one of only a handful that does not refer to revelation directed toward humanity, and it is the only one in which the recipient of the message is not a human or an angelic being.

The other animal whose habits are described in uncharacteristic detail is the spider, but here the example is a negative one. The spider's capacity to weave a web is compared to unbelievers who depend upon something other than God to sustain them. In both cases, the result is a flimsy structure that lacks strength and is easily destroyed. Here, too, the spider's actions are a sign for people, but in this case it is a reminder of what not to do: "People who take protectors other than God are like the spider making itself a house. The spider's is the flimsiest of all houses, if only they knew. God knows what things they call upon beside Him—He is the mighty One, the wise One. These are the comparisons We make for people, but only those who know understand them" (29:41-43).

The clearest distinction the Qur'an makes among land animals is based on their mode of locomotion—it distinguishes among those that crawl on their bellies, those that move on two legs, and those that get around on four legs (24:45). The colorful array of shades and tones found among the animals is further evidence of the diversity that God has introduced into the world. "Do you (Muhammad) not see how God sends water down from the sky and that We bring forth with it fruits of varied colors? In the mountains there are streaks of white and red in various colors, while others are jet black. There are also various colors among humans, wild animals, and livestock. It is only the knowledgeable ones among His servants who fear God. Truly, God is mighty and forgiving" (35:27-28).

According to the Qur'an, livestock and other animals serve a variety of functions for people, including providing warmth and food, carrying loads, and being a form of transportation: "God has made livestock for you, some for you to ride upon and some for you to eat. They provide other benefits for you as well—with them you can fulfill any need you have in your hearts, and, like ships, they carry you." (40:79-80; cf. 6:142; 16:5-8; 23:21-22). People may take advantage of such benefits, but they should not become so focused on animals and other things in their day-to-day lives that they lose sight of their transitory and temporary nature. "The love of attractive things is hard to resist. Women, children, heaps of great fortunes of gold and silver, well-marked horses, cattle, and farmland—all these may be the pleasures of this life, but with God is the best final abode" (3:14).

People are permitted to eat animals, provided they consume only what is lawful, a category sometimes referred to as "good things" (2:57, 172; 7:160; 23:51). The Qur'an contains some basic dietary regulations, but it does not present a comprehensive system that covers every aspect of what is permissible to eat and how animals are to be slaughtered. Details on such matters were eventually worked out in Islamic law through study of the ḥadith and other extra-qur'anic sources. Animal products like furs and skins can be used by people (16:80), and hunting is permitted in the Qur'an except when one is in a state of consecration as, for instance, during the pilgrimage ritual (5:2, 95). Fishing, on the other hand, is permissible at any time (5:96; 16:14). There are only a few references to aquatic creatures in the Qur'an, with one of the most well-known being its account of Jonah's being swallowed by a great fish (137:139-48; cf. 21:87-88).

*Jonah is mentioned by name five times in the Qur'an, and the account of his life there is similar to the one found in the Bible. Chapter 10 of the Qur'an bears his name, and the fullest version of Jonah's story is found in 37:139-48.*

As with the other elements of creation, God both cares for and has supreme power over all animals: "There is not a creature on earth whose sustenance does not depend on God. He knows where it resides and where it will end up—it is all found in a clear record" (11:6; cf. 11:56). They, like everything else that exists, are manifestations of God's presence and concern for all of creation.

For this reason, animals are referred to as "signs" in the Qur'an. According to the text, humans are literally surrounded by divine signs wherever they look, even in their encounters with the animal world. The purpose of these signs is to elicit a response—many of the texts that speak of animals as signs go on to remind people that they must be thankful. "Do they not see that, among the things

*According to the Qur'an, King Solomon had the ability to communicate with animals. Conversations he had with birds and ants are mentioned in 27:16-28.*

*One of the miracles of Jesus found in the Qur'an describes how he made a bird-shaped form out of clay and breathed into it, making it a real bird (3:48-49; 5:110). This tradition has things in common with a similar one found in the* Infancy Gospel of Thomas, *an extracanonical Christian writing.*

Our hands made, We created the livestock they own? We made them obedient so that some can be used for riding, and others for food, some for another advantage, or for drink. Are they not thankful?" (36:71-73).

One text that speaks of animals as signs is particularly striking because it states that animals are on an equal footing with humans since they both share something basic that has been instilled in them by God. "They say, 'Has no sign been sent down to him [Muhammad] from his Lord?' Say, 'God is certainly capable of sending down a sign,' though most of them do not know. All creatures that live on the earth and fly with their wings are, like you, communities. We have left out nothing from the book—then they will be gathered to their Lord" (6:37-38).

According to this passage, animals are like humans in that they form communities or groups that band them together. The Arabic term used here is *umma*, a word that has special significance in Islam because it refers to the worldwide community of Muslims. Something that people tend to miss—a sign they ignore—is that there is a communal dimension to the animal world that is analogous to what humanity experiences. All creatures, human and animal alike, are designed to live in communities until they die and return to the source of their existence. This neglected "sign" is an important component of the Qur'an's view of how humans should interact with other inhabitants of the natural environment.

In some texts, the animal community sets an example for the human *umma* on how to live in accordance with the divine will. The birds join with the mountains and King David to sing God's praises. "Remember Our servant David, a man of great power who always turned [to God]. We compelled the mountains to join him in singing praise at sunset and sunrise. The birds also gathered together and turned in praise" (38:17b-19; cf. 34:10). Another passage describes the flight of birds as a form of prayer that is known to God, as are all the unique ways every part of creation acknowledges its creator (24:41).

The Qur'an sometimes speaks of animals and the rest of creation submitting to God. In a verse discussed earlier in this chapter, a distinction is made between the nonhuman parts of creation, including animals, which all prostrate before God, and humans, not all of whom do so. "Do you (Muhammad) not know that everything in the heavens and earth prostrates before God—the sun, the moon, the stars, the mountains, the trees, and the animals? Many people do as well, but many others deserve the punishment they receive. The one disgraced by God will not be honored by another. God does what He wishes." (22:18; cf. 16:48-50). The underlying message is that humans can learn much from animals and other parts of creation about how to submit.

## Nature as Muslim

A key point that emerges from this overview of the created world as it is conceived in the Qur'an is that nature is semiotic. Everything that exists—heavens, earth, light, darkness, sun, moon, stars, water, animals—is a sign that points beyond itself. Furthermore, it all points in the same direction—toward God. Time and again, the Qur'an repeats the theocentric message that everything was created by God and is controlled by God. Most of nature accepts that situation and does not try to rebel or deny God's authority. Only humanity attempts to wrestle control from God and assert its independence. Nowhere in the Qur'an does it say nature disobeys God's will. That is humanity's doing, and for this reason people must read the signs of creation to learn what true submission is.

Its complete conformance to the divine will has led some scholars to suggest that nature is Muslim. They and others refer to Islam as the religion of nature because the act of submission that is central to the faith is something that nature does naturally. The passages in the Qur'an that speak of creation submitting to God, using words etymologically related to "Muslim" and "Islam," support this idea. Humans are capable of submitting to God's will, and when they do so they are Muslims. But nature can do only God's bidding and nothing else. In this way, it serves as an example for humanity to emulate and strive for.

## Angels and *Jinn*

The Qur'an's cosmology also includes other beings that, while not human, are capable of interacting with humanity. These beings are not part of the physical environment people inhabit as normally conceived, and so they are less relevant for this chapter. But they deserve some brief consideration because they are frequently mentioned in the Qur'an, and they continue to play an important role in Islam. The two main categories of these beings are angels and jinn.

### Angels
(Q 35:1; 6:30-34; 7:11; 15:29-30; 2:28-39; 7:10-25; 2:97-98; 66:4; 19:16-26; 6:9; 3:42-51; 32:11; 6:93; 13:23; 6:66; 43:77; 69:17; 89:22)

The Arabic term for an angel is *malak*, a word found thirteen times in the Qur'an. Most angels in the text remain unnamed, but some, like Gabriel and Michael, are identified by name. The primary distinction among them is the number of wings they possess. "Praise be to God, the

Creator of the heavens and earth, who made angels messengers with two, three, four [sets of] wings. He adds to creation as He wishes. God has power over everything" (35:1). This difference in the number of wings is often understood to be a reference to the various functions and responsibilities that angels have. The verse indicates that angels in the Qur'an, like their counterparts in the Bible, are primarily messengers. They often function this way in the text, but they also appear in a number of contexts in which their role as heralds is not to the fore.

The Qur'an teaches that angels were with God when humanity was first created. According to 6:30-34, the angels balk at God's plan to create humans because of the problems that will result, but God shows a special preference for humanity. After creating Adam, God tells him the names of things but does not share this information with the angels. God then asks for the names, and only Adam is able to recite them. When God then commands the angels to bow down before Adam, all but one do so, indicating humanity's superiority over the angels (cf. 7:11; 15:29-30).

*The Qur'an's most detailed accounts of the creation of humanity are found in 2:28-39 and 7:10-25.*

The messenger function of angels is found in a number of places in the Qur'an. The most prominent example is Gabriel, who is mentioned three times in the text and is responsible for communicating to Muhammad the revelation that constitutes the Qur'an. One passage, in which he is named twice, identifies him as the agent of revelation and acknowledges the high regard in which angels are held. "Say (Muhammad), 'Who is an enemy of Gabriel? By God's leave he brought it [the Qur'an] down to your heart verifying the previous books as a guide and good news for the faithful. Who is an enemy of God, His angels, His messengers, Gabriel, and Michael? God is truly an enemy of the unbelievers'" (2:97-98; cf. 66:4). This is the only explicit reference to Michael in the Qur'an, but both he and Gabriel are mentioned in other Islamic literature, where they sometimes play prominent roles in key events of Muhammad's life like his night journey to Jerusalem and trip through the seven heavens.

Another scene in which angels play a prominent role as messengers in the Qur'an is when Mary is told she is pregnant and will give birth to Jesus. This story is told in two different places, and the angelic role is slightly different in each. In 3:42-51, a group of angels appears to her to announce that she will bear a child, and they then go on to explain some of the things Jesus will teach and do after he is born. Just prior to this, the angels appear to Zechariah to inform him that he and his wife will also have a son—John, known as the Baptist in Christianity—despite their advanced age.

The story has a somewhat different form in chapter 19, where the angels are now a single figure—God's spirit in the form of a human being. He is never described as an angel, but he refers to himself as a "messenger" (*rasūl*). The message he delivers is similar to what Mary is told in chapter 3, and so most commentators understand him to be an angel like those found in the earlier chapter (19:16-26). Supporting this interpretation is a reference in 6:9 to angels appearing in human form.

> *Mary is the only woman mentioned by name in the entire Qur'an, and chapter 19 is named after her.*

A third context in which angels are found in the Qur'an is in references to death and the end time. There is an angel of death, who is responsible for delivering each person to God for judgment. "Say, 'The angel of death who is in charge of you will summon you, and then you will be returned to your Lord'" (32:11). Angels will taunt unbelievers, who are punished in the afterlife (6:93), and they will attend to those who are rewarded in paradise (13:23). They stand guard over hell (6:66), and the one who is primarily charged with that task is named Mālik (43:77). At the end time, eight angels will hold up God's throne (69:17), and row upon row of angelic beings will be present for the cataclysmic events that will occur then (89:22).

## Jinn

(Q 68:51; 15:6; 37:35-36; 44:14; 52:29; 68:2; 81:22; 6:10; 7:179; 15:27; 55:15; 51:56-58; 6:112, 128; 41:29; 32:13; 11:119; 46:29-31; 18:50a; 2:34; 7:11; 15:31-32; 17:61; 20:116; 38:73-74; 2:30-39; 7:11-25; 20:116-23; 55:33)

Another group of supernatural beings is the *jinn*, from which the English word *genie* comes. *Jinn* are mentioned approximately twenty-five times in the Qur'an, and belief in them among the Arabs predated Islam. They were invisible creatures, sometimes associated with animals or other parts of the natural world, who interacted with humans and influenced their lives in both positive and negative ways. Many of the references to them in the Qur'an are found in the phrase "*jinn* and humans" (or vice versa), showing the close connection between their two spheres of existence even though people are incapable of seeing the *jinn*.

It was believed that *jinn* could possess people and cause them to act erratically, and the word describing an insane or possessed person (*majnūn*) comes from the same Arabic root as *jinn*. Evidence of this belief is found in the Qur'an in a number of places when the people of Mecca believe Muhammad to be insane and possessed by *jinn* because of the message he is preaching: "The unbelievers nearly trip you up with their looks when they hear the Qur'an. They say, 'He is truly mad [*majnūn*]!'" (68:51; cf. 15:6; 37:35-36; 44:14; 52:29; 68:2; 81:22).

According to the Qur'an, the *jinn* were created by God from fire (6:10; 7:179; 15:27; 55:15), and their main purpose is to acknowledge their creator: "I created *jinn* and humanity only to worship Me. I do not want them to provide for Me or to feed Me. God is the One who provides, the Lord of power, the strong One" (51:56-58). This text reflects the Qur'an's tendency to put the *jinn* in a subordinate position to God in a way that limits the power and abilities they had in the pre-Islamic period. Nonetheless, they are capable of leading people to ruin (6:112, 128; 41:29), and will themselves experience eternal punishment. "If We had wished, We would have given every soul its proper guidance. But My words are true—I will surely fill Hell with *jinn* and people together" (32:13; cf. 11:119).

However, the *jinn* can also guide people in the proper way and remind them to follow God's will. The first fifteen verses of chapter 72, which has the title "The Jinn," urge Muhammad to tell his people about a group of *jinn* who hear the Qur'an and immediately express their belief in it. They go on to profess their faith in some of the basic tenets of Islam while acknowledging that not all of their fellow *jinn* have been as receptive to the message of the Qur'an and will consequently suffer in hell for their lack of faith.

This is clearly meant to be a warning to Muhammad's audience to not follow the way of the unbelieving *jinn*. A similar message is conveyed in an abbreviated form in 46:29-31: "We sent a group of *jinn* to you (Muhammad) to listen to the Qur'an. When they were there they said to one another, 'Be quiet!' When it was over they warned their fellow *jinn*. They said, 'Oh our people, we have been listening to a revelation sent down after Moses that validates what came before it and gives guidance to the truth and the straight path. Oh our people, respond to the one who summons you in God's name and believe in Him! He will forgive your sins and will protect you from a painful punishment.'"

The only one of the *jinn* named in the Qur'an is Iblīs, the one mentioned earlier who refused God's command to prostrate before Adam. "When We said to the angels, 'Bow down before Adam,' they all bowed down except Iblīs. He was one of the *jinn*, and he disobeyed his Lord's command" (18:50a). Iblīs is mentioned eleven times in the Qur'an, and his name derives from the Greek term describing the personification of evil (*diabolos*), from which the English "devil" comes. This is the only time he is identified as one of the *jinn*, as the other references to the scene with Adam simply identify him as an angel (2:34; 7:11; 15:31-32; 17:61; 20:116; 38:73-74).

This has led to much discussion by commentators as to whether Iblīs was an angel or one of the *jinn*, without any clear agreement on the matter. He eventually became associated with the figure of Satan in later Islamic thought. The qur'anic basis for this identification is found in those passages (2:30-39; 7:11-25; 20:116-23) describing human creation and the garden story that see a shift in the name of Adam's antagonist from Iblīs to Satan (*shayṭān*). Some have suggested that his name was changed as a result of his disobedience of God's command to bow down.

*According to tradition, Iblīs's name comes from an Arabic verb that means "he was made to be full of despair," a reference to his being punished by God.*

As already noted, in its presentation of the *jinn*, the Qur'an describes them in a way that is consistent with how it views all other elements of the created order. They are creatures who are completely dependent upon God for their existence, and they can do nothing but submit themselves to the divine will. In this way, the *jinn* reinforce the theocentric view of creation that permeates the entire Qur'an, and they are a sign of God's supreme power. "Oh company of *jinn* and humanity, if you are able to pass through all the regions of heaven and earth, then pass through. But you cannot pass through without [Our] authority" (55:33).

## Humanity's Place in Creation

(Q 18:37; 35:11; 40:67; 30:20; 3:59; 23:12; 6:2; 7:12, 61; 32:7; 38:71, 76; 55:14; 15:26; 28:33; 22:5; 23:12; 16:4; 36:77; 53:45-46; 76:2; 80:18-19; 24:45; 25:54; 77:20-22; 86:5-7; 24:43-44; 25:47-50; 26:7; 31:10; 18:7; 6:165; 11:7; 71:15-20; 16:12, 65-69, 79; 20:53-54; 25:61-62; 30:30; 30:41; 2:30; 6:165; 27:62; 35:39; 10:24)

The Qur'an's description of human creation has much in common with that found in Genesis 2 in the Bible—God formed Adam and Eve (who is unnamed in the Qur'an) from the earth. The material that is used to create them is identified in several different ways. In some texts, it is referred to as *turāb*, Arabic for "dust" or "soil": "Among His signs is that He created you from dust, and then you became humans who are scattered about" (30:20; cf. 3:59; 18:37; 35:11; 40:67). Elsewhere, humans are created from *ṭīn*, or clay: "We created humanity from a portion of clay" (23:12; cf. 6:2; 7:12, 61; 32:7; 38:71, 76). In still other texts, it is described as dry clay, or *ṣalṣal*: "He created humanity out of clay, like pottery" (55:14; cf. 15:26; 28:33). The imagery of the last verse is similar to Genesis 2:7, where the Hebrew verb used to describe Adam's creation can refer to the work of a potter.

FIGURE 15 *Adam and Eve.*

Some passages list a sequence of stages of growth that appear to describe the development of the fetus in the womb. "Oh humanity, if you are in doubt regarding the resurrection, [know that] We created you from dust, then a drop of fluid, then a clot, then a lump of flesh, both formed and formless, in order to make it clear to you. We cause what We wish to remain in the womb for a set period, then We bring you out as infants and you attain maturity" (22:5a; cf. 23:12ff). The "drop of fluid" mentioned here is a reference to semen, which is referred to in other passages in the Qur'an (16:4; 36:77; 53:45-46; 76:2; 80:18-19). Elsewhere, the creative material is simply referred to as "water" (*mā'*), which could be another way of referring to semen (24:45; 25:54; 77:20-2; 86:5-7).

All these passages agree that humanity comes from the earth and has an intimate relationship with the rest of creation. The Qur'an sometimes portrays this relationship as a dependent one. As already noted, humans depend on other parts of creation for light, warmth, sustenance, transportation, and other necessities of existence. But the Qur'an also encourages people to admire creation and to learn from it. Humans are dependent upon the rest of the world like a student is dependent upon his or her teacher.

Earth is full of many marvelous things that teach lessons to humanity (24:43-44; 25:47-50; 26:7; 31:10). Sometimes these lessons take the form of a test: "We have made everything on the earth an adornment so that We might test them to learn which of them do best" (18:7; cf. 6:165; 11:7). In these passages, creation is a test in the sense that it is a vehicle through which people can demonstrate that they have heard and understood the message of the Qur'an as it pertains to humanity's place in the larger scheme of things.

What do humans learn when they observe the world around them? Because the universe is full of signs that point to God, the main lesson they learn is that creation is theocentric. Wherever one looks, one should be reminded of God's presence and authority over everything that exists. What makes it possible for people to learn that lesson is the thing that sets us apart from all other living beings—our capacity to think and reason. The Qur'an urges us not to observe the world but also to study it, reflect on it, ponder it. Such reflection will inevitably lead us back to God as the source and creator. "Have you not seen how God created the seven levels of heaven, and made the moon a light within them and the sun a lamp? God made you grow forth from the earth like a plant—He will return you to it and then bring you out again. God has made the earth wide so that you may walk along broad spacious paths" (71:15-20; 16:12, 65-69, 79; 20:53-54; 25:61-62).

The Qur'an teaches that humans must conform to the laws of nature; they cannot change or replace them. When they act as they should, they submit to God's will as revealed to them in the world they are a part of. A term used to describe this condition of submission is *fiṭra*, which is found only in 30:30 and refers to the original state of humanity. "Set your (Muhammad) face toward religion devoted to the pure faith, the natural state (*fiṭra*) with which God endowed humanity. God's creation cannot be changed. This is the true religion, but most people do not know it." The prohibition against altering creation is at the heart of the Qur'an's view of the natural environment. It is God's creation, not humanity's. To modify or somehow interfere with creation is to usurp God's role and to set oneself up in God's place. Consequently, those who abuse and harm the environment are guilty of the unforgivable sin of *shirk*, or associating themselves with God.

As noted at the outset, as an ancient text, the Qur'an does not refer to modern environmental concerns like pollution and global warming. Nonetheless, it acknowledges that humans must have a proper relationship with the environment, and it reminds them of the consequences if they fail to do so. Sometimes these passages have a modern ring to them even if, in keeping with its aims as a religious text, the Qur'an interprets such abuses in strictly theological terms. "Corruption has appeared on land and sea because of people's actions. He will have them taste some of the results of what they have done so that they might turn back" (30:41).

The Qur'an recognizes the enormous responsibility humans bear in relation to the rest of creation. In several places, they are described with terms that come from the Arabic root kh-l-f, which can refer to an act of succession, as when someone takes another's place. According to one of the creation accounts, humans were created for the purpose of being God's successors on earth (2:30). The

> The word "caliph" (khalīfa) comes from the Arabic root kh-l-f and is used as a title to designate one who succeeds the Prophet Muhammad as leader of the Muslim community.

exact nature of that role is not spelled out in the text, but the use of the Arabic word in other contexts indicates that the one who takes another's place should function with the objectives and desires of the predecessor in mind.

This means that humans, in their capacity as God's successors on earth, must treat the natural environment with the respect and dignity God intended it to have according to the Qur'an. In other words, they should be good stewards of the signs of God. "God made you successors [khalā'if] on the earth and has put some of you above others in rank to test you through what He has given you. Your Lord is quick to punish, but He is truly forgiving and merciful" (6:165; cf. 27:62; 35:39).

This chapter ends as it began, with a parable that succinctly summarizes the Qur'an's theocentric view of the natural environment. In 10:24, the Qur'an offers a simile for "the life of this world." It describes an earth in which all the elements of creation function in harmony and peace until the humans begin to think they are in charge and try to dominate things. It is a reminder that only God has authority over the works of creation, and it closes with a call for humanity to reflect on the world they are but a part of: "The life of this world is like this—the water We send down from the sky irrigates the earth's vegetation, from which humans and animals eat. Just when the earth is in its most colorful and beautiful state, its people think they have control over it. Then our command comes to pass, by night or by day, and We cut it down as if it had not been flourishing the day before. In this way We explain the signs for a people who reflect."

## key TERMS

mathal; shirk; tawḥīd; muḥīṭ; al-fātiḥa; waḥdat al-wujūd; mi'rāj; astrolabe; umma; jinn; Iblīs; shayṭān; fiṭra

## QUESTIONS for discussion

1. What are some of the strengths and weaknesses of the Qur'an's theocentric view of the natural world?

2. Can the Qur'an provide the framework for a coherent system of ecological ethics?

3. How is the Qur'an's understanding of the natural world similar to that found in the Bible or other sacred texts? How is it different?

4. What is your reaction to the idea that nature is Muslim?

## further READING

Jamal A. Badawi, "The Earth and Humanity: A Muslim View," in *Three Faiths—One God: A Jewish, Christian, Muslim Encounter* (Albany: SUNY Press, 1989), 87–98.

Saadia Khawar Khan Chishti, "*Fiṭra*: An Islamic Model for Humans and the Environment," in *Islam and Ecology: A Bestowed Trust*, ed. Richard C. Foltz, Frederick M. Denny, and Azizan Baharuddin (Cambridge: Center for the Study of World Religions, 2003), 67–82.

Mawil Izzi Dien, *The Environmental Dimensions of Islam* (Cambridge: Lutterworth, 2000).

Seyyed Hossein Nasr, "Islam, the Contemporary Islamic World, and the Environmental Crisis," in *Islam and Ecology: A Bestowed Trust*, ed. Richard C. Foltz, Frederick M. Denny, and Azizan Baharuddin (Cambridge: Center for the Study of World Religions, 2003), 85–105.

Ibrahim Özdemir, "Toward an Understanding of Environmental Ethics from a Qur'anic Perspective," in *Islam and Ecology: A Bestowed Trust*, ed. Richard C. Foltz, Frederick M. Denny, and Azizan Baharuddin (Cambridge: Center for the Study of World Religions, 2003), 3–37.

Lutfi Radwan, "The Environment from a Muslim Perspective," in *Abraham's Children: Jews, Christians and Muslims in Conversation*, ed. Norman Solomon, Richard Harries, and Tim Winter (London: T & T Clark, 2006), 272–83.

## 2
# Family Matters

Kinship relations are mentioned often in the Qur'an. Passages that present the stories of prior prophets and other figures of the past sometimes refer to spouses, parents, siblings, children, and other family members. The domestic life of the Prophet Muhammad is occasionally mentioned, especially the role of his wives within his family and the wider Muslim community. Elsewhere, various relationships are discussed in legal texts that control and regulate behavior in such areas as marriage, divorce, inheritance, adoption, and breastfeeding. These passages provide a glimpse into views regarding social relations and the family within early Islam that sometimes continue to be influential in the modern day.

## Kinship

(Q 106:1; 53:19-23; 49:10)

Muhammad was born into an environment in which tribal affiliation was central to one's personal identity and social status. The Quraysh tribe of which he was a member played a dominant role in the Hijaz region of the Arabian Peninsula, but it is mentioned by name only one time in the Qur'an (106:1). It is alluded to in other places, especially in verses that depict its members as resistant to the monotheistic message Muhammad was preaching. One passage criticizes the Quraysh for their belief that God has three daughters (53:19-23). It is commonly claimed that Islam revolutionized the social context of Arabia by making faith, rather than one's tribe, the focus of one's allegiance. There is some support in the Qur'an for this claim, but much attention is still paid in the text to those related by blood or marriage.

Conclusions about life in ancient Arabia are sometimes drawn from study of modern societies that are organized along tribal lines. Any such method that attempts to draw parallels between groups of people living many centuries apart is highly problematic. In recent times, ethnographers and anthropologists have pointed out the flaws in this type of approach, and they urge caution when comparing modern societies with ancient ones. This is useful advice to keep in mind when trying to make sense of qur'anic teachings in light of the modern world.

Many terms in the Qur'an convey various degrees of relationship among people. Some of these are general, including *nasab* ("lineage"), *qurbā* ("affinity"), *'ashīra* ("clan"), *arḥām* ("kindred"), *ḥamīm* ("close relative"), and *ṣihr* ("in-law"). Others are more specific in that they define the relationship more precisely, like *ab* ("father"), *umm* ("mother"), *akh* ("brother"), *ukht* ("sister"), *ibn* ("son"), *ibna* ("daughter"), *zawj* ("husband"), and *zawja* ("wife"). In keeping with the shift mentioned above, on occasion some of these terms are used in a less literal way in the Qur'an to describe people who are joined not by consanguinity or marriage but by faith. For example, the term "brothers" is sometimes used to refer to fellow Muslims. "The believers are brothers. Make peace with your brothers and be mindful of God, and you will be shown mercy" (49:10).

Islam, like other religions, is often associated with a patriarchal view of human relations that tends to be centered on and to privilege the male experience and perspective. This can be seen in many sections of the Qur'an, suggesting that the text took shape within and responded to a context in which males had much control and influence. How the Qur'an understands gender difference is a topic that is treated in detail in the next chapter, but for now it is important to note that a significant portion of the society the Qur'an first addressed had just recently become a more patriarchal one.

The evidence suggests that, prior to the time of Muhammad and into the early days of Islam, the culture of many Arabian tribes was matriarchal and matrilineal. This is seen in a number of ways. To identify but a few, family lineage was typically traced through the mother's side, married couples usually resided with or near the woman's family, and women had certain rights when it came to matters related to divorce and inheritance. These and similar practices were common features of the nomadic societies that were found throughout Arabia in the pre-Islamic period. But by Muhammad's lifetime, some of these groups had become more sedentary and had settled in towns and villages like Mecca, and this new environment contributed to the shift from a matriarchal framework to a predominantly patriarchal one. From that point on, a patrilineal and patrilocal system became the norm, and this is the social structure that is assumed throughout the pages of the Qur'an.

## Love

(Q 42:11; 2:187a; 60:3; 35:18; 3:14; 42:23; 59:9; 30:21; 12:8; 12:30; 60:1a; 3:119; 58:22; 5:82; 60:7; 9:24; 2:165; 3:31; 2:195; 3:134, 148; 5:13; 2:222; 9:108; 3:76; 9:4,7; 3:146; 3:159; 5:42; 49:9; 60:8; 11:90; 85:14; 19:96)

The most basic social unit mentioned in the Qur'an is the nuclear family, comprising a husband, his wife or wives, and their offspring. "The Creator of the heavens and the earth made mates for you from among yourselves—and did the same with animals—so that you might multiply. Nothing is like Him—the One who hears, the One who sees" (42:11). Family relations are to be marked by closeness and intimacy, and this is most clearly seen in the conjugal relationship between spouses. In a simile that is striking for its imagery and simplicity, one verse refers to a couple as each other's clothing as it gives permission to engage in sexual activity during the month of Ramadan: "During the night of the fast, sexual intercourse with your wives is permitted for you. They are like garments to you, and you are like garments to them" (2:187a). Despite the benefits such close relationships can afford, however, they will not save one because each person is responsible for his or her own actions. "Neither your relatives nor your children will be any help to you on resurrection day. He will judge among you. God sees everything you do" (60:3; cf. 35:18).

Words conveying ideas related to love derive primarily from two Arabic roots, w-d-d and ḥ-b-b, with the great majority of them coming from the latter root. Very few of these occurrences describe love between human beings, which is mentioned only a handful of times in the Qur'an. There are a few general references to loving those one is related to (3:14;

42:23) and fellow Muslims who have journeyed from Mecca to Medina (59:9), but these are quite rare.

The most explicit positive comment on human love is a statement that affection between spouses is something that has its origin in God and is therefore a natural part of the order of things: "Among His signs is that He created spouses from among yourselves that you might live with them in comfort. He placed love (*mawadda*) and mercy between you. These are truly signs for a people who reflect" (30:21).

The only two references to love between particular people are both found in the story of Joseph—which is the Qur'an's longest single narrative, constituting all of chapter 12—and in

FIGURE 16 *Islamic love.*

both cases love has a negative connotation because it leads to trouble for Joseph. Early in the story, his father Jacob's love for him and one of his brothers results in jealousy on the part of his other brothers, who sell him into Egypt (12:8). Later on, it is said that Joseph's Egyptian master's wife loves him, and when he does not respond in kind he is thrown in prison (12:30).

In several passages, Muslims are urged to love only other Muslims and not to love unbelievers, even if they are members of their own families. "Oh believers, do not take My enemies and yours as your allies, being their friends when they have denied the truth that has come to you and have driven out the Messenger and you because you believe in God, your Lord" (60:1a; cf. 3:119; 58:22). However, some texts adopt a more positive view of relations with non-Muslims, including one that says Christians are deserving of love. "Truly, the ones closest in affection [*mawadda*] toward believers are those who say, 'We are Christians.' That is because among them are priests and ascetics, and they are not boastful" (5:82b; cf. 60:7). Such passages are an important corrective for those who believe the

Qur'an has only negative things to say about non-Muslims, a topic discussed more fully in a later chapter.

In a few places, the Qur'an states that humans should love God. Their love of God should be greater than the love they have for any person or object, and if this is not the case they are not members of the community of believers: "Say (Muhammad), 'If your parents, children, siblings, spouses, families, the wealth you have accumulated, the business that you fear will falter, and the dwellings that please you are dearer to you than God and His Messenger and the struggle in His cause, then wait until God brings about His punishment.' God does not guide transgressors." (9:24; cf. 2:165).

The love people are to have for God is not one-way but is reciprocated by the deity, who loves them in return. "Say (Muhammad), 'If you love God, follow me. God will love you and forgive your sins—God is forgiving and merciful'" (3:31). In fact, God is the most common subject of the verb "to love" in the Qur'an. More than twenty of these texts have a negative connotation when they describe the people God does not love, including those who are aggressive, ungrateful, unbelievers, evildoers, proud, traitors, corrupt, transgressors, and wasteful.

But elsewhere, other types of people are the recipients of divine affection. Those loved by God in the Qur'an include those who do good (2:195; 3:134,148; 5:13), the repentant (2:222), the clean (2:222; 9:108), the God-fearing (3:76; 9:4, 7), the patient (3:146), those who trust (3:159), and the just (5:42; 49:9; 60:8). It is therefore not an exaggeration to say that God is the great lover in the Qur'an, and the many references to those who will receive and be denied divine love are a clear indication of its importance in the text. In two places, the deity is given the title "the lover" (al-wadūd), and this is one of the ninety-nine names Muslims use to pray to God (11:90; 85:14).

Like most other things, love is understood in the Qur'an in primarily theocentric terms. References to love between humans are relatively rare and tend to be general in nature. However, passages that discuss love in relation to God, as both subject and object, are more numerous and detailed. This emotion, which is at the core of family life, therefore serves to support the theological agenda of the Qur'an, which highlights God as love's source and perfect manifestation. "The merciful One will bestow love on those who believe and do good deeds" (19:96).

# Family Ties

(Q 4:23; 24:61; 33:50)

The various relationships that constitute a family are discussed throughout the Qur'an. As noted already, some terms describe the extended family in a general way, like *nasab* ("lineage"), `ashīra* ("clan"), and *ṣihr* ("in-law"). In a few places, more precise relationships within the extended family are identified through the use of words that refer to paternal and maternal uncles and aunts (4:23; 24:61; 33:50). But these latter terms are not very common in the Qur'an, and so the focus here will be on relationships within the immediate family, which are treated in more detail. Spouses, parents, children, and siblings are all mentioned, and the text at times describes how these various groupings are to relate among themselves.

## Parents

(Q 7:189; 4:1; 39:6; 2:223; 31:14; 46:15; 31:33; 28:7-13; 17:23-24; 2:215; 4:36;
6:151; 2:179-80; 29:8; 9:23; 31:15; 9:114; 19:41-48; 21:51-70; 37:83-98)

Nowhere in the Qur'an is it explicitly stated that producing offspring is the goal of marriage, but it is assumed in some texts that parenthood is a natural outcome of the married state. "He created all of you from one individual, and from it made its mate so that he might find comfort with her. When one lies with his wife, she conceives a light burden and goes about with it. Then when she becomes heavy with it, the two of them call upon God, their Lord, 'If You give us a healthy child we will be truly thankful'" (7:189; cf. 4:1; 39:6). Very little is said about the details of bearing and raising a child beyond a few references to the difficulties of pregnancy and matters related to weaning (2:233; 31:14; 46:15).

*An important difference between the Qur'an's and Bible's versions of the story of Moses' birth is the prominent role God plays in the Islamic tradition while being virtually absent from the biblical one. In several places in the Qur'an, God intervenes to allay the concern that Moses' mother feels, affecting the outcome of the story.*

The Qur'an understands the care and responsibility at the heart of the parent-child relationship to be reciprocal (31:33), but it has more to say about how children should treat their parents than vice versa. Nonetheless, there are some noteworthy examples of parental concern in the text. Jacob's affection for his son Joseph has already been mentioned. Similarly, Moses' mother is described as anxious and worried when she is forced to adopt extreme measures in an effort to save her infant son (28:7-13).

Children are urged to respect their parents and to be kind to them, just as their parents took care of them when they were young: "Your Lord has commanded that you worship only Him, and that you treat your parents kindly. If either or both of them reaches old age with you, do not speak harshly to them or rebuke them. Rather, speak to them with respect and treat them with humility and kindness. Say, 'My Lord, show them mercy, just as they took care of me when I was young'" (17:23-24; cf. 2:215; 4:36; 6:151). If a parent outlives a child, he or she is entitled to a portion of the estate of the deceased offspring (2:179-80).

The reference in the verse quoted above to worshiping only God relates to an important point about the parent-child relationship that the Qur'an addresses in a number of places. Loyalty and obedience are required of children only as long as their parents remain faithful to God. Should parents hold beliefs or engage in practices that are not in conformance with Islam, their children should reject them. "We have commanded people to be good to their parents. But if they try to get you to serve anything besides Me about which you have no knowledge, disobey them. All of you will return to Me, and I will inform you about what you have done" (29:8; cf. 9:23; 31:15). This is a good example of the shift in emphasis from tribal loyalty to religious affiliation that was mentioned earlier. Texts like this illustrate how faith, rather than genetics, became the dominant factor in determining where one's allegiance should be placed.

The choice to reject one's parents is dramatically illustrated in several passages that describe the relationship between Abraham and his father. Abraham is celebrated in the Qur'an as a *ḥanīf*, a morally upright person who was a true monotheist. His father did not share that faith, so Abraham made the difficult decision to break from his family and remain true to his beliefs. "Abraham asked forgiveness for his father only because he had made a promise to him. But when it became obvious that his father was an enemy of God, he disowned him. Abraham was sensitive and patient" (9:114). Elsewhere,

*The Qur'an sometimes shares themes or stories with Jewish and Christian writings not in the Bible. An example is the tradition about Abraham's rejection of his father's idolatry, which is not in Genesis but is found in Jewish extra-biblical sources.*

the Qur'an describes scenes in which Abraham unsuccessfully attempts to convince his father and his neighbors to put aside false worship (19:41-48; 21:51-70; 37:83-98). The latter two passages are particularly vivid because they underscore the unbelievers' inability to accept Abraham's message despite clear demonstrations of God's superiority over the idols they worship.

When these stories of tragic family breakups are read in context, they serve an important purpose. These Abraham passages, and others like them that show the earlier prophets being rejected and misunderstood by their contemporaries, legitimate and affirm Muhammad's prophetic status. Their experiences are not unlike those of the Prophet of Islam, who was rebuffed by many of the people of Mecca and, like Abraham, forced to flee in order to survive. To be a prophet sometimes means to be shunned by those closest to you, and the fact that Muhammad had to endure what his predecessors went through validates him as one of them. Such texts also respond to the situation of the early Islamic community, many of whom had to make a clean break from their family members and friends after they decided to become Muslims. They left behind what was comfortable and familiar to enter into uncharted waters, and the traditions about their monotheistic predecessors who did a similar thing were undoubtedly a source of comfort and strength.

### Children

(Q 42:49-50; 17:6; 26:132-33; 71:12; 25:74; 16:72; 16:58-59; 81:8-14; 6:140, 151; 17:31; 18:46; 64:15; 31:14; 46:15; 4:23; 2:233; 65:6; 28:7, 12; 24:31; 24:58-59; 6:152; 12:22; 17:34; 18:82; 22:5; 28:14; 40:67; 46:15; 33:5)

According to the Qur'an, whether or not one has offspring and what gender they are is a matter decided by God: "God has dominion over the heavens and the earth. He creates whatever He wills. He gives female offspring to whomever He wishes, and male offspring to whomever He wishes, or both male and female. He makes whoever He will be childless. He knows and is powerful" (42:49-50; cf. 17:6; 26:132-33; 71:12).

Children bring great joy to a person's life (25:74), but the text is insistent that one should never forget that God is the source of that happiness: "God has given you spouses from among yourselves, and through them He has given you children and grandchildren and has provided you with good things. Do they then believe in empty things and reject God's favor?" (16:72). This verse is a rare reference to grandchildren in the Qur'an, although some commentators prefer to translate the Arabic word (ḥafada) as "daughters" and give the meaning "sons" to the word translated here as "children."

> A patrilineal society traces the family history through the father's side. The opposite system, which establishes ancestry through the mother, is called matrilineal.

It has been claimed that the Qur'an expresses a clear preference for male offspring over female, but the evidence is more ambiguous than is sometimes acknowledged. The text undoubtedly reflects its patrilineal context in places, but it is sometimes difficult to determine the precise sense of the original Arabic. This is so because, like in other languages, the Arabic word for "son" (*ibn*), especially in its plural form, can sometimes refer to both sons and daughters. One therefore needs to keep in mind that a word that is translated into English as "sons" might actually be a more inclusive term that refers to both males and females, as in 16:72, mentioned above.

The fact that the Qur'an clearly outlaws female infanticide, which was practiced by pre-Islamic Arabs, indicates that it does not place the value of a male child's life above that of a female child. One text speaks of the anguish that accompanies the birth of a daughter for an unbeliever and the horrific option that is contemplated. "When one of them is given news of the birth of a girl, his face darkens and he is distressed. He avoids other people because of the bad news that has been announced to him. Will he keep it and endure humiliation or bury it in the dust? How evil is their judgment!" (16:58-59; cf. 81:8-14). Other texts prohibit infanticide with no reference to the child's gender, and they sometimes cite poverty as a motivation (6:140, 151; 17:31).

Despite the overwhelmingly positive understanding of children throughout it, the Qur'an nonetheless cautions that offspring can distract a person from what is most important in life. In this way, they are a temptation for parents to lose focus and not put their faith into practice. "Wealth and children are adornments of the life of this world, but enduring good works are better before God in terms of reward and hope" (18:46; cf. 64:15). Equating children with one's possessions, as this and similar verses do, reflects a mindset typical of antiquity, in which offspring were regarded as one's property.

The Qur'an understands weaning to be part of the life cycle (31:14; 46:15), and so breastfeeding is discussed in several different contexts. Wet nurses and milk sisters are included in a lengthy list of women that a man is forbidden to marry, suggesting that this creates a relationship between them that would be incestuous if they were to engage in sexual relations (4:23). The responsibilities of the father to provide for the mother and child during breastfeeding are spelled out in detail in a verse that is sensitive to the needs of both parents: "Mothers should suckle their children for two whole years, for those who wish to complete the term. The father must provide food and clothing in an acceptable manner. Neither one should be overburdened with more than they can bear—the mother should not suffer hardship because of her child, nor should the father suffer hardship because of his. The same responsibility falls on the father's heir. If they agree to wean the child, there is no fault in that. Nor is there any blame if you want to use a wet nurse, as long as the pay is acceptable. Fear God, and know that He sees what you do" (2:233; cf. 65:6). Nursing is mentioned twice in the scene discussed earlier that features Moses and his mother (28:7, 12).

The Qur'an refers to puberty in a few places. Twice in chapter 24 reference is made to a prepubescent child's unawareness of sexual matters, which allows him or her to be with an adult whose state of dress would preclude more mature individuals from being present. One includes children who have not yet reached puberty in a list of those before whom a woman may adopt a more relaxed standard of dress than what is normally stipulated in the Qur'an (24:31). The other makes a distinction between children who have reached puberty and those who have not, with the latter having access to parents who might be in a state of undress. "Oh believers, your slaves and any who have not yet reached puberty should ask your permission on three occasions—before the dawn prayer; when you take off your clothes in the noon heat; and after the evening prayer. These are the three times you are undressed. During other times, neither you nor they should be blamed if you interact with one another freely. In this way God makes clear the revelation for you—God knows and is wise. When your children attain puberty, they should ask for your permission like those before them did. In this way God makes clear His revelation for you—God knows and is wise" (24:58-59). For other texts that mention puberty, see 6:152; 12:22; 17:34; 18:82; 22:5; 28:14; 40:67; 46:15.

Adoption was practiced in pre-Islamic Arabia, but the Qur'an forbids it. It allows for the possibility of a child to be brought into another family and raised, but it does not permit legal adoption in which the child takes the name of the new family. "Name your adopted sons after their biological fathers—it is more just before God. If you do not know who their fathers are, consider them to be your brothers in faith and your wards. You will not be blamed if you are mistaken on the matter, but [you are responsible for] what your hearts intend. God is forgiving and merciful" (33:5). The passage goes on to say these children

> The Qur'an's ban on adoption illustrates the importance society in seventh-century Arabia placed on blood ties. Biological relationship brought with it privileges and status that were unavailable to those outside the family lineage.

may receive benefits from their new status, but they are still inferior to blood relations.

## Siblings

(Q 4:23; 24:31; 33:55; 58:22a; 9:23-24; 2:220; 6:87; 26:106; 7:65; 7:73, 85; 3:103; 9:11; 15:47; 33:5, 18; 49:10; 59:10; 17:26-27; 4:23; 24:31; 33:55; 4:12, 176; 24:61; 7:38; 43:48; 19:28; 7:148-54; 20:86-98; 5:17-32; 20:40; 28:11-12; 7:122; 10:75; 28:34-35; 7:148-57; 20:83-98; 4:163; 19:53)

When considering how terms that refer to siblings function in the Qur'an, a couple of things should be kept in mind. Like the word that describes a son, the term for a brother, especially in its plural form, can have a wider semantic sense to include sisters. Unless the context clearly requires that the text be interpreted as a reference to only males, the possibility that the term is being used in an inclusive way must be considered. Similarly, as noted previously, sibling terms are sometimes used metaphorically. In some cases, such metaphorical usage is readily apparent, but occasionally it is less clear or obvious.

The word "brother" (*akh*) is found more than eighty times in the Qur'an. Sometimes it is used in stories about sons of the same father. Some examples of this are considered below. In other passages, it still describes biological relationship but is used in a general way without reference to particular individuals. This is seen in legal texts that set guidelines on matters like who may marry whom and who may see whom in circumstances that permit only certain people to be present (4:23; 24:31; 33:55).

Elsewhere, the literal meaning of the word "brother" is found in passages that instruct Muslims to reject members of their own family if they do not follow the teachings of Islam. "You (Muhammad) will not find a people who believe in God and the Last Day loving those who oppose God and His Messenger, even though they may be their fathers, sons, brothers, or other relations. These are the ones in whose hearts He has inscribed faith, and whom He has fortified with a spirit from Him" (58:22a; cf. 9:23-24). This is an example of a verse in which the terms "fathers," "sons," and "brothers" have a wider sense to include mothers, daughters, and sisters.

Sometimes the term *akh* is found in texts that discuss members of the extended family or other social groups. It is used in reference to orphans (2:220), the relatives of the prophets (6:87), and the people to whom a prophet is sent (26:106). When discussing the careers of pre-Islamic Arabian prophets like Hūd, Ṣāliḥ, and Shuʿayb, it is used to refer to their relationship with the members of their respective tribes: "To the people of ʿĀd We sent their brother, Hud. He said, 'My people, worship God! You have no god other than Him. Will you not be mindful?'" (7:65; cf. 7:73, 85).

The most common metaphorical use of the term "brother" in the Qur'an is found in texts describing other Muslims with that familial term. This is an example of the tendency that was mentioned earlier to highlight faith connections and downplay biological ties. As already noted, family relations are not dismissed as irrelevant, especially in legal matters. Rather, sometimes the terms that denote them are expanded to incorporate individuals who normally would not be included within them.

According to 3:103, one of the benefits of being part of the Muslim community is that it can join together people who previously had been at odds, and do so to such a degree that it is as if they are members of the same family: "Hold on to God's rope all together, and do not become divided. Remember God's favor to you. You were enemies and then He joined your hearts together so that you became, by His grace, brothers. You were on the edge of a pit of fire, but He rescued you from it. This is how God makes His revelations clear to you so you might be guided" (cf. 9:11; 15:47; 33:5, 18; 49:10; 59:10).

*A particularly egregious example of non-Muslim bias against the Qur'an was seen in a widely circulated hoax about the text of 9:11 (cited on this page). Exploiting public fear after September 11, 2001, and seeking to justify American military action against Afghanistan and Iraq, it was alleged that the passage in 9:11 speaks of an "eagle cleansing the land of Allah." In fact, those words are not found in that verse or anywhere else in the Qur'an.*

There is an interesting metaphorical use of *akh* in 17:26-27, where it has a negative sense to describe those who use their resources irresponsibly. They are called brothers of Satan rather than brothers of their fellow Muslims. "Give to relatives their due, as well as to the poor and travelers. But do not squander your wealth frivolously— those who fritter away their money are the brothers of Satan, and Satan is ungrateful to his Lord."

The word "sister" (*ukht*) appears fourteen times in the Qur'an. The majority of those occurrences are found within legal texts, including those mentioned above that also refer to brothers and treat topics like marriage and who is permitted to be present in certain places (4:23[4x]; 24:31; 33:55). Other texts that mention sisters do so in the context of discussions of inheritance (4:12, 176) and eating in the homes of relatives and acquaintances (24:61).

There are several examples of metaphorical usage of the word "sister" in the Qur'an. One describes various crowds of people entering hell, with each group cursing its "sister" group (7:38). Another verse describes the signs that Moses worked in the presence of Pharaoh, and says that each sign was greater than its "sister" (43:48). Such examples of metaphor are usually missed in translation because *ukht* is normally not rendered "sister" is these contexts. One that is more easily identified is in 19:28, where Mary the mother of Jesus is called "sister of Aaron" by her people, a presumed reference to Moses' brother. This title has generated some debate among Muslim commentators throughout history, and on occasion Christians have cited it as evidence that the Qur'an contains errors since Mary lived long after Aaron and Moses. It is most commonly under-

*Moses' brother Aaron plays an important role in the Qur'an, where he is identified as a prophet. The story of the golden calf, in which he is a central figure, is recounted twice in the text (7:148-54; 20:86-98).*

stood to be a reference to Mary's being a descendant of Aaron, with whom she shares the same lineage, but some have suggested that Mary had an otherwise unknown biological brother named Aaron.

The most well-known sets of siblings in the Qur'an are also found in the Bible, and there are many similarities in how the two texts present their relationships. The story of the two sons of Adam and Eve—Cain and Abel in Genesis 4, but unnamed in the Qur'an—is found in 5:17-32. One kills the other, but in the Qur'an the murderer expresses a degree of remorse not found in his biblical counterpart.

As already mentioned, the story of Joseph and his brothers takes up virtually the entirety of chapter 12, and it is the longest single narrative in the Qur'an. As in Genesis 37–50, it is a tale full of family friction and mistaken identity. Joseph is sold into Egypt by his brothers, who convince their father that he has been killed by an animal, only to be reunited with them when they come to Egypt seeking food during a famine. An interesting difference in the Qur'an's version of the events is that God's role is much more visible and apparent than it is in the Bible.

Moses' brother Aaron and sister, who remains nameless, are the only set of male and female siblings depicted in the Qur'an. His sister plays a key role in Moses' return to his mother after he is found in the river by members of Pharaoh's household (20:40; 28:11-2). Aaron's character is well developed in the Qur'an, where he is mentioned by name twenty times and is Moses' helper (7:122; 10:75) and spokesman (28:34-35). The two brothers work together to try to convince Pharaoh to allow the Israelites to leave Egypt, and once they depart, Aaron is implicated in the golden calf episode, which is also mentioned in Exodus 32 (7:148-57; 20:83-98). Unlike in the Bible, Aaron enjoys status as a prophet in the Qur'an (4:163; 19:53).

## Widows and Orphans

(Q 2:234-35; 2:240; 4:12; 93:6; 2:215; 2:83, 177; 4:8, 36; 8:41; 76:8-9; 17:34; 6:152; 89:17; 93:9; 107:2; 4:10)

Two groups mentioned in the Qur'an because they have lost important members of their family are widows and orphans. All of the references to widows are found in the context of legal texts. The Qur'an does not use a particular term to refer to widows, describing them as "the wives you leave behind." In 2:234, the period of time a widow must wait before she can remarry after her husband's death is given as four months and ten days. This is longer than the three-month period of waiting that is required of a woman after a divorce. The text goes on to say that after the prescribed waiting period widows are free to do as they wish, indicating widowhood was not an impediment toward a woman being fully incorporated into the community. This is supported by the next verse, which is directed toward men who wish to marry widows and urges them to wait until the waiting period has expired before publicly acknowledging the marriage even if they have already spoken to others about it (2:235).

A widow's independence is affirmed in 2:240, which stipulates she is to be taken care of for a year with funds from her husband's estate and permitted to stay in the home they shared. The text does not indicate whether her housing is provided for only that year or if it is a permanent arrangement, but it does state that she is free to reject this provision and go off on her own at any time if she prefers to do so. Another text that refers to a widow's financial status is 4:12, an inheritance law stating she is entitled to one-quarter of her husband's property if he leaves no children and one-eighth if there are children.

*Yatīm*, the Arabic word for an orphan, is found twenty-three times in the Qur'an in both early and late texts. Muhammad himself was orphaned at a young age, and that status is alluded to in 93:6, when he is asked, "Did He not find you an orphan and give you shelter?" The protection that God extended to Muhammad the orphan is to be duplicated by members of the Muslim community in their relationships with children who have lost their parents. The orphan is the quintessential vulnerable person in the Qur'an, and many texts include orphans among other members of society who must be cared for by those in a position to help them. "They ask you (Muhammad) what they should give. Say, 'Whatever you give should be for parents, relatives, orphans, the poor, and travelers. God is aware of whatever good you do'" (2:215; cf. 2:83, 177; 4:8, 36; 8:41; 76:8-9).

*Muhammad's parents are not named in the Qur'an. According to Islamic tradition, his father, Abdullah, died soon after the Prophet was born in 570. His mother, Amina, passed away when he was six, and after spending two years with his paternal grandfather, he was raised by his uncle Abu Talib.*

The Qur'an contains explicit warnings against misappropriating the property of orphans and using it for one's own gain (17:34; 6:152), and it expressly forbids dishonoring and oppressing them (89:17; 93:9; 107:2).

Whoever does not heed the Qur'an's call to respect orphans will suffer harsh punishment. "Those who unjustly devour the property of orphans are consuming fire into their own bellies, and they will burn in a blazing fire" (4:10).

## Marriage

(Q 24:32; 57:27; 2:235, 237; 4:4, 24; 4:19; 4:25; 4:3; 4:129; 4:22-24a; 2:230; 5:5; 2:221; 24:26; 24:3)

The Qur'an holds up marriage as the norm for believers and encourages all people to enter the married state: "Marry off the single ones among you, as well as your male and female slaves who are virtuous. If they are poor, God will enrich them from His favor. God embraces all and knows all" (24:32). The text goes on to say that the unmarried should remain chaste, but this should be only a temporary situation until they are in a position to marry. The Qur'an does not endorse voluntary celibacy as an appropriate way of life, and 57:27 is sometimes interpreted as a rejection of monasticism that contains an implicit critique of celibacy.

The Arabic word for marriage is *nikāḥ*, and words related to it appear approximately twenty-five times in the Qur'an. It has a semantic association with sexual intercourse, indicating that the Qur'an understands marriage to be the proper context in which human sexuality is expressed. The most common terms for a husband and wife are *zawj* and *zawja*, respectively. They are best translated as "mate" and so convey a sense of equality and partnership. However, other words that refer to the husband, like *sayyid* ("lord," "chief") and *ba'l* ("master," "owner"), underscore the fact that in the Qur'an, marriage is a legal contract whereby the husband owns the wife.

That legal dimension is captured by the term `uqdat al-nikāḥ*, the "marriage knot," which expresses the contractual nature of the relationship (2:235, 237). Before the contract can be entered into, it is necessary that each party be of marriageable age, which in antiquity was considered to be puberty. A legal guardian, often a relative, functions as the intermediary between the man and the woman, acting as the woman's representative (2:237). A formal proposal of marriage is required, and it is usually directed to the legal guardian. In speaking about marriage to widows, the Qur'an states that it must be a public union that is out in the open. "There is no blame on your part whether you state that you wish to marry these women or you keep it to yourselves. God knows that you intend to marry them, but do not make a secret arrangement with them. Speak to them in the prescribed way and do not confirm the marriage until the appointed period has come to its end" (2:235).

The man is obligated to give the woman a bride-gift, or dowry, which then becomes her property that she is free to dispose of as she wishes: "Give women their bride-gift upon marriage, and if they are pleased to give some of it to you freely, you may accept it without feeling guilty" (4:4, 24). The Qur'an makes it very clear that the man is forbidden from trying to recover the gift he has given to the woman (4:19). The amount of the dowry is not stated in the Qur'an, but one text suggests that it is tied to the woman's status within society: "If one of you does not have the means to marry a believing chaste woman, he may marry a believing slave. God best knows your faith. You are part of one another, so marry them with the consent of their people and give them their proper bride-gifts. They are chaste women, not fornicators or lovers" (4:25a).

The Qur'an's endorsement of polygamy—more properly, polygyny—is well known and often commented upon by non-Muslims. The issue is addressed in 4:3: "If you fear that you will not treat orphans justly, then marry whichever women seem good to you, two, three, or four. If you fear that you cannot be fair, then marry one or what your right hands possess. That is more likely to keep you from going astray." The reference to

*Polygyny describes a situation in which a man has more than one wife at the same time. Its opposite, when a woman has more than one husband, is known as polyandry.*

"what your right hands possess" is usually understood to be a reference to slaves, with the verse giving a man permission to marry female servants he owns.

While the passage appears to permit marriage to up to four women at the same time, several things must be kept in mind. The text singles out a particular group of women when it focuses on orphans. Some commentators have argued that orphans remain the topic throughout the entire verse, so when the text gives permission for multiple marriages it is limiting the pool of potential wives to only that group. The reason orphans are identified specifically is because of their vulnerable status within society.

This text comes from the Medinan period, when a number of battles occurred, and it may be responding to a situation in which many Muslim men had lost their lives in battle. Their daughters and young wives were therefore alone and unprotected. The verse might therefore be telling the surviving men that if they cannot treat these women honorably as their guardians without marrying them, then they are allowed to marry them. Despite this more restricted way of understanding the verse, however, it is not uncommon to see translations widen it to include marriage to other women besides the wives and daughters of those killed in war.

It is also important to note that the second part of the verse contains a qualification on the permission to marry up to four women. If the man does not think he can be equitable and treat all his wives the same, he should marry only one. As many scholars have pointed out, this disclaimer needs to be read in light of what is stated later in the same chapter in 4:129: "You will not be able to treat your wives with equal justice, no matter how much you want to do so. Do not turn away from one of them, leaving her suspended. If you repair the situation and continue to be aware of God, He is forgiving and merciful." Many commentators believe that this categorical denial of the possibility of being impartial in a situation of multiple marriages is a virtual abrogation of the other verse and therefore nullifies the practice of polygyny. At the very least, 4:129 expresses a strong preference for monogamy and discourages marriage to more than one person.

It has already been observed that the Qur'an forbids marriage between certain people. The most detailed discussion of this issue is found in 4:22-24a, a lengthy passage that lists those with whom marriage is prohibited. "Do not marry women your fathers married, except for what has already occurred. It is an indecent thing that is hateful and leads to evil. You are forbidden to marry your mothers, daughters, sisters, paternal aunts, maternal aunts, the daughters of your brothers, daughters of your sisters, women who nursed you, women who were nursed by the same woman as you were, your wives' mothers, stepdaughters under your guardianship— those with whose mothers you have consummated marriage, if you have not consummated marriage with them you will not be blamed—wives of your biological sons, two sisters at the same time, except for what has already occurred—God is truly forgiving and merciful—or women who are already married, except for your slaves. God has decreed this for you."

The phrase, "except for what has already occurred," which is repeated twice, refers to those marriages that were entered into prior to this passage being revealed. There is no need for the spouses in such marriages to divorce. According to this listing, several types of relationships create an impediment to marriage, including being a blood relation, having a foster or milk relationship, affinity by marriage, and attempting to marry two sisters. The male perspective is privileged in this passage, and the Qur'an contains no legislation for women with the same detail and scope.

In addition to those listed here, a number of other categories of women are unmarriageable according to the Qur'an. It is illegal to marry a woman who would become a man's fifth wife. A man is not allowed to marry a woman he has divorced twice until she marries another man and obtains a divorce from him (2:230). Muslim men may marry women from among the People of the Book (5:5), a category referring primarily to Jews and Christians, but they are not to marry other non-Muslims (2:221). Muslim women, however, are not granted permission to marry men from the People of the Book. According to 24:3, Muslims are not to marry those who have committed adultery. "The adulterer may only marry an adulteress or an idolatress, and only an adulterer or an idolater may marry an adulteress. Such behavior is forbidden to believers." Later in the same chapter, it is stated that evil people should marry each other and good people should marry each other (24:26).

## Divorce

(Q 2:224-42; 4:19b; 4:35; 2:231; 2:228a; 2:226; 65:1; 33:49; 2:237; 65:6; 2:241; 65:1; 65:2; 2:229-30; 2:226-27; 24:6-9; 4:130-31; 4:24)

Divorce (ṭalāq) is permitted in the Qur'an, and four chapters (2, 33, 65, and 66) refer to it specifically. The most detailed discussion of divorce is found in 2:224-42. The first seven verses of chapter 65, which has the title "Divorce," also treat various legal dimensions of the dissolution of a marriage. Although it is permissible for a couple to end their marriage, the Qur'an sees it as a last resort after all attempts at saving the relationship have failed. There is a well-known ḥadīth that has the Prophet Muhammad say that, among the things permitted by God, the most detestable is divorce.

Even if a man no longer has affection for his wife, the Qur'an urges him not to mistreat her because marriage, in and of itself, is beneficial for people: "Live with them in an honorable way. If you loathe them, it could be that you dislike something in which God has put much good" (4:19b). Fairness extends to the act of divorce itself, which can be an expression of kindness under the proper circumstances: "When you divorce women and they have fulfilled the waiting period, then either keep them in a fair way or release them in a fair way. Do not keep them to harm them and be hostile. The one who does this harms himself" (2:231a). Prior to the decision to divorce formally, however, the Qur'an holds out hope that mediation will be able to keep the couple together. Family members are to play an important role in that process: "If you fear that a couple may break up, appoint an arbiter from his family and one from hers. Then, if the couple wants to reconcile, God will bring about agreement between them. God knows and is aware" (4:35).

Once a husband declares the *ṭalāq*, or his intention to divorce his wife, they have to wait three months, or menstrual cycles, to ensure the woman is not pregnant. This is the "set time" mentioned in 2:231 above. Another reason for this three-month delay in formalizing the divorce, in addition to establishing the paternity of any children, is that it functions as a cooling-off period during which the couple may be able to work out their differences and reconcile, which the Qur'an hopes is the outcome: "Divorced women are to wait for three monthly periods before remarrying, and they are not allowed to hide what God has created in their wombs if they really believe in God and the Last Day. Their husbands would do better to take them back during this time if they wish for a reconciliation" (2:228a; cf. 2:226; 65:1). If the marriage has not been consummated prior to the divorce, there is no waiting period since the possibility of pregnancy does not exist (33:49), and in such a case the woman is entitled to one-half of the agreed-upon bride-gift (2:237).

During the waiting period, the man must provide for the woman and allow her to stay in the house. Here, too, one reason for their close proximity is the hope that they will be able to repair the damage to their relationship and remain married, although the primary motive is the support and protection of the woman and her offspring: "House them [the wives you are divorcing], as your means allow, where you yourselves live. Do not harass them and make their situation difficult. If they are pregnant, maintain them until they give birth. If they are nursing compensate them for it, and encourage one another in a good

*Shi`a Islam permits mut`a, or temporary marriage, by which a man and woman legally agree to marry for a set period of time after which they are divorced. Some have supported the practice with 4:24, a section of which reads "If you wish to enjoy women, you are required to give them their bride-gift."*

way. If there are problems between you, another woman may nurse the child for him" (65:6; cf. 2:241; 65:1). A divorce is considered official when, after the waiting period, it is proclaimed in the presence of two witnesses (65:2).

The qur'anic legislation about divorce may seem one-sided in that it gives too much control to the man and leaves the woman in a relatively vulnerable situation. Some have responded to that seeming imbalance by claiming that the wedding gift the man presents to the woman gives her some leverage the man does not enjoy. Because the dowry becomes her property and she does not have to return it to him, a divorced man suffers a double loss—he no longer has his wife, and he has lost the gift he gave to her when they were married. According to this line of thinking, if a woman had the authority to initiate a divorce, she would then have control over her husband's property, including herself.

Nonetheless, there is a verse in the Qur'an that suggests that under certain conditions a woman may be able to release herself from an unhappy marriage by buying her way out of it: "Divorce may occur twice, and after that either keep her in a way that is acceptable or kindly let her go. It is not permissible that you take back something that you have given them [your wives] unless both parties fear that they cannot stay within the limits established by God. If you fear the two of them will not stay within the limits established by God, there is no blame on them if the woman gives something to release herself from the marriage. These are the limits established by God, so do not transgress them. Those who do so act unjustly" (2:229).

The mention at the beginning of this verse that divorce can occur twice is another way of giving the woman a measure of protection. A man cannot continue to divorce and reconcile with his wife as many times as he likes. After the second divorce, he may not remarry her until she marries another man and then divorces him (2:230).

The process outlined above is the usual way divorce is enacted according to the Qur'an, but other, less common methods exist to dissolve a marriage. One passage explains that if a man makes good on an oath not to have sexual relations with his wife, they are divorced after four months: "For those who vow that they will abstain from sexual relations with their wives there is a four-month waiting period. If they return to them, God is forgiving and merciful. But if they are determined to divorce, God hears and knows" (2:226-27). Once again, the text holds out the possibility that the marriage will survive.

Although divorce is not the stated outcome, it is the most logical result in another situation mentioned in the Qur'an in which a man accuses his wife of adultery. Normally, four witnesses must attest to an act of adultery for someone to be found guilty, but in the absence of witnesses, a man may swear four times that his wife was unfaithful to him. A fifth time he calls God's punishment upon himself if he is lying. If the woman goes through the same five steps to claim her innocence, she will not be punished (24:6-9). Since, as noted already, Muslims may not be married to adulterers, divorce is the only option if the woman does not protest her innocence. If she does, it is a probable result nonetheless since the accusation of adultery likely will irreparably harm the marriage.

Like every other aspect of human life discussed in the Qur'an, divorce comes under the authority of God, and details regarding how to initiate and carry out the dissolution of a marriage are spelled out in the text.

The most beneficial outcome for all concerned would be survival of the marriage, but if that is not possible, God continues to be present with the couple: "But if they separate, God will give to both out of His abundance. God embraces all, and is wise" (4:130).

Something missing in the Qur'an, which strikes the modern reader as unusual, is the lack of discussion regarding what constitute legitimate grounds for seeking a divorce. This absence is partly a result of the context in which the text took shape. Because a wife was considered to be a man's property, the issue of the reasons why the marriage contract could be nullified was less important than the man's right to dispense with his property as he saw fit to do. Consequently, his motivations, as well as the woman's perspective, are of little interest.

## Inheritance

(Q 8:75; 33:6; 89:19; 4:5; 4:19a; 4:7-8; 2:140; 5:106-8; 2:180-82; 4:33; 4:11-12; 4:176; 15:23; 3:180b; 19:40; 57:10; 19:77-80)

Rules regarding the transfer of property from one individual to another are mentioned in a number of places in the Qur'an. They are most commonly found in sections that treat the laws of inheritance, an aspect of Islam that is notoriously intricate and difficult to understand. Other passages treat the topic in a less complex way and function more as guidelines that should be followed in matters related to property transfer.

It is stated, for example, that blood relations have a greater claim to one's wealth than fellow believers who are not kin, although the latter may be the recipients of gifts (8:75; 33:6). Elsewhere, there is a warning about misusing one's inheritance (89:19), a command not to trust property to fools (4:5), and a prohibition against inheriting wives from deceased relatives (4:19a). Another text states that both men and women are entitled to receive inheritances: "Men will receive a portion of what their parents and close relatives leave, and women will receive a portion of what their parents and close relatives leave. Whether the amount is small or large, it is obligatory. If other relatives, orphans, or poor people are present at the division of the property, give them something and speak to them gently" (4:7-8).

A distinction should be made between texts that speak of bequests, whereby an individual designates that a particular portion of his or her wealth should be given to another person, and those that treat inheritance, in which one's relationship to the deceased determines the amount he or she receives as a beneficiary. Among the former group are a passage that stipulates that widows are to be provided with a year's worth of financial support and are not to be expelled from the home (2:140) and another that gives instructions on how to ensure that a bequest is properly witnessed to when one is near death (5:106-8).

The necessity to take care of one's family members through bequests is stressed in 2:180-82, which also spells out the community's obligation to honor the wishes of the deceased person: "When death is near to one of you who possesses wealth, it is required that he make a proper bequest to his parents and close relatives. This is an obligation incumbent upon all who are mindful of God. Whoever changes the bequest upon hearing it, the guilt of the change is only upon them. Truly, God hears and knows. But if someone fears that the testator has been unfair or done something wrong, and therefore corrects the situation among the parties, that person is not guilty of anything. Truly, God is forgiving and merciful."

Other passages specify the amount each heir is to receive, based on his or her relationship to the dead person. These verses are the basis for Islamic laws of inheritance, which the Prophet Muhammad referred to in a ḥadīth as containing one-half of all useful knowledge. "To each person We have established heirs for everything that parents and close relatives leave behind. Give their share to those to whom you have pledged your hand [in marriage]. Truly, God is a witness over all things" (4:33).

The three verses that lay out the Qur'an's teaching on inheritance are 4:11-12 and 4:176. This is a relatively small number of passages treating the topic, but they have generated much discussion among commentators because there are inconsistencies within them, and they do not always agree with what the verses that discuss bequests have to say. The second problem is often addressed by appealing to the Qur'an's chronology. According to the most widely accepted understanding of the reception of the text, the inheritance verses were received by Muhammad after the ones that mention bequests, so they abrogate the previous ones and provide the text's definitive teaching on property transfer.

The share that children and parents receive is the main topic of 4:11. The verse begins with the statement that a son should receive an amount equal to what two daughters receive. This has sometimes led to the formulation of a general principle that a brother will always receive twice as much as his sister(s), but the rules elsewhere in the inheritance verses reveal this not to be the case because, depending on the number of heirs and who they are, the amount the sister(s) receives could be more than one-half that of the brother. This is just one example of the mathematical anomalies that have made the inheritance laws in the Qur'an such a challenge to understand fully. Verse 12 discusses the share of the inheritance a spouse receives, and the amount varies depending on how many offspring, parents, and siblings the deceased had.

The laws in 4:176 complicate matters further because they do not agree with what is stated in 4:12. According to 4:176, siblings of someone who dies with no children or parents are entitled to anywhere between 50 and 100 percent of the deceased person's estate, but in 4:12 siblings in the same situation would receive only a maximum of one-third of the inheritance, and as little as one-sixth if there is only one brother or sister. Commentators have often addressed this inconsistency by making a distinction between the siblings in 4:12, who share the same mother but have different fathers, and those in 4:176, who are full siblings and are therefore entitled to a larger portion of the inheritance. However one attempts to resolve this issue, it is representative of the problems and challenges related to the Islamic inheritance system that are well documented throughout history in the various sources.

While they are different from the passages that have been discussed so far, it is worth noting that some texts speak of God as the recipient of an inheritance. In fact, "the Heir" (al-wārith) is one of the ninety-nine names by which God is known in Islam. According to 15:23, God inherits everything, an idea that is captured well in the references in the Qur'an to God's inheriting the heavens and earth: "God is the heir of the heavens and earth, and is aware of what you do" (3:180b; cf. 19:40; 57:10).

This is a natural extension of the belief central to the Qur'an that all of creation belongs to God and will return to God. This idea is vividly portrayed in a brief passage that describes a man who foolishly thinks he will pass on his possessions to the next generation, not realizing that he is part of the inheritance passed on to God: "Have you seen the one who does not believe Our revelation and says, 'I will certainly be given wealth and children'? Has he entered into the unknown or received a pledge from the merciful One? No! We will write down what he says and extend his punishment. We will inherit from him what he is speaking about, and he will come to Us all alone" (19:77-80).

## The Family of the Prophet Muhammad

(Q 33:6a; 33:28-34; 33:33b; 33:37; 33:50-52; 33:53b; 66:1-5)

The Qur'an does not have a great deal to say about Muhammad's family life, and most of the material that treats this topic has to do with his wives. Tradition claims that the Prophet had thirteen wives or concubines, but the extant lists do not agree on their names. All but three of them outlived him, and among those who died before him was Khadija, his first wife, who passed away a few years before the *hijra* to Medina. She was about fifteen years older than the twenty-five-year-old Muhammad when they married, and he was in her employ-ment at the time. She was his earli-est supporter and among the first to become a Muslim when he began to experience the revelations that became the Qur'an. Muhammad mar-ried no other women while Khadija was alive. Together they had four daughters and two or three sons, but none of the boys lived past child-hood. Among Muhammad's other wives, the most prominent is `Aisha, who died childless.

*`Aisha is often referred to as Muhammad's favorite wife. She was the daughter of Abu Bakr, who succeeded Muhammad as leader of the Muslim community at his death, and many ḥadīth are traced through Aisha.*

None of the Prophet's wives are mentioned by name in the Qur'an, although a number of texts address them directly. Almost all references to them are found in chapter 33, which comes from the Medinan period. Many passages indicate that these women enjoyed special status within early Islam, and they continue to be honored into the present day by the Muslim community with the title "mothers of the believers." That des-ignation is based on what is said about them in 33:6a, which is the first mention of Muhammad's wives in the chapter: "The Prophet has a greater claim on the believers than they have on themselves, and his wives are their mothers."

Verses 28 through 34 of chapter 33 touch on a number of themes regarding how Muhammad's wives should conduct themselves. The sec-tion opens with Muhammad being told to give his wives a choice between the fleeting luxuries of the present world or the eternal reward of the life to come (vv. 28-29). As usual, the text provides no context for the passage, but here and elsewhere, the *ḥadīth* and "occasions of revelation" (*asbāb al-nuzūl*) provide an historical framework that identifies the situation being addressed. In this case, some of Muhammad's wives began to seek more possessions and provisions from him as his reputation and status grew, and the passage is meant to remind them about what should matter most in their lives.

Muhammad's wives are addressed directly in the next five verses, where they are urged to obey God and the Prophet and told that they will experience a double punishment or double reward based on their ability to do so (vv. 30-31). This is followed by a statement that they are different from all other women, and they must act accordingly by speaking appropriately, engaging in the practices of the faith, and paying attention to the revelations received by Muhammad (vv. 32-34). "Maintain prayer, give alms, and obey God and His Messenger. God wishes to keep impurity away from you, People of the House, and to completely cleanse you" (33:33b).

An interesting episode involving members of Muhammad's extended family is mentioned in 33:37: "You (Muhammad) said to the man who was favored by God and by you, 'Keep your wife and be mindful of God.' But you hid within yourself what God

*Some, particularly within the Shi'a community, believe the term "People of the House" refers to members of Muhammad's immediate family, namely his daughter Fatima, son-in-law and cousin Ali, and their sons Hasan and Husayn.*

later disclosed. You feared the people, but it is better that you should fear God. When Zayd ended his marriage with her, We gave her to you so that there would be no blame if believers marry the wives of their adopted sons after they no longer want them. God's command must be followed."

The Zayd mentioned in this verse was Muhammad's adopted son, who married the Prophet's cousin Zaynab. After they divorced, Muhammad married her despite his concern about how people would react to the marriage. The verse immediately following this one absolves Muhammad of any guilt in the affair and repeats the notion that it all took place because this was God's will. The reference that it is permissible for a man to marry his adopted son's former wife is anticipated in 33:4, where it says that God does not consider adopted sons to be real sons.

Muhammad is addressed in 33:50-52 about several matters regarding his relationships with his wives. He is told which women it is permissible for him to marry (v. 50), and then he is instructed that he is free to arrange conjugal relations with his wives in whatever way he wishes (v. 51). The section concludes with a limit set on the number of wives he may have, and he is advised not to marry anyone else or divorce a wife to replace her with another. This ruling did not apply to female servants, who were his own personal property. "You (Muhammad) are not allowed to take any additional wives, nor may you exchange your current wives for others even if their beauty pleases you. Your slave-girls are an exception to this. God watches over everything" (33:52).

There is a shift of addressee to the community of believers in the next verse, which begins by telling them that they should respect Muhammad's privacy by not entering his living space unless they are invited and not overstaying their welcome when they visit him. The text then turns to his wives and how Muslims should interact with them. "When you ask them (Muhammad's wives) for something, ask from behind a curtain. That is purer for your hearts and theirs. You should not trouble God's Messenger,

*A favored man*

and you should not ever marry his wives after him. That would be a great offense before God" (33:53b).

The Arabic word translated "curtain" is *ḥijāb*, a word that is found seven times in the Qur'an and usually describes a partition or barrier that separates some people from others. It later came to have the meaning of a veil that is worn by a woman to cover some portion of her head and/ or face. This verse is frequently cited to support the practice of veiling, but the context makes clear that it is describing some partition between Muhammad's wives and other Muslims rather than how the women are dressed. This is an issue that will be addressed more fully in the following chapter. The prohibition against marrying Muhammad's wives reflects the respect the community is to have for the Prophet and his family, and is also understandable in light of their status as "mothers of the believers."

Reading between the lines of this verse offers a glimpse into what Muhammad's home life might have been like at times. As a focal point of the early community, his residence was a place that was frequently visited by Muslims who wished to spend time with the Prophet and consult him on a variety of matters. This undoubtedly placed certain demands and strains on all members of the household, and this text helped to establish guidelines on issues like when it was appropriate to visit and how Muslims should conduct themselves in the presence of the Prophet and his wives. Having these rules communicated in the form of divine revelation served to legitimate them and to guarantee they would be observed.

The only other passage in the Qur'an that treats Muhammad's family in any detail is 66:1-5. The first two verses refer to something allowed by God that Muhammad prohibited in order to please his wives. It is a mysterious text that describes a vow or oath made by the Prophet, but its content is unknown. It has been suggested in traditions and commentaries that it might be an allusion to an abstention from something, maybe a particular type of food or sexual relations with one or more of his wives. Verses 3-5 relate an episode in which Muhammad tells one of his wives something in confidence that she does not keep to herself. God informs the Prophet of this violation of trust, and Muhammad confronts his wife about it. The two guilty wives are then encouraged to repent, and all his wives are warned of the possibility of divorce if they engage in similar behavior.

In places, the Qur'an broadens the concept of kinship because it teaches that faith unites people into a family of believers, which gives them a sense of identity and common purpose. Nonetheless, it has much to say about the family as normally conceived, and this chapter has considered some texts that speak of various dimensions of the relationships existing among members of the same household and more distant relatives. Many of these passages are legal in nature, and they are meant to normalize and regulate behavior in the domestic realm in such areas as marriage, divorce, and inheritance. Nonlegal texts often speak of the affection and commitment that are at the core of a healthy family, but some passages acknowledge that families are sometimes, to use a modern term, dysfunctional.

The Qur'an does not use family-based language to speak about God, which is different from what is found in the Bible. Like the Qur'an, the Judeo-Christian scriptures sometimes refer to fellow believers as brothers and sisters, but the Bible also speaks often of God as a father, and less commonly as a mother. The main reason for this difference is tied to Islam's understanding of the deity, who is completely transcendent and beyond human understanding or experience. Several texts state that it is impossible for God to have offspring, and language that would present God as a parent in relationship to humanity is not present in the Qur'an.

## key TERMS

Quraysh; Hijaz; patrilineal; ḥanīf; polygyny; ṭalāq; Khadija; ʿAisha; People of the House; ḥijāb

## QUESTIONS for discussion

1. What is your reaction to the way the Qur'an favors faith ties over biological relationships?

2. Does the Qur'an's male-centered perspective make it a problematic source for discussing family matters?

3. Does the Qur'an's theocentric emphasis transform family relations in a positive or a negative way?

4. How do you respond to the presence of biblical figures in the Qur'an?

## further READING

Zainab Alwani, "The Qur'anic Model for Harmony in Family Relations," in *Change from Within: Diverse Perspectives on Domestic Violence in Muslim Communities*, ed. Maha B. Alkhateeb and Salma Elkadi Abugideiri (Peaceful Families Project, 2007), 33–65.

Azizah Y. al-Hibri, "The Nature of the Islamic Marriage: Sacramental, Covenantal, or Contractual?" in *Covenant Marriage in Comparative Perspective*, ed. John Witte Jr. and Eliza Ellison (Grand Rapids: Eerdmans, 2005), 182–215.

Richard C. Martin, "Marriage, Love, and Sexuality in Islam: An Overview of Genres and Themes," in *Covenant Marriage in Comparative Perspective*, ed. John Witte Jr. and Eliza Ellison (Grand Rapids: Eerdmans, 2005), 217–38.

Khaleel Mohammed, "Sex, Sexuality, and the Family," in *The Blackwell Companion to the Qur'ān*, ed. Andrew Rippin (Chichester: Blackwell, 2006), 298–307.

Th. J. O'Shaughnessy, "The Qur'anic View of Youth and Old Age," *ZDMG* 141 (1991): 33–51.

David S. Powers, *Studies in Qur'an and Hadith: The Formation of the Islamic Law of Inheritance* (Berkeley: University of California Press, 1986).

# 3
# Gender and Sexuality

In recent times, some of the most hotly debated issues related to Islam have centered on the question of gender. How are relationships between men and women understood and articulated? On what should that understanding be based? What are the resulting practical implications for everyday life and social interaction? These and similar questions have been discussed frequently both within and outside of the Muslim community.

Some non-Muslims consider Islam to be a misogynistic or backward religion due to their perception that it mistreats women and relegates them to an inferior status in relation to men. Others are less negative in their assessment, and they argue that it is unfair to generalize in this way because gender relations is a very complex issue that varies from place to place and comprises a range of factors beyond religion that need to be kept in mind.

Similar debates take place among Muslims. Some prefer to maintain and perpetuate a view of gender that took shape centuries ago in a world very different from our own that tended to privilege males, while others call for the replacement of that system with one that stresses the gender equality they claim is at the heart of Islam. Among the most vocal proponents in favor of such a change are those associated with the feminist movement within Islam that has developed over the past few decades.

The Qur'an is at the very center of these discussions and debates, and this chapter presents an overview of what the text teaches about gender and sexuality. Passages that have been particularly influential in shaping opinions and behavior regarding how men and women should relate to one another are cited and analyzed. Other texts that have played a role in determining attitudes toward things like menstruation and how women should dress are also considered. Additional topics treated include sex outside of marriage and homosexuality. With the recent emergence of feminist scholarship, new voices have entered the conversation, and they have proposed interesting and insightful readings of some of these texts, thereby introducing fresh ways of interpreting them. The aims and methods of these feminist readings of the Qur'an are explained and examined.

## Terminology

(Q 33:25; 3:195a; 4:124; 16:97; 40:40; 11:81a; 3:35, 40; 11:71; 12:21; 27:57; 28:9; 11:69-83; 15:61-77; 52:21; 8:24; 24:11; 70:38; 74:52; 78:40; 80:37)

Arabic has words for "gender" and "sex" that are relatively new and not found in the Qur'an. Nonetheless, the text acknowledges the differences between men and women in a number of ways. One is by virtue of the way the Arabic language works. All nouns and many verbs are grammatically either masculine or feminine, and so there is a dimension of gender often present within a word itself. Similar to what is found in other languages, like Italian and Spanish,

*The feminine-singular noun ending in Arabic is the letter tā' marbūṭa, which is written ﺔ when attached to the letter before it and ﺓ when unattached. Not all feminine nouns have this ending, so the gender of a word is not always immediately apparent.*

Arabic has two distinct plural endings for nouns, one masculine and the other feminine. As with those other languages, the Arabic masculine plural can be used to speak of a group of males or a mixed group of both males and females.

The former usage that refers exclusively to males is most clearly seen in texts that contain both a masculine plural and a feminine plural in succession as a way of speaking of the males and females in a given category. An example of this is seen in 33:35, which contains a string of ten such pairs: "For Muslim men and women, believing men and women, devout men and women, truthful men and women, perseverant men and women, humble men and women, charitable men and women, fasting men and women, modest men and women, and men and women who remember God often, God has prepared for them forgiveness and a great reward." To anticipate a discussion that will be taken up later in this chapter, the presence of passages like this that make no distinction between men and women is one reason why some argue that the Qur'an's view of gender is essentially egalitarian.

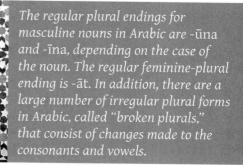

*The regular plural endings for masculine nouns in Arabic are -ūna and -īna, depending on the case of the noun. The regular feminine-plural ending is -āt. In addition, there are a large number of irregular plural forms in Arabic, called "broken plurals," that consist of changes made to the consonants and vowels.*

The differences between men and women are also acknowledged in the Qur'an through its use of separate terms for male and female. The word for a male is *dhakar*, which is found eighteen times in the Qur'an, while the term designating a female (*unthā*) appears thirty times. In all but two of the eighteen passages that contain the word *dhakar*, the word *unthā* also appears, as in 3:195a, another passage that reflects gender equality: "Their Lord answers them, 'I do not allow to go to waste the deeds of any one of you, whether male or female—the two of you are like each other'" (cf. 4:124; 16:97; 40:40).

A common word for "woman" in the Qur'an is *imra'a*, which can carry the sense of "spouse, wife" when it is found in a context that calls attention to the relationship that exists between the woman and a man. An example of this is seen in 11:81a, which describes the fate of Lot's wife: "They said, 'Lot, we are your Lord's messengers. They will not reach you.

*In the Qur'an, Lot is a prophet who was sent to the people of Sodom. His story is recounted in several places, including 11:69-83 and 15:61-77.*

Leave with your household during the night, and let none of you turn back except for your wife [*imra'ataka*]. She will suffer the fate that befalls the others.'" (cf. 3:35, 40; 11:71; 12:21; 27:57; 28:9).

The masculine form of *imra'a* is used on a few occasions to refer to a man, but in some cases the term is better translated "person" since these passages speak of both men and women. "We join together the believers and their offspring who share their faith, and we do not diminish any of their deeds. Each person [*muri'*] is bound to what he or she does" (52:21; cf. 8:24; 24:11; 70:38; 74:52; 78:40; 80:37). A much more common designation for a man is the word *rajul*, which appears more than fifty times in the Qur'an. Like *imra'a*, it is usually found in its plural form (*rijāl*).

The plural form most often used to describe women is *nisā'*, which appears twice in the related form *niswa*. The title of chapter four of the Qur'an is *al-nisā'* ("The Women"), which is so named because the word appears twenty times in the chapter, more than one-third of its total occurrences.

A number of terms in the Qur'an are grammatically masculine but refer to both men and women, sometimes in the collective and sometimes as an individual. The most common of these words are *nās* ("humanity"), *ahl* ("people"), *bashar* ("person"), and *insān* ("human being"). Of this group, *nās* is by far the most frequently used, with nearly 250 occurrences of it throughout the Qur'an.

## Feminist Readings of the Qur'an

Prior to the 1990s, commentary upon and analysis of the Qur'an was, with rare exceptions, an exclusively male activity. During the first few centuries of Islam and into the medieval period, all of the classical works of exegesis that helped give shape to Islamic theology and law, many of which continue to be influential into the present day, were written by men. Likewise, virtually all of the key thinkers and scholars of the early modern era and on into the latter part of the twentieth century were male.

Sources outside the Qur'an suggest that things were different in the earliest years of Islam, when women were consulted on matters related to the content of the text. According to tradition, some of the women who were closest to the Prophet Muhammad, including his wives, `Aisha and Hafsa and his companion Umm Waraqa, played significant roles in the compilation and transmission of the written text.

A feminist movement began to emerge within Islam during the nineteenth century, but most of its organizers and supporters lacked formal training in theology and related fields and were consequently unable to engage in serious scholarship. This began to change in the twentieth century, when the education of women became a significant component of the reform efforts of many Muslim-majority countries, and by the end of the century women were making important contributions to the study of the Qur'an and in other scholarly areas from which they previously had been excluded.

During the 1990s, a feminist hermeneutics of the Qur'an began to be articulated that offered innovative alternative readings of passages and called into question long-held assumptions about the text that had contributed to the oppression and marginalization of women. This method of analysis is built on three interrelated principles. The first is that interpretation of the Qur'an has tended to rely on what commentators have had to say about the text rather than on the text itself. The authors of the commentaries that constitute the body of writings known as the *tafsīr* have become the supreme authorities, and their opinions, rather than the words of the Qur'an, have formed the basis for Muslim belief and practice. The main problem with such reliance on the views and opinions of these scholars is that their interpretations of the Qur'an reflect the biases and limitations of the contexts in which they were living and writing. Their patriarchal environments, which privileged males, were often reflected in and validated by their reading of the Qur'an. The feminist critique posits that such a situation only perpetuates and canonizes antiquated interpretations that are not relevant for later contexts.

The second principle of feminist hermeneutics is that, at its core, the text of the Qur'an is inherently egalitarian in its view of relations between men and women. All people are equal in God's eyes and all have the same basic rights regardless of gender or any other differences that might exist among them. Unfortunately, women and others have sometimes been denied those rights because of the above-mentioned overreliance on interpreters at the expense of the Qur'an itself or because of unjust political systems that claim to be based on Islam. But such situations are due to the mistakes and manipulations of human beings, and they should not be used to malign or call into question the Qur'an, whose message of equality is clear and consistent.

The third principle recognizes that the Qur'an contains texts that are not in agreement with its egalitarian core. It states that a distinction must be made between two different types of material in the Qur'an—those passages and messages that are universally relevant for all times and places, and those that are more limited in their scope and application. The first group contains the eternal essence of the Qur'an that transcends time and space, while the second is context-specific and meant to be directed to a particular moment and location. In the view of feminist scholars, it is crucial to keep this distinction in mind because without it one might mistakenly assume that texts that were originally directed to the circumstances of seventh-century C.E. Arabia are also addressed to us in the twenty-first century. They claim that this is precisely what has happened throughout history since the *tafsīr* literature has tended to focus more on the patriarchal, context-specific passages of the Qur'an and has downplayed the egalitarian ones that are universal in nature.

With these principles in mind, feminist interpreters attempt to point out the flaws in traditional exegesis of the Qur'an while proposing new ways of thinking about passages that have often been used to subjugate women or to justify patriarchal attitudes and behavior. The field is ever-expanding, but among the most prolific

> *The three principles of feminist interpretation of the Qur'an: (1) prior interpretation has relied on commentators rather than the text itself; (2) at its core the Qur'an is egalitarian in its view of gender relations; (3) some texts are not in agreement with that egalitarian core.*

and influential of these scholars are Asma Barlas (Pakistan, b. 1950), Riffat Hassan (Pakistan, b. 1943), Fatima Mernissi (Morocco, b. 1940), and Amina Wadud-Muhsin (United States, b. 1952). The results of their scholarship are reflected in some of the analysis presented in this chapter.

## The Egalitarian Core

(Q 9:71-72; 4:124; 16:97; 24:12; 33:35-36; 40:40; 48:4-5, 25; 57:18; 71:28; 85:10; 9:67-68; 33:73; 48:6; 2:34-36a; 7:20-22; 20:120-23; 7:22; 20:121; 4:1; 6:98; 7:189; 35:11a; 36:36; 53:45; 75:39; 78:8; 92:3; 51:47-49; 30:21; 7:189; 49:13; 7:26; 20:132; 47:17; 49:3; 58:9; 74:56)

The equality of men and women is stressed throughout the Qur'an in many texts that are addressed to or mention both males and females. The obligations and duties required of men and women are identical, and they will all be rewarded in the same way if they remain faithful and carry out those responsibilities. The use of gender terms in these verses is a subtle way of reinforcing the idea that all people are full and equal members of the Islamic *umma*. "Believers, both male and female, are protectors of one another. They command what is right, and they forbid what is wrong. They maintain prayer, give alms, and obey God and His Messenger. God will grant mercy to such as these. Truly, God is powerful and wise. God has promised the believers—both male and female—gardens under which rivers flow where they will remain forever, and lovely dwellings in the eternal gardens. But the greatest thing of all will be God's approval—that is the supreme victory!" (9:71-72; cf. 4:124; 16:97; 24:12; 33:35-36; 40:40; 48:4-5, 25; 57:18; 71:28; 85:10).

Elsewhere, unbelievers and sinners are spoken of in a similar way, by identifying the men and women among their ranks and the punishments that await them: "The hypocrites, both male and female, are like each other. They command what is wrong, and they forbid what is right.

They are tight-fisted. They have forgotten God, so He has forgotten them. Truly, the hypocrites are transgressors. God has promised the hypocrites, both male and female, and the disbelievers that they will reside in the fire of hell forever. It is what they deserve. God rejects them, and an enduring punishment is theirs" (9:67-68; cf. 33:73; 48:6).

The fact that both believers and unbelievers are spoken of in this way indicates that the Qur'an understands gender equality to be an inherent part of humanity that is not contingent upon having faith or being a good person. This idea is expressed in a number of texts that speak of creation and the origin of humanity in which men and women are viewed to be on equal footing. The story of the first couple, for example, does not privilege Adam over Eve in any way: "When We told the angels, 'Prostrate yourselves before Adam,' they all prostrated except Iblīs, who refused and was proud. He was one of the unbelievers. We said, 'Oh Adam, live with

FIGURE 17  *All the angels except Iblīs*
*(upper right) bow down to Adam.*

your mate in this garden, and you may both eat freely from it as you wish. But do not approach this tree, or you will both become transgressors.' But Satan caused them to slip up, and removed them from the state they were in" (2:34-36a; cf. 7:20-22; 20:120-23).

Eve remains unnamed in this passage, as she does throughout the entire Qur'an. In fact, the only woman referred to by name in the Qur'an is Mary the mother of Jesus. Something else not explicitly mentioned in the text is Eve's creation. There is no equivalent in the Qur'an to the biblical tradition that Eve was created from some part of Adam's body, usually understood to be a rib. That mode of creation in the book of Genesis has sometimes been cited as support for the belief that Eve was inferior to Adam and therefore, by extension, men are superior to women. There are many reasons why such an interpretation is incorrect, but the lack of this tradition about Eve's creation in the Qur'an shuts off the possibility of such an understanding of human origins. The Islamic text does not describe the creation of either Adam or Eve, so it is not possible to compare their origins in a way that places one above the other.

Another difference between the qur'anic and the biblical accounts of the garden story is in the way the eating of the fruit is described. In Genesis, Eve eats from the tree first after being deceived by the serpent, and then brings some fruit to Adam, who eats it. This has caused many readers to place the blame on Eve as the one primarily responsible since she was the first to disobey the order not to eat. Consequently, she is often seen as the cause of humanity's "fall." This interpretation is not possible with the Qur'an's version of

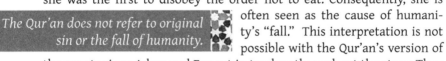
*The Qur'an does not refer to original sin or the fall of humanity.*

the events since Adam and Eve act in tandem throughout the story. They both are deceived, and although it is not stated in this text, elsewhere in the Qur'an it says that they both ate of the fruit, with no indication that one ate before the other or caused the other to eat (7:22; 20:121). In the Qur'an, the first man and first woman are created as equals, and they disobey God's command as equals. There is nothing in the text that suggests one is superior to the other.

This view of gender equality is reinforced in other passages that speak of human origins without recounting the story of the first couple. For example, the Qur'an's egalitarian view is clearly articulated in the first verse of chapter four ("The Women"): "Oh people, be mindful of your Lord, who created you from a single soul, and created from it its mate. From them spread out many men and women. So be mindful of God, by whom you request things of one another, and [be mindful of] your kinship relations. God watches over you" (4:1; cf. 6:98; 7:189).

According to this verse, all people have a common point of origin in the same *nafs*, an Arabic word that is often found in the Qur'an. It appears almost 150 times, and it is sometimes difficult to know how it should best be translated in a given verse. Among its possible meanings are "self," "mind," "heart," "person," and "soul." Many translators favor the last alternative for 4:1, and that is how it is rendered here. Although the precise sense of the word is somewhat ambiguous, the meaning of the text is not in doubt—men and women come from the same source and ultimately trace their creation back to God.

The reference to a mate in 4:1 is an important aspect of the Qur'an's view of the male-female relationship. The Arabic word used here is *zawj*, which can refer to two things that are connected in some way or to one of the two components of such a pairing. When used in reference to human beings, it therefore describes a couple or one member of that couple. The idea that people are created in couples is mentioned in several places in the Qur'an. "God created you from dust, then from a drop of fluid, and then made you pairs" (35:11a; cf. 36:36; 53:45; 75:39; 78:8; 92:3). Such passages highlight the relational dimension of human life, and they never privilege one member of the couple over the other. All of creation, including humanity, is paired in mutual relationships, a situation that is meant to remind people of their unity and equality under God. "We built the heavens with power, spreading them wide, and We laid out the earth—how great is the One who spread them out! We created everything in pairs so that you might reflect" (51:47-49).

The Qur'an sometimes explains why humans have been paired in relationships: "Among His signs is that He created spouses for you from among yourselves so that you might find comfort in them. He put love and compassion between you. There truly are signs in this for a people who reflect" (30:21; 7:189). The Arabic verb translated here as "find comfort" is *sakana*. When it is followed by the preposition *illā*, as it is in this verse, it can mean "to rely upon," "to be reassured by," "to trust in," and "to feel at home in." This passage offers one of the Qur'an's most tender and moving descriptions of the bond that exists between spouses. Each should be for the other a source of comfort, security, and support. It is to be an equal partnership in which love and compassion are ever present. This is an image of domestic harmony that can be attained only if each partner treats the other with dignity and respect.

Asma Barlas has suggested that the meaning of *sakana* in this verse should extend into the area of sexuality. She believes that the text is describing a situation in which both partners are sexually satisfied since this is an essential dimension of a happy and mutually fulfilling relationship. She points out that, if her reading is correct, the Qur'an articulates a message of equality between spouses related to sexuality that will not become a part of other religious traditions until centuries later.

A final aspect of 30:21 to consider is the double reference to "signs" at the beginning and end of the verse. Like so many other facets of life mentioned in the Qur'an, human coupling is first and foremost a sign of God's power and authority over creation. This transforms a relationship between spouses into something much more than the shared life of two individuals who have chosen to come together. It becomes an opportunity for them to learn something about God if they, as the text urges, take the time to reflect on their shared experiences.

The texts examined here and others like them constitute what feminist scholars believe to be the egalitarian view of gender relations that is at the heart of the message of the Qur'an. This is the universal teaching of the text that is relevant for all times and places and must form the basis for an authentically Islamic understanding of how men and women should relate to one another. The text does not discriminate or show prejudice based on one's gender, but considers equality among all people to be something instilled in creation by God.

The only distinction the Qur'an makes among people is based on belief, not biology. It is one's faith, or lack of faith, that ultimately determines one's fate. This idea is present in 49:13, one of the Qur'an's most eloquent statements on the need to celebrate diversity and respect differences: "Oh humanity, We created you male and female and made you into peoples and tribes so that you might know one another. The most honorable of you before God are the ones who are most pious. Truly, God knows and is aware."

Here, too, the common origin of all people is recognized, and there is no attempt to make distinctions among them based on gender. The determining factor is rather one's ability to be "mindful" of God. The Arabic term for the quality being called for here is *taqwā*, a theological concept that is central to the Qur'an and Islam. It comes from a verb that carries the meaning of being mindful or conscious of something, and when used in reference to God, it describes an attitude of piety that is constantly aware of one's complete dependence upon and submission to the deity. Such a person, whether male or female, is the one who will be, in the words of 49:13, most honored. "Children of Adam, We have given you garments to cover your nakedness as an adornment. But the garment of piety (*taqwā*)— that is the best. This is one of God's signs, so that people may reflect" (7:26; cf. 20:132; 47:17; 49:3; 58:9; 74:56).

# Problematic Passages

Certain other verses have sometimes been cited, especially by non-Muslims, as evidence that the Qur'an is a misogynistic text and teaches that women are inferior to men. Feminist interpreters have criticized this analysis with the claim that it is too simplistic because it does not take into account the cultural context of the passages in question or the meanings of certain key terms found within them. They argue that a thorough study of these texts indicates that some of them are relevant only for their original seventh-century-c.e. audience and are not meant to be universally applied. In other cases, a careful consideration of their vocabulary reveals that they actually reflect and support the egalitarian ethos that is central to the Qur'an. In the following sections, some of these passages are examined and discussed.

### Legal Witnesses
(Q 2:282a; 6:117; 10:108; 20:52; 39:41; 27:20-44)

The number of witnesses the Qur'an stipulates as necessary for a legal proceeding is sometimes considered to be indicative of a negative view of women. The relevant text is found in 2:282a: "Oh believers, if you contract a debt for a stated term in your dealings with one another, put it in writing. Have a scribe write it down between you fairly. A scribe cannot refuse to write as God has taught him. Let the debtor dictate—he should fear God, his Lord, and not reduce [the amount] a bit. If the debtor is mentally deficient, feeble, or cannot dictate, then let his guardian dictate justly. Have two of your men act as witnesses. If two men are not available, then use one man and two women out of those you deem acceptable as witnesses. If one of the two women makes an error, the other can remind her. The witnesses should not refuse when they are called."

This passage has led some to conclude that the Qur'an's view of the relative worth of men and women can be summed up in the formula "one man equals two women." It has even been suggested on occasion that the verse reflects the view that women are not as intelligent as men. This reading may be influenced by the reference to the feeble-minded debtor who needs to rely on the help of a guardian just prior to the mention of witnesses. According to this reading of the text, two women are required because one by herself would not be the intellectual match of her single male counterpart.

In response to this reading, it should be noted that the text does not state that both women are to function as legal witnesses. Only one of them is a witness, and the other plays a role in the proceeding only in the event that the first woman needs assistance in recalling the details of the case. The Arabic verb that is used to describe the state of the woman who needs assistance is *ḍalla*, which can mean "to lose one's way," "to stray," and "to err" (cf. 6:117; 10:108; 20:52; 39:41). It is translated here as "to forget," but the semantic connection to these other meanings should be apparent. If she becomes confused and lost, her companion is to remind her and help her to get back on track in her testimony.

The text stipulates that two women attend the proceeding to ensure that the outcome is fair and just, but it is not making a disparaging comment on their capacity to reason and think for themselves. It is simply acknowledging a sociological fact of the time—that the world of business and commerce was a primarily male-centered one with which women had little experience and familiarity. Because this was the situation in seventh-century Arabia, it was necessary to have a system in place that would guarantee a fair outcome in the event that two people from the group that had the most knowledge of such transactions—males—could not be present.

The two women are able to consult one another and collaborate to make sure the case is properly decided. But, in the view of feminist scholars, such an arrangement is necessary only under those conditions. If, in other circumstances, women are skilled and experienced in business matters the arrangement outlined in 2:282 is unnecessary and does not apply. This is therefore a context-specific passage that should not be universally applied and is not making a blanket statement about the relative value of men and women. The fact that the Qur'an holds up a woman like the Queen of Sheba as a preeminent model of political leadership, a field dominated by men, illustrates the same point.

> The Queen of Sheba is known as Bilqīs in Islamic sources. In the Qur'an, she becomes a believer after a visit to King Solomon's court. Her story is told in 27:20-44.

## Gender Ranking

(Q 4:95; 9:20; 57:10; 2:253; 58:11; 20:75; 46:19; 6:132; 2:228; 2:226-39)

A recurring theme in the Qur'an is the idea that God ranks some people above others. The Arabic term that is used in these passages is *daraja*, which conveys the meanings "level," "degree," and "step." According to these texts, God raises the status of certain individuals, thereby privileging them and setting them apart. One passage states that anyone God chooses will be raised in rank, but more commonly groups are singled out because of some quality they possess. Among the groups that are ranked

FIGURE 18 *The Queen of Sheba (far right)*
*approaches Solomon's throne.*

ahead of others are those who put forth effort on behalf of the faith (4:95; 9:20; 57:10), messengers to whom God's word is revealed (2:253), believers (58:11), and those who perform good deeds (20:75). It is said elsewhere that this will be an experience that all people will have because each person will be ranked based on his or her actions: "All will be ranked [*darajāt*] based on their deeds, and He will repay them for what they have done. They will not be treated unjustly" (46:19; cf. 6:132).

One passage is different from the others because it appears to make a distinction among people based on their gender. This idea is mentioned at the end of 2:228, a lengthy verse that must be quoted in full because the topic of its earlier part must be kept in mind to properly interpret it: "Divorced women are to wait for three monthly periods before remarrying, and they are not allowed to hide what God has created in their wombs if they really believe in God and the Last Day. Their husbands would do better to take them back during this time if they desire reconciliation. Women have [rights] similar to those [of men] over them, according to what is acceptable, and men have a degree [*daraja*] over them. God is strong and wise." As the words in brackets indicate, the precise meaning of the latter portion of this verse is somewhat difficult to understand. The context suggests the passage is a reminder that, like men, women enjoy certain rights that are well-known and beyond dispute. In other words, there is equality between men and women when it comes to the rights they have.

But the use of the word *daraja* in reference to men seems to indicate that they are somehow privileged above women, not unlike the way the groups mentioned earlier are ranked above other people. This part of the verse does not specify why this is the case since it does not identify what it is that sets men apart from women. This has sometimes led interpreters to argue that the verse is simply describing the state of things as they are. They understand it to be a blanket statement that expresses God's preference for men over women and therefore an endorsement of male superiority.

To read the verse in this way is to misinterpret it because its wider context has been ignored. According to Amina Wadud-Muhsin and other feminist scholars, the first part of the verse identifies the area in which men have an advantage over women. It and the two verses prior to it describe the process a man must follow when he wishes to dissolve a marriage by pronouncing the decree of divorce. The mention later in the verse of the degree that men have over women is in reference to this practice since women are not permitted to obtain a divorce by pronouncing the decree. For Wadud-Muhsin and others, 2:228 is not issuing a general statement about male superiority over women. It is limiting the man's *daraja* solely to the area of divorce, but even then it is quick to point out that women, like men, enjoy certain rights that are well-known to all and must be granted.

The wider literary context of 2:228 supports this understanding of the verse. It comes at the beginning of a lengthy section (2:226-39) whose primary topic is divorce. It contains many instructions to men about the need to treat women honorably and fairly, and it reminds them repeatedly about the rights women have in the divorce process. The point seems to be that even though men have been granted an advantage in this one area, they are to act responsibly and not abuse it.

Throughout the section are warnings about the need to adhere to the teachings of the Qur'an and not transgress the rules. "Those are God's limits—do not transgress them. Those who transgress God's limits are evildoers" (2:229b; cf. 2:230b, 231b, 232b, 233b, 234b, 235b, 237b). Given the explicit focus on divorce throughout the section, it is clear that the reference to the *daraja* of men in 2:228 is confined to that one area and should not be seen as a broader comment about men and women in general.

## Physical Abuse

(Q 4:34; 4:135; 5:8; 2:47, 122; 7:140; 45:16; 2:253; 6:86; 17:55; 27:15; 4:95; 17:70; 4:32-33; 4:7; 33:31, 35; 66:5; 2:238; 3:17; 33:35; 2:116; 30:26; 16:120; 3:43; 66:12; 4:128)

If any text qualifies as "ground zero" in discussions regarding the Qur'an's view of gender, that designation would have to go to 4:34. It is a very important verse that has generated much controversy, not least of all because it appears to give husbands permission to physically abuse their wives. As with other texts discussed in this section, though, a thorough analysis of the verse and its key terms demonstrates that the message of male superiority it is held to espouse is not as certain as it might first appear to be. Nonetheless, this text presents a challenge for those who assert that the Qur'an's essential view of gender is an egalitarian one.

"Husbands are providers [qawwāmūna] for their wives, since God has favored [faḍḍala] some with more than others and they spend out of their wealth. Good women are devout [qānitāt], guarding during the absence [of their husbands] what God would have them guard. If you fear antagonism [nushūz] from them, admonish them, then leave them alone in bed, then hit [iḍribū] them. If they obey you, do not mistreat them in any way. God is most high and great." To facilitate analysis of this key verse, it will be divided into two sections. The first part comprises the first two sentences, which explain certain obligations for each party in the relationship between spouses. The second part offers instructions on how to respond to a particular set of circumstances that threaten the stability of the relationship. Key words in each section are at the center of the interpretive debate over the verse's meaning.

The text begins by stating that husbands are supposed to provide for their wives. The Arabic word used to describe this is qawwāmūna, which is found in two other verses of the Qur'an. In 4:135, it is used to speak of those who uphold or defend justice, and in 5:8 it describes those who are committed in their faith in God. Looking at these three occurrences, it appears that 4:34 is instructing men to be steadfast as they take care of and protect their wives. They are to provide for them as intently as they seek justice or believe in God. Some interpreters give the word a sense that privileges men over women by suggesting that husbands are to exercise authority over their wives by dominating and controlling them. This is partly due to the use of the preposition ʿalā after qawwāmūna, which can carry the meaning "over" or "against." But there is nothing in the meaning of the word qawwāmūna that requires it have this connotation. The word is used here to remind men of their responsibility to provide for and protect the women in their care.

The first part of the verse speaks of God having a preference when it says that God has preferred, or favored (*faḍḍala*), some over others. This idea is expressed a number of times in the Qur'an, and it is similar to the notion of God raising the rank (*daraja*) of some people that was mentioned earlier in this chapter. Other passages that use the verb *faḍḍala* speak of divine preference for the Israelites (2:47, 122; 7:140; 45:16), prophets and/ or messengers (2:253; 6:86; 17:55; 27:15), those who strive for the faith (4:95), and humans in general (17:70).

It is important to note, however, that 4:34 is not claiming a universal divine preference for all males, as is sometimes claimed, which would place men in a position of superiority vis-à-vis women. The Arabic of the passage is ambiguous because it can mean, "God has preferred some [males] over others [females]," but it is also grammatically acceptable to read it as, "God has preferred some [males] over others [males]". There are good reasons for opting for the second possibility over the first, and if it is adopted, the verse is making a comment about some males in relation to others rather than discussing males in relation to females.

The first part of this verse states that husbands are *qawwāmūna* over their wives only when they are among the group of men who are singled out by God to play this role. But how is God's preference for them manifested, and does it somehow privilege men over women? The two previous verses help to answer these questions. The beginning of 4:32 anticipates a theme in 4:34 by using the verb *faḍḍala* to indicate that some have received more than others, and the implication is that men and women do not receive the same amount of compensation: "Do not covet that by which God has favored [*faḍḍala*] some of you more than others. To men the portion they have acquired, and to women the portion they have acquired. Ask God for some of His bounty—He has knowledge of everything."

The reason for the disparity between men and women is suggested in 4:33, which mentions the topic of inheritances: "To each person We have designated heirs for what parents and close relatives leave behind. Give their portion also to those to whom you have pledged your hands [in marriage]. God is a witness over everything." As noted in the chapter on family matters, according to the Qur'an, male heirs are entitled to more money than female heirs (4:7). Inheritance is the only area in which a divine preference for men over women is stated in the Qur'an, and this plays a critical role in how 4:34 should be interpreted.

The first sentence of 4:34 is referring in part to inheritances when it explains what makes some men *qawwāmūna* over women. "Husbands are providers [*qawwāmūna*] for their wives, since God has favored [*faḍḍala*] some with more than others and they spend out of their wealth." Not all men receive inheritances, but those who do must use some of that money to support the women who are dependent upon them. This is the reason why men receive more inheritance than women, who are permitted to keep their inheritance for themselves. Men who do not support their wives from their means are not *qawwāmūna* over them, so the text is not saying that men, as a group, are superior to women. Neither is the verse implying that women are incapable of providing for themselves. It is simply stating that women are normally not expected or required to be the breadwinners and provide for the family.

Some scholars, like Amina Wadud-Muhsin, have argued that this verse also acknowledges the woman's role in childbearing and perpetuating the human race. It places additional responsibilities on the man to provide for her so that she is not further burdened by being required to find the means to support herself, thereby giving each spouse certain obligations and duties.

Another key term in the first part of 4:34 is *qānitāt*, an adjective that describes women and is translated here as "devout." It is sometimes rendered as "obedient," and some have suggested that this word stresses the deference wives are to show to their husbands, but there is no support for this interpretation. In a few other texts, the word is used to describe women (33:31, 35; 66:5), and elsewhere the context suggests that it is used in reference to men (2:238; 3:17; 33:35). In a couple of passages, it is stated that everything on earth and in heaven, presumably including the non-human elements of creation, is *qānit* (2:116; 30:26).

In every one of these texts, the obedience being described is directed toward God, not to another person. It is therefore an expression of one's humility and submission to God rather than an indication of one person's deference to another. This is clearly seen in the passages that mention the only two individuals who are said to be *qānit* in the Qu'ran. One is Abraham, the quintessential monotheist and model for all believers: "Abraham was truly an example, devout [*qānit*] to God and upright in faith. He was not an idolater" (16:120).

The other is Mary the mother of Jesus, who is told by the angels who announce the birth of her son that she is to express her obedience to God by bowing down: "Mary, be devout [*uqnutī*] to your Lord, prostrate yourself, and bow down with those who bow down" (3:43; cf. 66:12). This usage, which understands *qānit* to be a form of obedient reverence toward God, is reflected in the other passages mentioned above that contain the word. It is therefore a term that describes the piety a woman should possess, and it does not support the idea that God wants wives to obey their husbands in all matters.

The second half of 4:34 is the more controversial part of the verse, and two words in particular have been at the heart of the debate over what the passage means. "If you fear antagonism [nushūz] from them, admonish them, then leave them alone in bed, then hit [iḍribū] them. If they obey you, do not mistreat them in any way. God is most high and great." After the description of the ideal relationship that should exist between spouses, this section offers guidance on what to do if the stability of the marriage is threatened. In fact, though, this hypothetical scenario is outlined in a one-sided way since it is directed to the man and discusses only a case that presents the woman as the blameworthy party.

The term that describes the woman's offense is nushūz, which can be translated as "haughtiness," "disloyalty," "antagonism," and the like. It is sometimes understood to be a uniquely feminine trait and therefore a description of a cause of marital disharmony that is found only on the disobedient wife's part. But to take this position is to ignore the fact that the word is found later in the same chapter to speak about a husband who disrupts the relationship between spouses. "If a wife fears antagonism [nushūz] or rejection from her husband, neither of them will be blamed if they can reconcile, for harmony is best. Pettiness is present in the human soul, but if you work toward good and are mindful of God He is truly aware of what you do" (4:128). The husband, too, can be guilty of engaging in nushūz, and so it is a mistake to consider it to be a quality that is found only among women.

While each member of the couple is capable of violating the relationship by committing the same offense, the Qur'an offers different counsel on how to deal with the matter, depending on whether the offending party is the man or the woman. The reference to nushūz on the man's part in 4:128 leads to a discussion of a "peaceful settlement" between the couple that, in light of the literary context of the surrounding verses, is best understood to be a reference to divorce and the dissolution of the marriage. If such is the outcome, the text assures the couple that neither of them will be at fault. But this does not appear to reflect the facts of the case, since it is the husband's nushūz that set in motion the end of the marriage.

The way the Qur'an addresses nushūz on the part of the woman is quite different. It calls for increasingly harsh measures against her, and it does not speak of the option of a peaceful settlement through divorce or other means. The different approaches to handling the situation are likely due to the originating context of the Qur'an, and they reflect a time and place in which issues of gender and social status were perceived in a way different from our own.

The Qur'an lists three responses for the husband whose wife has engaged in *nushūz*, with each successive one to be implemented only if the previous one does not work. The first is verbal in nature, as the man is instructed to admonish or warn the woman about the damage she is causing to their relationship. If this fails, the man is to refrain from sexual relations with her (literally, "forsake them in bed"). In both these scenarios, the hoped-for outcome is reconciliation between the man and woman or an amicable separation, and in this sense the verse is similar to 4:128, which urges the couple to seek a peaceful settlement.

The third response has been the subject of much controversy because it employs the verb *ḍaraba*, whose primary meaning is "to hit, strike." There have been two main ways of addressing the Qur'an's apparent approval of domestic violence in this verse. The first is to accept it at face value, but to interpret it in a way that softens its initial harshness. This is done primarily by arguing that the text is calling for a very light slap or tap rather than the use of extreme physical force. Some have even suggested that the hit should be symbolic rather than an actual strike. Those who opt for this interpretation often point out that the verse uses the first form of the Arabic verb (*ḍaraba*) rather than the second form (*ḍarraba*), which intensifies the meaning and describes a harsh physical beating or repeated blows. In this reading, the passage is actually trying to reduce domestic violence by limiting it and presenting it as only a last resort after all other measures have been exhausted. In other words, it is restricting spousal abuse rather than giving permission for it.

> *In the Arabic verb system, there are ten forms. The first is the three-letter root with no changes made to it. The other nine all entail modifications of that root, including the doubling of letters, lengthening of vowels, and insertion of additional consonants.*

The other way of understanding the verb is to say that it has an entirely different meaning that has nothing to do with physical violence. Arabic is a very rich language whose words often have multiple meanings that are not semantically close to one another, and that is the case with *ḍaraba*. Among its possible other meanings are "to set an example" and "to go on a journey," and it is sometimes suggested that one of these alternatives is really what the text is calling for. With the first, the man is being advised to somehow use the situation as an example for the couple to learn from, and with the second the passage is calling for some physical distance between them to allow for a cooling-off period in the relationship.

There are good reasons why modern readers of the Qur'an should not consult 4:34 for guidance on marital relations. In the first place, because this verse is ambiguous and its meaning is unclear, particularly regarding the word *ḍaraba*, it should not be used as a norm for how spouses should relate to one another. The passage can mean more than one thing, and that vagueness cautions against choosing one meaning as the correct one to the exclusion of others.

Another issue that lessens the relevance of 4:34 for today's readers is the difference in context between our own day and that of the text's original audience. Modern notions of what marriage is and how spouses should relate to one another differ significantly from seventh-century Arabia, where women were subjugated to men and physical abuse was permitted. Marriages of subjugation are becoming a thing of the past, and so this text does not speak to our circumstances. If we take *ḍaraba* to have its basic meaning of "to hit," we must understand the verse as an attempt to limit and control violent behavior in a context in which a man's physical abuse of a woman was tolerated. Because such behavior is unacceptable today, the text should not serve as a guide for us.

Put another way, 4:34 is one of those context-specific texts mentioned earlier that should not be universally applied to later times and places. Unfortunately, as many feminist scholars have pointed out, that is not the way the text is usually understood. The exegetical writings found in the *tafsīr* tradition have formulated and passed down interpretations of the verse that reinforce stereotypes about male superiority and perpetuate the oppression of women in many places. Because the views of the exegetes have become canonized over time and form the basis of many Islamic laws and attitudes, views that highlight the egalitarian nature of the Qur'an's message on gender or that point out the ambiguities in the text have often been downplayed or ignored.

## The Veil

(Q 7:46; 17:45; 19:17; 38:32; 41:5; 42:51; 33:53; 33:59; 24:31; 21:91; 33:35; 33:5; 66:12)

How Muslim women should dress is one of the most frequently discussed topics related to Islam in the modern world. Stories that treat various aspects of the issue are regularly covered by the media in North America, Europe, and other parts of the world where Muslims are in the minority. These debates have also taken place in Muslim-majority countries, where some of the religious and cultural dimensions of women's dress have been discussed and dissected. Much of the controversy has surrounded the wearing of a veil, often referred to by its Arabic term *ḥijāb*. Non-Muslims often assume that the practice of donning a veil is something that can be traced to the Qur'an, but that is not the case. In fact, the Qur'an has surprisingly little to say about the subject of women's dress.

The word *ḥijāb* is found seven times in the Qur'an, and in none of those cases does it refer to an article of clothing that is meant to cover some part of a woman's (or a man's) body. It comes from an Arabic root whose primary meanings are "to screen," "to seclude," and "to cover." All of the references to *ḥijāb* in the Qur'an describe a barrier or partition that is meant to form a separation between those on one side and those on the other. An example is seen in 7:46, which speaks of a barrier that separates those in heaven from those in hell. "Between the two groups is a barrier [*ḥijāb*], with men on the heights recognizing them by their marks. They call out to those in the garden, 'Peace be with you!' They do not enter, but they long to" (cf. 17:45; 19:17; 38:32; 41:5; 42:51).

Another text in which it is used is 33:53, discussed in the previous chapter in reference to Muhammad's family, where the word *ḥijāb* is sometimes wrongly associated with women's dress: "Oh believers, do not enter the Prophet's dwellings for a meal unless you are given permission to do so, and do not linger there until it is ready. When you are invited, enter. After you have eaten, depart. Do not stay to engage in idle chatter, for that bothers the Prophet. He is embarrassed to ask you to leave, but God is not embarrassed by the truth. When you ask them [Muhammad's wives] for something, ask from behind a curtain [*ḥijāb*]. That is purer for your hearts and theirs. You should not trouble God's Messenger, and you should not ever marry his wives after him. That would be a great offense before God." This verse is one of the rare times the Qur'an discusses some aspect of the Prophet Muhammad's personal life in some detail. The mention of a *ḥijāb* is in reference to a partition or screen behind which Muslims were to stand when they spoke to Muhammad's wives, and is not speaking about something the women were wearing on their bodies.

The two primary texts in the Qur'an that discuss women's clothing are 33:59 and 24:31. The first is directed to Muhammad and puts forth a general guideline for how female members of the Islamic *umma* should dress. "Oh Prophet, tell your wives, your daughters, and women believers to have their outer garments [*jilbāb*] hang low over them. That way, they will be recognized and not be harassed. God is forgiving and merciful." The word used for the garment referred to is *jilbāb*, and this is the only place it is mentioned in the Qur'an. It is generally understood to be a loose-fitting article of clothing that covers the upper part of the body, including the neck and bosom, as a type of cloak.

The verse does not describe the garment in any detail, so it is difficult to know precisely how it was worn, but it is not referred to as a *ḥijāb* and therefore did not function as a type of veil. The verse explains the reason why women are to wear the *jilbāb*, and this is an important point to keep in mind—it is not meant to cover them up or render them invisible, but to make them visible to others, especially non-Muslim men. It is a marker that calls attention to their status as Muslim women and protects them from unwanted advances.

Some feminist scholars, like Asma Barlas, have argued that because the verse is directed to Muhammad, it is relevant only for his time period and is not meant to be universally applied to later contexts. Because his environment was a patriarchal one in which sexual abuse and sex for pay were common among non-Muslims, Muslim women needed to identify themselves to ensure they would not be mistaken for slaves or prostitutes. In other situations in which this is not a concern, according to Barlas and others, wearing the *jilbāb* is not necessary.

As is the case with other passages already discussed, the history of interpretation of this verse found in the *tafsīr* material introduced new ways of reading it that are not supported by the text of the Qur'an. In this case, commentators came to see it as a statement about the importance of covering up women rather than the need to identify them. This led to calls for their veiling and more extreme forms of rendering them invisible, like covering their faces and hands, that persist in some quarters today but have no basis in the Qur'an.

The other verse that discusses how women should dress is 24:31: "And tell believing women to lower their gazes, guard their private parts, and not show their adornments except what is [normally] visible. They should draw their head-scarves over their bosoms and not show their adornments except to their husbands, their fathers. . . . They should not stomp their feet so as to reveal their adornments they have hidden. Oh believers, turn to God so you may prosper." The missing section identified by the ellipsis contains a lengthy list of other people to whom women may "reveal their adornments."

Three times in this verse the word "adornments" (Arabic, *zīna*) is used, but the precise sense of the term is unclear. Its most common meanings are "charm" and "decoration," but the context here suggests that this fits only the third occurrence, where it is probably a reference to jewelry that is otherwise unseen but might be heard if a woman stomps her foot. The other two times *zīna* appears are most likely speaking about the parts of the body that only some people are allowed to see. Those areas of the body are not identified, but the text states that it is normal and acceptable to reveal certain "adornments," so it is clearly not calling for a woman to cover up completely. The only part of the body that is specified in the verse is the *furūj*, a euphemism for the sexual organs that is translated here as "private parts" (cf. 21:91; 33:35; 33:5; 66:12).

The article of clothing mentioned in this verse is the *khimār*, a type of head-scarf or shawl that the text says should also cover the skin that is exposed above the neckline of the woman's garment. It does not function as a veil and is clearly not meant to cover the entire face because, if so, the command for women to avert their eyes and lower their gazes would not make any sense. The fact that a *khimār* can also refer to a man's turban also argues against its functioning as a type of veil.

An interesting aspect of 24:31 is that its first part is found almost verbatim in the verse before it, which is directed toward men. "Tell believing men to lower their gazes, and guard their private parts—that is better for them. God is aware of all they do." This is significant because it shows that the Qur'an expects every person to act and dress modestly, regardless of gender. Such modesty requires that a person's body be covered in a way that is socially acceptable, but it does not stipulate that a woman must cover her face or hands. Those practices stem from commentaries on the Qur'an rather than from the Qur'an itself. Very often, these commentaries put forward a view of the female body as something dirty and polluting that must therefore be covered up and rendered invisible. But this idea is at odds with the text, which values the body to a high degree and says that it must be treated with dignity and respect.

*Only two verses in the Qur'an discuss how women should dress.*

## Menstruation

(Q 2:222; 4:43; 5:6; 65:4; 2:223)

The Qur'an's most detailed statement on the subject of menstruation is found in 2:222: "They ask you (Muhammad) about menstruation [*maḥīd*]. Say, 'It is a hardship ['*adhā*], so keep away from women during it. Do not approach them until they are cleansed. When they are cleansed, approach them as God has commanded. God loves those who turn to Him, and He loves those who cleanse themselves." The reference to menstruation putting a woman in an unclean state is probably the main reason why Islamic law holds that contact with menstrual blood makes a person impure. Other passages in the Qur'an list a number of bodily functions—including urination, defecation, and sexual intercourse—that render one unclean for prayer and require an ablution (4:43; 5:6). Menstruation is not mentioned explicitly in those texts, but the presence in 2:222 of words from the Arabic root *t-h-r,* which describes ritual purity, is likely a reason why it came to be viewed as one of the bodily functions that make one impure.

The English translation of 2:222 can give the impression that men are to completely avoid their wives during their menstrual periods, but that is not what the text is saying. The Arabic expressions used in the verse make it clear that they are only to refrain from having sexual relations with their wives during this time. Other forms of interaction and physical contact are permissible, and so the couple should behave as they normally do in every area of their relationship except for the sexual.

> *Contact with certain bodily discharges like blood, urine, and semen renders a Muslim ritually impure and therefore not in the proper physical state for prayer. Depending on the circumstances, the impurity is removed by either a full bath or a simple ablution.*

Even if her menstrual blood is seen as impure or polluting, there is nothing in the Qur'an that says the woman herself, or her body, should be viewed in this way.

In the verse, menstruation is referred to as a "hardship." The Arabic word used to describe it is *'adhā,* which describes a disease, ailment, painful condition, or inconvenience. However it is translated, the passage is acknowledging the painful effects that typically accompany menstruation, and it urges a man to put his wife's situation and needs above his own. The word used for menstruation is *maḥīḍ,* and some have suggested that it is a noun of place and that therefore the text is calling for avoidance of the location where menstruation occurs, the woman's genital area. If this reading is adopted, it further supports the idea that the verse is not calling for complete avoidance of the woman but simply refraining from sexual contact. The only other place in the Qur'an where *maḥīḍ* is found is in 65:4, which discusses the period of time a divorced woman must wait before remarrying to determine if she is pregnant.

The reference in 2:222 to having marital relations "as God has commanded" has been taken by some commentators to be a comment about the sexual practices the couple might engage in. They think the verse could be a statement in favor of vaginal intercourse that is opposed to other sexual positions and techniques. In other words, the passage is advising people about not just when to have sexual relations but how to have them. They cannot engage in sexual activity whenever and however they wish, but they are to express themselves sexually as God intends.

This is an important point because it has a bearing on how to understand the verse that follows immediately after it, which has sometimes been interpreted in a way that denigrates and objectifies women: "Your wives are fields for you. Go into your fields as you wish, and send forward [something] for yourselves. Be mindful of God, and remember that you will meet Him. (Muhammad), bring good news to the believers" (2:223). The description here of wives as fields has sometimes led to the accusation that the Qur'an considers women to be the property of men.

But to adopt this view is to read a modern assumption into the text and to impose on it a notion of land ownership that would have been foreign to those living in seventh-century Arabia. Land at that time was not something to be parceled out and owned by individuals; it was something to be cultivated and nurtured for the good of society. This is precisely the point behind the use of the metaphor "fields." It is in their capacity to bring forth new life through childbirth that women are like fields, and this verse encourages men to do their part in perpetuating the human race and helping to bring about the next generation. Working together in their distinct but complementary roles in conceiving and raising children, this is what men and women are to "send forward" for themselves.

The reminder at the end of the passage to be mindful of God recalls the statement in the previous verse that men are to engage in sexual relations as God intends. Reading that as an acknowledgment of divine preference for vaginal intercourse supports the interpretation that 2:223 describes women as fields in order to underscore the connection with human reproduction, and it has nothing to do with women's inferiority or subjugation. So when the text tells men they may "go into your fields as you wish" it is not giving them license to be selfish or forceful in their relationships with their wives. It is meant to remind them of the creative and life-giving dimension of human sexuality.

## Sexual Activity

(Q 30:21; 7:189; 2:187a; 2:197a; 4:15; 4:22, 25; 17:32; 33:30; 65:1; 7:80; 27:54; 29:28)

The Qur'an teaches that sexual expression is a natural and essential part of human existence. As already seen, the text sometimes uses the verb *sakana*, which can mean "to feel at home" and "to trust in," to describe the peace and harmony that result from the physical intimacy enjoyed by a couple. "Among His signs is that He created spouses from among yourselves that you might live with them in comfort [*litaskunū*]. He placed love and mercy between you. These are truly signs for a people who reflect" (30:21; cf. 7:189). This is one of several signs of God's involvement as creator of the physical world that are mentioned in this section of the Qur'an (30:20-25), which underscores the text's positive view of sexuality as a gift from God that is meant to be celebrated.

Islamic law stipulates that sexual relations are not permitted in daytime during Ramadan, the month of fasting, but the Qur'an allows it in the evening hours of the month. "During the night of the fast, sexual intercourse with your wives is permitted for you. (2:187a). There is a possible prohibition against sexual activity during the pilgrimage ritual in 2:197a: "The pilgrimage takes place during the well-known months. Let there be no sexual intercourse, aberrant behavior, or arguing for anyone doing the pilgrimage. God knows about any good you do." In both verses the Arabic word for "sexual intercourse" is *rafath*, a term that clearly has that meaning in the first text because of the presence of the phrase, "with your wives." In the second passage, the word might have its other meaning of "to engage in obscene or sexually explicit talk," and the verse could be forbidding such behavior during the pilgrimage.

The Qur'an typically does not refer to particular forms of sexual activity, and so it is difficult to know with certainty what it is referring to when it uses the word *rafath* or other terms. It does not, for example, refer specifically to anal intercourse or oral sex. It is commonly assumed that the references to a man and a woman engaging in sexual relations are speaking of vaginal intercourse, but it should be kept in mind that many other forms of sexual expression are not explicitly mentioned or prohibited in the Qur'an.

Improper sexual activity is often termed *fāḥisha* or *faḥshā'*, two related words that can describe any indecent or immoral act. The exact nature of the offense is usually left unexpressed, but the general context of some passages suggests that these are sometimes references to adultery or fornication. "If any of your women engage in lewdness [*fāḥisha*], call four witnesses from among you. If they testify against them banish the women to their houses until they die, or until God shows them another way" (4:15; cf. 4:22, 25; 17:32; 33:30; 65:1). In a few passages, the term is used in reference to homosexuality, a topic discussed below (7:80; 27:54; 29:28).

*The Prophet Muhammad is castigated in 66:1 for refraining from engaging in sexual relations with his wives.*

## Extramarital Sexual Relations

(Q 24:23-24; 5:5; 23:5; 24:4, 33; 33:35; 70:29; 66:12; 21:91; 3:35-36; 4:25; 5:5; 17:32; 25:68; 17:32; 3:135; 6:151; 7:28, 33; 42:37; 53:32; 4:15; 24:2; 24:4; 24:6-9; 12:22-29)

The Qur'an teaches that Muslims should observe modesty and refrain from inappropriate sexual activity. Some words that convey this notion of chasteness come from the Arabic root ḥ-ṣ-n, which in certain forms means "to guard, preserve," and others come from the root ḥ-f-ẓ, which has similar meanings. The idea behind this usage is that good people protect themselves from immorality by guarding their genitals and refraining from all improper sexual activity. "Those who accuse chaste [al-muḥṣanāt] and innocent believing women are cursed in this life and the next. A great punishment will be theirs on the day when their tongues, hands, and feet

*The Qur'an refers to Mary's birth in 3:35-36, a chapter whose title ("The Family of 'Imrān") mentions her father's name.*

testify against them about what they have done" (24:23-24; cf. 5:5; 23:5; 24:4, 33; 33:35; 70:29). The individual who personifies this quality most clearly in the Qur'an is Mary, who guarded her virginity and gave birth to Jesus without having had sexual relations with a man. "Mary, daughter of 'Imran, guarded [aḥṣanat] her private parts, so We breathed Our spirit into her. She accepted the truth of the words of her Lord and His books—she was one of the devout ones" (66:12; cf. 21:91).

The Qur'an forbids taking a lover and having sex outside of marriage (4:25; 5:5; 17:32; 25:68), and extramarital sexual activity is often described by words that come from the Arabic root z-n-y, as in 17:32: "And do not go near adultery [zinā]. It is a vile deed, and a path to evil." Another word that is often identified with extramarital relations is fāḥisha, discussed above, but since this term refers to various types of indecent and immoral acts, it is sometimes difficult to know precisely what kind of activity is being condemned (3:135; 6:151; 7:28, 33; 42:37; 53:32). As already noted, it appears in 4:15 in a text that is often held to be prescribing the punishment for women who have committed adultery: "If any of your women engage in lewdness [fāḥisha], call four witnesses from among you. If they testify against them banish the women to their houses until they die, or until God shows them another way." According to this verse, the guilty party is to be consigned to her home until death, unless she is otherwise rehabilitated by divine means.

One reason why it is believed that this passage is speaking about adultery is that there is another verse in the Qur'an that also refers to the need for mulitple witnesses to charge a woman with a violation, and there the offense is clearly adultery because the verse uses words from the root z-n-y to describe both the man and the woman: "Flog the adulteress and the adulterer one hundred times. Do not let compassion for them prevent you from carrying out God's demand, if you believe in God and the Last Day. Make sure a group of believers witnesses their punishment" (24:2). Most commentators claim that this verse abrogates 4:15, and that is why whipping is sometimes a punishment for adultery in those places that strictly follow Islamic law. It should be noted that the Qur'an does not make a distinction based on gender but says that both parties are equally guilty. The practice of stoning adulterers has no basis in the Qur'an, and derives from the hadīth traditions associated with the Prophet Muhammad.

A punishment of eighty lashes is prescribed in 24:4 for those who accuse a woman of adultery but are unable to garner four witnesses. In point of fact, it would be extremely difficult, if not impossible, to assemble four people to testify to the offense because they each would have to witness the act of penetration. This means it is highly unlikely that the scenario imagined in 24:2 could occur and its punishment be enforced.

The Qur'an refers to another set of circumstances whereby a man can accuse his wife of adultery without witnesses, but there the woman has the right to defend herself and has the last word on the matter: "Those who accuse their wives of adultery and have no witness but themselves should swear by God four times that they are telling the truth. A fifth time he should call God's curse upon himself if he is lying. The punishment will be averted from the woman if she witnesses by God four times that her husband is lying and, the fifth time, calls God's wrath upon herself if he is telling the truth" (24:6-9).

The most dramatic passage related to adultery is found in 12:22-29, which is the Quran's account of the biblical story in Genesis 39 that describes the encounter between Joseph and his master's wife after his brothers sold him into Egypt. Almost all of the one hundred verses in chapter 12 relate the story of Joseph, making it the longest single narrative in the Qur'an. Its version of what happened between Joseph and his master's wife is similar to the Bible's, but with some important differences. In the Islamic text, her husband comes home to find them together only to exonerate Joseph when it is pointed out that his shirt is torn from behind, indicating Joseph

> Although she is unnamed in the Qur'an, the wife of Joseph's master is identified as Zulaykha in other Islamic sources.

was trying to flee and the woman is the guilty party. The most notable difference is the important role God plays in the Qur'an while being completely absent from Genesis 39. The moral of the story is clear—Joseph was able to resist temptation only because of his belief and trust in God, and

# GALLERY

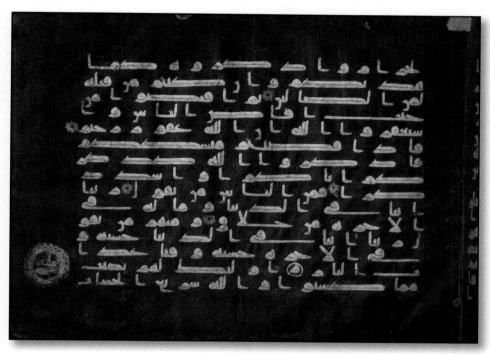

FIGURE A

Ninth-century Qur'an in Kufic script. This version of the Qur'an, from Kairouan, Tunisia, is
distinctive for its dramatic contrast of gold on
blue parchment. Verses are marked off by small
circles within the text, which itself contains no
vowel signs, points, or other diacritical marks.

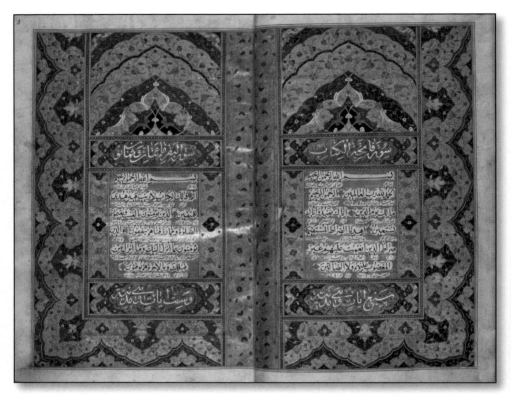

FIGURE B

Seventeenth-century Qur'an leaf. The text of the Qu'ran's first chapter (right) and the beginning of the second chapter (left) is written in the central portion of the page. Above it is written the chapter's title and below it the number of verses it contains and whether it is from the Meccan or Medinan period.

FIGURE C
Miniature Qur'an. This Shiite man holds the Qur'an on his head during prayers on the twenty-seventh day of Ramadan known as Lailat al-Qadr (Night of Power), which marks the night on which the Qur'an was first revealed to Muhammad.

FIGURE D
World's largest Qur'an. At the King Abdulaziz al-Saud library in Medina (Saudi Arabia), the library's director poses in front of the the world's largest copy of the Qur'an. While the Qur'an comes in a variety of sizes and forms, the text is always the same regardless of its dimensions.

FIGURE E
Reading the Qur'an. This photograph shows an Indonesian Muslim woman reading the Qur'an during Ramadan.

FIGURE F
Father and son reading the Qur'an. All Muslims are expected to read the Qur'an on a regular basis, a practice that typically begins at a young age. This father and son read the Qur'an in an Indonesian mosque during Ramadan.

in this he serves as a model for others to follow. "She made a play for him, and he would have done the same if he had not seen the proof of his Lord. We did this in order to keep him free of evil and lewdness—he was truly one of Our pure servants" (12:24).

FIGURE 19 *Joseph flees from Zulaykha, as depicted in this fifteenth-century manuscript.*

## Homosexuality

(Q 7:80-84; 11:77-83; 15:61-77; 26:160-75; 27:54-58; 29:28-35; 54:33-40; 4:15-16)

The Qur'an does not have much to say on the subject of homosexuality. Most of the references to it are found in passages discussing the visit of God's messengers to Lot, which have much in common with the biblical account found in Genesis 18 and 19 that describes the fate of Sodom and Gomorrah (7:80-84; 11:77-83; 15:61-77; 26:160-75; 27:54-58; 29:28-35; 54:33-40). Upon the messengers' arrival at the unnamed town in the Qur'an, its inhabitants seek to engage in activity described as *fāhisha* (7:80; 27:54; 29:28), which leads to their destruction.

As noted above, the term *fāḥisha* is somewhat vague since it can refer to any immoral or indecent act. But in several of these passages, the nature of the offense is identified as the men's sexual desire or lust for other men. In 26:165-66, Lot chastises the men of his town, "Of all humankind, do you come to the males and reject the spouses God has created for you? You are a people who exceed the bounds!" (cf. 7:81; 27:55; 29:29). In these texts, same-sex activity is criticized and condemned, but it is important to keep in mind that nowhere does the Qur'an consider it to be a greater offense than other forms of sexual transgression. The terminology found in the stories associated with Lot's people is also found in passages that are critical of opposite-sex transgressions like desiring a man or woman one is not married to, fornication, adultery, and having sexual relations while a woman is menstruating. It is therefore incorrect to claim that the Qur'an considers same-sex activity to be a greater sin than those committed within heterosexual relationships.

The punishment of Lot's people is not solely or primarily due to their sexual practices or preferences. As with all the stories in the Qur'an that describe a community's punishment, the main cause is their failure to heed a prophet's message and, ultimately, their refusal to submit to God's will. The Lot stories are about a people's alienation from God, and their same-sex desires are considered to be one manifestation of that estrangement. This idea is well expressed in 54:33-35: "The people of Lot rejected the warnings. We sent a storm of stones against all of them, except the family of Lot. We saved them just before dawn as a favor from Us. Thus We reward those who are thankful."

In recent times, some Bible scholars have argued against the traditional view that the main purpose of the story in Genesis 19 is to condemn homosexuality. They offer an alternative interpretation that focuses more on hospitality than sexuality. In ancient Near Eastern societies, guests were treated with a great deal of respect and honor, and this practice continues in many cultures into the present day. When the townspeople of Sodom and Gomorrah tried to break into Lot's home and kidnap his visitors for their own purposes, they violated one of the basic principles of social interaction—hospitality toward the stranger. According to this reading, their lack of respect, more than anything else, is why the people of Sodom and Gomorrah were punished.

Reading the Qur'an passages about Lot with this interpretation in mind reveals some intriguing connections because his concern with hospitality appears to be present in a couple of places. In 11:78, Lot reacts to the men's attempt to forcibly take his visitors: "His people hurriedly came to him, and previously they had committed evil deeds. He said, 'Oh my people, these are my daughters—they are purer for you. Be mindful of God, and do not shame me before my guests. Is there not a sensible man among you?'" Lot's offer of his daughters as a substitute in place of his visitors strikes the modern reader as repugnant, but it reflects the cultural norms of a time that was markedly different from our own. In antiquity, children were a man's possession, and he could use them as he liked. As strange as it may sound to us, Lot was actually trying to protect his people by offering them his daughters. This becomes apparent when it is observed that the word translated here as "purer" comes from the Arabic root t-h-r, which is commonly used to convey the idea of purity, especially in ritual matters. Lot does not want his people to pollute themselves, and so he offers them his daughters because he knows if the men have relations with them they will not render themselves impure.

But what may be driving his actions most of all could be his awareness of the hospitality norm, as evidenced by his desire not to be shamed and disgraced before his visitors. A similar note is sounded in 15:68-69, where he utters a double plea in an effort to avoid embarrassment: "He [Lot] said, 'These are my guests, do not humiliate me. Be mindful of God, and do not shame me.'" The presence of the hospitality theme in the Qur'an, as in the Bible, adds an important nuance that suggests the story has broader social implications and that the people of Lot are punished for reasons beyond their sexual practices.

Another passage that is sometimes considered to be speaking about homosexuality is 4:15-16, the first verse of which was discussed earlier in connection with adultery: "If any of your women engage in lewdness, call four witnesses from among you. If they testify against them banish the women to their houses until they die, or until God shows them another way. If two men commit a lewd act, punish them both. If they repent and mend their ways, leave them alone. Truly, God accepts repentance, and is merciful." Although many commentators maintain the passage is concerned with improper heterosexual relations, it has been suggested on occasion that it is actually treating same-sex relationships. If so, it would be the Qur'an's only explicit statement on lesbianism. As already noted, the word describing the offense in these verses is *fāḥishah*, which refers to any indecent act. But some of the Arabic words in the second sentence are grammatically masculine dual, which underscores the fact that the verse is speaking about the actions of two men and lends support to the interpretation that it is discussing homosexuality.

> *The Qur'an does not say anything specific about topics like abortion, birth control, or masturbation.*

The Qur'an addresses many topics related to gender and sexuality, and in recent times new ways of thinking about this ancient text's meaning and relevance for today's world have been put forward. Some have warmly embraced these newer approaches, and others have denounced them. The debates and discussions will undoubtedly continue as Muslims wrestle with issues like male-female relations, appropriate dress, homosexuality, and other forms of sexual expression. Just as Jews and Christians disagree on the role the Bible should play in modern society, it would be unrealistic and unfair to assume that all Muslims should be of the same opinion when it comes to the Qur'an. Diverging views and disagreement are essential to any healthy, vibrant community. What remains to be seen is which perspective will exert the most influence by shaping Islamic attitudes and behavior in the future. The answer to that question is unknown, but that perspective will certainly be informed by the Qur'an, however its message is understood and interpreted.

## key TERMS

*tafsīr; umma; nafs; zawj; sakana; taqwā; daraja; qawwāmūna; faḍḍala; qānitāt; nushūz; ḍaraba; ḥijāb; jilbāb; zīna; furūj; khimār; 'adhā; maḥīḍ; rafath; fāḥisha; zinā*

## QUESTIONS for discussion

1. What are some of the benefits and drawbacks of relying on an ancient text like the Qur'an for guidance on matters like gender relations and sexuality?

2. What is your reaction to the aims and method of feminist readings of the Qur'an?

3. Do the problematic passages in the Qur'an that can be interpreted as privileging males negate the egalitarian core that some claim is its essential message?

4. Why do interpretations of texts sometimes become more influential than the texts themselves?

## further READING

Kecia Ali, *Sexual Ethics and Islam: Feminist Reflections on Qur'an, Hadith, and Jurisprudence* (Oxford: Oneworld, 2006).

Asma Barlas, *"Believing Women" in Islam: Unreading Patriarchal Interpretations of the Qur'an* (Austin: University of Texas Press, 2002).

Scott Siraj al-Haqq Kugle, *Homosexuality in Islam: Critical Reflection on Gay, Lesbian, and Transgender Muslims* (Oxford: Oneworld, 2010).

Mohamed Mahmoud, "To Beat or Not to Beat: On the Exegetical Dilemmas over Qur'ān 4:34," *JAOS* 126, no. 4 (2006): 537–50.

Barbara Freyer Stowasser, *Women in the Qur'an, Traditions, and Interpretation* (Oxford: Oxford University Press, 1996).

Amina Wadud, *Qur'an and Woman: Rereading the Sacred Text from a Woman's Perspective* (Oxford: Oxford University Press, 1999).

Tim Winter, "Gender from an Islamic Perspective," in *Abraham's Children: Jews, Christians and Muslims in Conversation*, ed. Norman Solomon, Richard Harries, and Tim Winter (London: T & T Clark, 2006), 236–43.

# Muslim/Non-Muslim Relations

An important question every religious community must address is how its members should relate to people of other faith traditions. Judging from the amount of attention the Qur'an devotes to it, this was a significant issue in the early years of Islam. The Arabian Peninsula, where the Prophet Muhammad spent his entire life, was also home to a variety of other religions, many of which predated Islam by centuries. As relative newcomers, Muslims had to learn how to interact with the followers of these faiths, who sometimes were suspicious of the new religion. The situation was complicated by the fact that prior to embracing Islam virtually all of the first generation of Muslims had themselves been adherents of one of these other religions. As a result, their newly formed identities as Muslims sometimes were in tension with long-established religious, tribal, and family ties that were now being challenged.

The Qur'an offers guidance on how Muslims were to negotiate this complex set of circumstances. It acknowledges the existence of other religious traditions, and it comments on how their relationship to Islam is to be understood. But the Qur'an's view is in some ways as complex as the situation to which it was responding. The text does not present a single position on how Muslims should relate to non-Muslims but offers a variety of possible responses that are at times in conflict with one another. This is due to the changing contexts of the early community, as Muhammad and his followers found themselves having to respond to many different situations and incidents. What was appropriate for one time and locale would not necessarily work for another, and so it was not possible to come up with a one-size-fits-all approach toward Muslim/non-Muslim relations.

This chapter provides an overview of what the Qur'an has to say about members of other religious communities and how Muslims should relate to them. After a treatment of some of the terminology associated with the concept "religion," the main religious groupings mentioned in the Qur'an will be identified and discussed. The chapter concludes with a section on religious pluralism that considers how four modern scholars interpret some of the passages that have been influential in shaping Muslim attitudes about the Other.

## The Language of Religion

(Q 4:125; 3:95; 6:161; 16:123; 22:78; 7:88-89; 14:13; 2:120a; 3:19a; 3:85; 5:3; 6:125; 9:74; 39:22; 49:17; 61:7; 2:135; 3:67; 6:79, 161; 16:120, 123; 10:105; 30:30)

The Qur'an uses a number of different terms to convey various aspects of what people today would identify as religion. Several of them are found in 4:125: "And who is better in religion [dīn] than the one who submits [aslama] his or her whole self to God, does good, and follows the creed [milla] of Abraham, the upright [ḥanīf]?"

The most frequently found word for religion in the Qur'an is dīn, which has a non-Arabic origin and appears almost one hundred times in the text. Related to cognate words in Akkadian (dānu) and Persian (dēn), its two primary senses are "judgment" and "ritual observance." Many of the texts that have the former meaning come from the earlier Meccan period, while those associated with ritual and cultic expression are from the Medinan period. This fits well with the general, if somewhat simplistic, distinction that is often made between the two sets of material that sees the Meccan chapters as primarily interested in conversion and the end times, with the Medinan ones being more concerned with community governance and practical matters.

> *Words of foreign origin—from languages like Syriac, Hebrew, and Persian—have attracted the interest of commentators since the earliest days of study of the Qur'an.*

The word *milla*, here translated as "creed," appears fifteen times in the Qur'an. It also entered Arabic from outside, being originally a Syriac term. It usually denotes a particular form of belief, and it is sometimes rendered into English as "sect" or "way." In eight places, as here, it is used in reference to the faith or community of Abraham, who is considered to be the quintessential monotheist in the Qur'an (cf. 3:95; 6:161; 16:123; 22:78). Despite this close identification with Abraham, *milla* does not describe only proper (that is, Islamic) belief, as seen in its use to refer to the religion of the people of pre-Islamic prophets like Shu'aib (7:88-89), the belief of polytheists (14:13), and Judaism and Christianity. "The Jews and Christians will never be satisfied with you (Muhammad) until you follow their way [*millatahum*]" (2:120a).

Two other terms are used in 4:125 to describe the religion of Abraham. First of all, the one who follows it is one who submits (*aslama*) to God's will. This verb comes from the same root as the word "Islam," which literally means "surrender, submission." While words from this Arabic root occur frequently in the Qur'an, the word *'islām* appears only eight times. It describes the perfect form of faith for humanity as intended by God and proclaimed by all the prophets from Adam to Muhammad. "Indeed, in God's eyes true religion is *al-'islām*" (3:19a; cf. 3:85; 5:3; 6:125; 9:74; 39:22; 49:17; 61:7).

There is a certain ambiguity in the term that will be discussed in detail later in this chapter. It is sometimes difficult to know if it is describing the specific form of religion proclaimed by Muhammad that included particular beliefs and practices and came to be known as Islam, or if it is a more general reference to any attitude of submission or surrender that puts one in a position of dependence upon God. How that ambiguity is resolved has a significant bearing on how one understands the Qur'an's view of Muslim/non-Muslim relations, an issue that will also be treated more fully below.

The other term in 4:125 that designates Abraham's faith and that helps to establish some basic parameters of the Qur'an's view of religion is *ḥanīf*. It is found twelve times in the text, and in most of those occurrences it is used in reference to Abraham, who is explicitly identified in the Qur'an as a *ḥanīf* (2:135; 3:67; 6:79, 161; 16:120, 123). It describes a devout person who is morally upright, a quality best seen in the person's rejection of polytheism and worship of the one God. The word comes from the Arabic root *ḥ-n-f*, meaning "to incline," which suggests that it describes someone who has abandoned polytheistic forms of religion and has inclined toward another form of faith. Scholars disagree over whether or not there were groups of such people who banded together as *ḥunafā'* during Muhammad's lifetime and what his association with such groups might have been, but there is evidence in the Qur'an that indicates that Muhammad should be thought of as a *ḥanīf* (10:105; 30:30).

## Religious Groups

(Q 22:17)

The Qur'an sometimes identifies particular religious communities, and six such groupings are listed in 22:17: "Regarding believers, Jews, Sabians, Christians, Magians, and idolaters, God will judge between them on the day of resurrection. Truly, God is a witness over all things." The first and last groups mentioned in this verse were the ones who had the most difficult and problematic relationship in the early years of Islam. "Believers" is another term for Muslims, those who accepted the message of Muhammad and adopted monotheism. The idolaters were people who chose not to follow Muhammad and continued to embrace polytheism. The Qur'an consistently presents the idolater or the one who associates (*mushrik*) as the antithesis and enemy of the Muslim.

An issue that is less clear to resolve is the Qur'an's attitude toward the other four groups mentioned in 22:17—Jews, Sabians, Christians, and Magians. Should they be classified with the believers? Are they among the idolaters? Do they occupy some intermediate category? As mentioned above, such questions are not easy to answer because the Qur'an does not present a consistent picture regarding how Muslims should view members of other faiths. This is especially true when it comes to Jews and Christians, who are mentioned more frequently in the Qur'an than Sabians and Magians, and are the two groups with whom Muhammad and his followers had the most contact.

Further complicating the situation is the fact that it is difficult to know exactly what the Qur'an means by "Jews" and "Christians" or "Judaism" and "Christianity." These religions took a variety of different forms, some more "orthodox" or mainstream than others, during this time period, and it would certainly be a mistake to equate them with their present-day manifestations. So what is the Qur'an speaking of when it refers to Jews, Christians, and their respective communities? To address these and similar questions, the Qur'an's treatment

> It is often difficult to know what the Qur'an is referring to when it mentions Judaism and Christianity.

of each of the non-Muslim groups mentioned in 22:17 will be considered, beginning with the ones mentioned less frequently.

## Magians

The Magians (*majūs*) are mentioned by name in the Qur'an only in 22:17. This is generally held to be a reference to Zoroastrians, the followers of an ancient Persian religious tradition that traces its roots to the first half of the first millennium B.C.E. The term originally applied only to the priestly class of Zoroastrianism, but it came to be used more generally to refer to all adherents to the faith. Their presence in the list has led to debates within Islam over whether or not the Magians are to be included among the members of the People of Book (see below), a designation extended to them by some commentators and legal experts. As noted above, a question remains regarding whether the Magians and the other groups identified in 22:17—Jews, Christians, and Sabians—are to be counted among the believers or the idolaters.

## Sabians

(Q 2:62; 5:69; 22:17)

The Sabians (*sābi'ūn*) are mentioned in three verses in the Qur'an (2:62; 5:69; 22:17). All three of these verses list them along with the believers, Jews, and Christians, with the third one including the Magians as well. The first two verses suggest that Sabians, along with Muslims, Jews, and Christians, will be blessed by God: "Regarding believers, Jews, Christians, and Sabians—those who believe in God and the Last Day and do good deeds—their reward is with their Lord. No fear will come upon them, nor will they grieve" (2:62; cf. 5:69).

It is unclear what group the Qur'an is referring to in these passages because it does not identify any details about Sabian practices or beliefs. Their inclusion in listings alongside Muslims, Jews, and Christians suggests that they may have had had some features in common with these other religious groupings. The Sabians should not be confused with the Sabaeans, who were the inhabitants of Sheba, an important South Arabian nation in antiquity that was famous for its trading activities.

## Jews

(Q 5:18; 2:113; 2:120; 5:51; 9:30; 5:64; 5:82; 2:62; 5:69; 22:17; 5:44; 6:146; 4:46, 160; 5:41; 16:118; 62:6; 61:6; 2:47; 2:122; 44:30-32; 2:63, 83-84, 93; 5:12, 70; 5:13a; 5:7; 2:75; 4:46; 5:13, 41-43; 6:91; 14:16, 26; 15:26; 16:7; 5:70; 2:61, 87, 91; 3:21, 112, 181, 183; 4:155; 2:85, 90, 94, 111; 62:5-6; 4:162; 4:46; 7:159; 2:142)

There were a number of Jewish tribes in Arabia during Muhammad's lifetime, particularly in Medina and its surrounding area. In fact, Jews were present in the Arabian Peninsula as early as the first century C.E., and so Islam emerged in a place that had long been familiar with Jewish traditions and practices. That familiarity is reflected in many passages of the Qur'an, which often assumes knowledge of biblical stories and other Jewish sources on the part of its audience.

The relationship between Muhammad and the Medinan Jews was sometimes a contentious one. The chapter on violence explains how efforts by the Jewish tribes of Medina to assist Muhammad's enemies in Mecca led him to adopt retaliatory measures that were sometimes harsh and included the mass execution of men and the enslavement of Jewish women and children. This uneasy relationship—and the political and social causes behind it—should be kept in mind when considering what the Qur'an has to say about the Jewish community and its relations with Muslims. Here, as elsewhere, the historical context and its "occasions of revelation" (asbāb al-nuzūl) have sometimes left its stamp on the tone and tenor of the Qur'an's message. This raises important interpretive issues, particularly in passages that are critical of Jews and Judaism. Are such passages making impartial theological statements about the legitimacy or efficacy of Judaism as a whole? Are they meant to be understood universally as relevant for all times and places? Or should they be understood as applicable only to the situation in Arabia more than a millennium ago?

> *The three most prominent Jewish tribes in the area of Medina during Muhammad's lifetime were the Nadīr, the Qaynuqā`, and the Qurayẓa. The origins of these groups are not certain. They are not mentioned by name in the Qur'an, but certain verses are often associated with them and their relationship with the early Muslim community.*

Jews (yahūd, sing. yahūdī) are mentioned explicitly nine times in the Qur'an. All of these texts are critical of the Jews, and in six of them the shortcomings of Christians are also mentioned. The longest passage is 5:18, which castigates both groups for claiming to be God's favorites and explains why they will be punished by God: "The Jews and the Christians say, 'We are the children of God and His beloved ones.' Say (Muhammad), 'Then why does He punish you for your offenses? You are merely among the human beings He has created. He forgives whomever He will and punishes

> *In 9:30, the Qur'an says that Jews take Ezra (`Uzayr) to be the son of God. This is sometimes interpreted as a reference to Ezra the priest, a Jewish leader during the return from the Babylonian exile in the sixth century B.C.E. It is an enigmatic verse whose meaning is unclear but best understood in light of the contentious relationship that sometimes existed between Muhammad and the Jewish community during the Medinan period.*

whomever He will. God has authority over the heavens and earth and everything between them. Everything leads to Him.'" Other passages say other negative things about Jews and Christians—that they accuse each other of wrongdoing (2:113), that they do not accept the Prophet Muhammad (2:120), that Muslims should not take them as allies (5:51), and that they violate monotheism by claiming someone is God's son.

Jews are mentioned without reference to Christians in 5:64, which adopts a very negative tone. It finds fault in them for not acknowledging the full extent of God's power, not recognizing the Qur'an as God's word, waging war, and spreading corruption. These allegations in a chapter coming from the Medinan period reflect and describe the tense situation that existed during that time when some Jewish tribes were questioning Muhammad's legitimacy and undermining his authority by cooperating with his enemies.

Another text that is very critical of the Jews equates them with idolaters and compares them unfavorably to Christians, who enjoy a warm and friendly relationship with Muslims: "You (Muhammad) will surely find that those most antagonistic to the believers are the Jews and those who associate other gods with God. You will also find that the ones closest in affection toward believers are those who say, 'We are Christians.' That is because among them are priests and ascetics, and they are not boastful" (5:82).

Elsewhere, the Qur'an identifies Jews without using the term *yahūd*. About a dozen times, it uses the verb *hāda* ("to be or become a Jew"), which is etymologically related to *yahūd* and may have entered Arabic via Hebrew. This is the form that is used in the texts mentioned above that refer to Jews, Christians, Sabians, and, in one instance, Magians (2:62; 5:69; 22:17). In those texts and in 5:44, they are spoken of in a positive way, but in other places Jews are evaluated in harsh terms. In 6:146, for example, the Jewish dietary restrictions are understood to be a punishment for lack of belief: "For the Jews [*hādū*] we prohibited animals with claws, and the fat of cattle and sheep, except what is on their backs and in their entrails or that attached to their bones. That is how We paid them back for their disobedience. Indeed, we are truthful" (cf. 4:46, 160; 5:41; 16:118; 62:6).

A common designation for the ancestors of the Jewish community, particularly those of biblical times, is "the Children of Israel" (*bānū isrā'īl*), a phrase found more than forty times in the Qur'an. Most of the references to them are associated with the time of Moses, but others relate to later periods of Israelite history, including up to the time of Jesus (61:6). There is an apologetic purpose to many of the passages that mention the Children of Israel since their main aim is to point out how the Israelites fell out of favor with God, thereby necessitating the rise of a new community—Islam—that would takes its place by conforming to the divine will.

In line with a central theme in the Hebrew Bible, several times the Qur'an makes reference to Israel's election as a people that enjoyed special status in God's eyes: "Oh children of Israel, remember how I favored you and privileged you over other people" (2:47; cf. 2:122; 44:30-32). The Arabic word that is used to describe this special relationship is *mīthāq*, a term that does not always refer to a bond between God and the Israelites in the Qur'an, but when it does it is often translated "covenant" (2:63, 83-84, 93; 5:12, 70). The Qur'an, like the Bible, maintains that Israel did not remain faithful to that covenant: "But they violated their covenant [*mīthāq*], so We rejected them and hardened their hearts" (5:13a).

This made possible the transfer of the covenant from the Israelites to Muslims, with whom God established a unique and special relationship: "Remember God's favor on you and the covenant [*mīthāq*] with which He bound you when you said, 'We hear and we obey.' Be mindful of God—truly, He knows the things of the heart" (5:7). As noted earlier, the apologetic nature of this theme is important to keep in mind. Behind the Qur'an's presentation of the Israelites as unworthy covenant partners is the uneasy relationship Muhammad had with his Jewish contemporaries, whose disloyalty to him led to his split from them. Their ancestors' earlier violation of their relationship with God sets the paradigm that explains and legitimates Muhammad's actions against them.

One of the serious charges leveled against the Children of Israel and Jews in the Qur'an is *taḥrīf*, falsifying or tampering with the divine revelations they received. Islam teaches that all the prophets from Adam through Muhammad were given the same message by God, but the followers of Judaism and Christianity distorted the teachings of their messengers. This explains why there are differences between the Bible and the Qur'an—they are not due to inconsistency or error on God's part but are solely of human origin. "How can you hope that they will believe you, when a group of them used to hear the word of God and then distorted it after they had understood it?" (2:75; cf. 4:46; 5:13, 41-3; 6:91). Some commentators have even argued that the

Some Muslims have claimed that Deuteronomy 18:18 alludes to Muhammad with its reference to a future prophet like Moses. Similarly, the advocate or helper that will come after Jesus and is mentioned several times in John's Gospel is sometimes considered to be an allusion to Muhammad (14:16, 26; 15:26; 16:7).

Bible originally contained references to the future coming of Muhammad that were removed by Jews and Christians who were opposed to Islam.

Related to this theme are those passages in the Qur'an that accuse the Jews or the Children of Israel of attacking and killing the prophets that have been sent to them: "We made a covenant with the children of Israel, and sent messengers to them. Every time a messenger brought them something they did not like, they accused some of lying and put others to death" (5:70; cf. 2:61, 87, 91; 3:21, 112, 181, 183; 4:155). Although some of these verses do not mention them specifically, their contexts indicate that it is the Jews who are the guilty parties. Other passages that view the Jews or Children of Israel unfavorably include 2:85, 90, 94, 111; and 62:5-6. It should be kept in mind that virtually all of these texts come from the Medinan period, which was precisely the time when Muhammad's relationship with the neighboring Jewish tribes was most fraught with difficulty.

As with many other topics treated in the Qur'an, its view of Jews and Judaism is not completely consistent. In addition to the negative assessments discussed above, there are other texts that speak in more positive terms. The clearest statement in support of Judaism is 2:62, mentioned earlier, which places Jews and members of other faiths on equal footing with Muslims before God's eyes: "Regarding believers, Jews, Christians, and Sabians—those who believe in God and the Last Day and do good deeds—their reward is with their Lord. No fear will come upon them, nor will they grieve" (cf. 5:69). In this verse, Jews will be rewarded if they are good people who have faith in God and recognize they will be judged at the end of time. They do not need to leave Judaism to be saved.

Elsewhere in the Qur'an, a distinction is made between Jews who are good and those who are not. After a listing of Jewish wrongdoings—including keeping others from God's way, practicing usury, unlawfully seizing property, and rejecting the truth—4:162 says that those Jews who do not engage in these activities will not be punished: "Those among them who are steeped in knowledge and are faithful, they believe in what has been revealed to you (Muhammad), and in what was revealed before you. Those who engage in prayer, pay alms, and believe in God and the last day—to them We will give a great reward" (cf. 4:46; 7:159). The reference here to belief in what was revealed to Muhammad can be interpreted as saying that only those Jews who embrace Islam will be saved, and if it is understood in this way the verse is less positive about Judaism than it at first appears to be. This is an important issue regarding some of the Qur'an's positive statements about other faiths that will be treated in more detail later in this chapter.

This overview has shown that most of the specific references to Jews and Judaism in the Qur'an tend to view them in a negative light. Those criticisms need to be read and interpreted with their originating contexts in mind. Such passages are often responding to a particular set of circumstances in which Muhammad was experiencing resistance and hostility from certain members of the Medinan Jewish community. Some commentators argue that their relevance is limited to those circumstances only and should not become a blueprint for how Muslims in later times should think about Jews and their faith. In

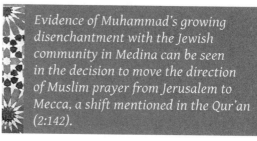

*Evidence of Muhammad's growing disenchantment with the Jewish community in Medina can be seen in the decision to move the direction of Muslim prayer from Jerusalem to Mecca, a shift mentioned in the Qur'an (2:142).*

other words, the attitudes and views reflected in these texts should not be seen as universal guidelines for Muslim/non-Muslim relations.

It should also be noted that there are quite a few other texts that are more positive about Jews even though they are not precisely identified. This is especially the case with passages about "the People of the Book," a category of non-Muslims that includes Jews and will be treated in a separate section below.

## Christians

(Q 34:18; 85:10; 5:46-47; 3:67; 2:62; 5:69; 5:82; 2:111, 140; 5:18; 2:113; 5:14; 2:120, 135; 5:51; 5:55; 6:14; 5:17; 5:72, 75; 3:37-47; 19:16-21; 3:59; 5:73; 4:171; 5:116-18; 5:72, 75; 4:157-59; 5:82-83; 9:31, 34; 57:27)

There is growing evidence of a fairly strong Christian presence in Arabia during the first century of Islam. The Christian community was probably not as large or unified as the Jewish one, but Muhammad and his early followers undoubtedly had contact with Christians. The fact that the Qur'an comments on Christian beliefs and individuals associated with Christianity testifies to this, as does the archaeological record, which shows that some parts of the Arabian Peninsula contained sizable numbers of Christians.

Perhaps the best example of this was Najran, a city in south Arabia that was an important economic and agricultural center (see Map, p. 8 above). By the fifth century, Christianity was so strongly established in Najran that it had its own bishop and had become a place of pilgrimage for Arab Christians, who traveled long distances to visit its shrine to martyrs. In 630, Muhammad established a pact with the Christians of Najran that guaranteed them freedom of worship, an arrangement that was the first treaty between Muslims and Christians. Najran is not mentioned specifically in the Qur'an, although it may be alluded to in 34:18, which speaks of several towns in southern Arabia, and in 85:10, where the reference to persecuted believers could be a comment about the martyrs of Najran.

Very little is known about the beliefs and practices of Arab Christians during this period. In all likelihood, they were members of subgroups like the Nestorians, Jacobites, and Melkites, Christian communities with a presence in Arabia whose roots could be traced to other parts of the Near East like Egypt and Mesopotamia, and whose principal languages were Greek, Coptic, and Syriac.

Influence from these languages, especially Syriac, can sometimes be seen in the Arabic of the Qur'an. A good example of this is the word commonly used for "Christians." Later forms of Arabic into the present day refer to a Christian by the term *masīḥī*, from the Semitic root also found in Hebrew and other languages that is the origin of the word "messiah." Although the word "messiah" (*masīḥ*) is found in the Qur'an, it is not used in reference to Christians. They are referred to as *naṣārā* (sing. *naṣrānī*), a word that likely stems from Jesus' connection with the town of Nazareth. The Qur'an calls Jesus' followers "Nazarenes," just as a cognate term in Syriac (*naṣrāyê*) is used in the same way. Drawing upon Syriac in this manner is a fairly common practice in the theological vocabulary of the Qur'an.

Most of the texts in the Qur'an about Christians include them—as well as Jews and others—in the category "People of the Book," which will be discussed below. With one or two exceptions where the term "People of the Book" is found, the discussion in this section of the chapter will be limited to those texts that refer explicitly to Christians as *naṣārā*. Christians are described once in the Qur'an as "People of the Gospel" in a passage that establishes the authority of the Bible: "We sent in their footsteps Jesus, son of Mary, confirming the Torah that had been sent before him. We gave him the Gospel, which contains guidance, light, and confirmation of the Torah sent before him—a guide and admonition for those who are mindful of God. So let the people of the Gospel [*ahl al-injīl*] judge by what God has revealed in it. Those who do not judge according to what God has sent down are transgressors" (5:46-47).

The term *naṣārā* is found fourteen times in the Qur'an. Its singular form (*naṣrānī*) is present only in 3:67, where it is stated the Abraham was neither a Jew nor a Christian. This is also the only verse in which the singular "Jew" (*yahūdī*) is found in the Qur'an. All fourteen of the occurrences of *naṣārā* are accompanied by a reference to Jews, and all but three of them evaluate Christians (and Jews) negatively. These three texts were all discussed above in the section on Jews. Two of them list Christians and Jews among those who will be rewarded by God (2:62; 5:69). The other is the only passage in this set of texts that privileges Christians over Jews: "You (Muhammad) will surely find that those most antagonistic to the believers are the Jews and those who associate other gods with God. You will also find that the ones closest in affection toward believers are those who say, 'We are Christians.' That is because among them are priests and ascetics, and they are not boastful" (5:82).

As noted above, among the shortcoming of Christians and Jews identified in the Qur'an are lying (2:111, 140; 5:18), bickering among themselves (2:113; 5:14), and trying to lead Muslims astray (2:120, 135). The negative assessment of them is summarized in 5:51: "Oh believers, do not take the Jews and Christians as allies. They are allies of one another. Anyone who takes them as allies is one of them. God does not guide an unjust people."

This verse has sometimes been cited in support of the argument that the Qur'an teaches Muslims to avoid Jews and Christians at all costs. This interpretation is based on a misreading of the Arabic word 'awliyā' (sing. walī), translated here as "allies." Some say that the word should be translated "friends," and they claim that the Qur'an is therefore prohibiting cordial, civil relations between Muslims and other monotheists.

In its singular or plural form, the word walī appears almost ninety times in the Qur'an, and it has a wide semantic range. Among its possible meanings are "ally," "friend," "protector," "patron," "follower," and "legal guardian." Each usage of the word has to be understood within its own unique literary and historical contexts in order to determine which meaning is most appropriate for that text. In this case, it is found in a chapter from the Medinan period in a section (5:51-60) that describes the mistreatment and lack of respect Muslims were experiencing from Jews, Christians, and others. It is therefore urging them to be cautious about whom they take as their allies or protectors and is not making a blanket statement about avoiding all contact with Christians and Jews. Given those circumstances, Muslims are being told to band together and lean on each other for protection and support. This point is reinforced a few verses later, when the importance of community ties is stressed: "Your allies [walī] are God, His Messenger, and the believers—those who engage in prayer, pay alms, and bow down in worship" (5:55; cf. 6:14).

Other texts criticize certain elements of Christian faith without always naming them as such. Two related Christian beliefs that are called into question by the Qur'an are the incarnation and the Trinity. The belief that Jesus is God in human

The term "messiah" is found eleven times in the Qur'an, and Jesus is the only person ever given that title. The Qur'an does not define what the word means or what the messiah's role is.

form is foundational to Christianity, and in several places, the Qur'an challenges this idea. "Those who say, 'God is the Messiah, the son of Mary,' are truly unbelievers. Say (Muhammad), 'Who would be able to stop God if he wanted to destroy the Messiah, son of Mary, his mother, and everyone else on earth? God has authority over the heavens and earth and everything between. He creates whatever He wishes, and God has power over everything'" (5:17; cf. 5:72, 75). The frequent references in the Qur'an to Jesus as "son of Mary," as in this verse, are probably meant to reinforce the idea that he is no different from any other person.

Despite its stress on the humanity of Jesus, however, the Qur'an teaches that he was conceived without a human father. In agreement with the Gospels of Matthew and Luke, the Islamic text mentions in two places that Mary maintained her virginity at Jesus' conception (3:37-47; 19:16-21). This is a miraculous event that gives him special status, but it does not raise Jesus to God's level according to the Qur'an. A precedent was established for this type of birth when the first human was created, and there has never been any attempt to ascribe divinity to Adam because of the unique circumstances of how he came to exist: "Before God, Jesus is like Adam. He created him from dust, and then said to him, 'Be,' and he was" (3:59).

*Joseph, the husband of Jesus' mother, Mary, is not mentioned in the Qur'an.*

The Christian belief in the Trinity, which holds God to be three persons in one, is also contested by the Qur'an as erroneous: "Those who say that God is the third of three are unbelievers. There is no god but the One God. If they do not desist in what they are saying, a painful punishment will come upon the unbelievers among them" (5:73; cf. 4:171). In a number of places, the Qur'an has Jesus himself refute the Trinity and other claims his followers have mistakenly made about him: "When God said, 'Oh Jesus, son of Mary, did you ever say to people, "Take me and my mother as two gods apart from God"?' He said, 'Praise be to You! Far be it from me to say what I have no right to say. If I had said such a thing You would have known it. You know all that is within me, but I do not know what is within You. Truly, only You know all hidden things'" (5:116; cf. 5:72; 5:117–18).

The reference to claiming divinity for Mary in the previous verse is interesting. This idea might also lie behind the curious statement in 5:75 that both Jesus and his mother ate food, a comment meant to stress their full humanity. Belief in Mary's divinity has never been a part of mainstream orthodox Christianity, and such passages may best be explained with reference to the diversity of groups and beliefs that constituted Arabian Christianity in the seventh century. Perhaps these verses reflect familiarity with and exposure to marginal segments of the Christian community that eventually were suppressed or died out. Related to this is the larger question of the precise form(s) of Christianity that Muhammad and his early followers came in contact with, an issue that continues to be debated. There is evidence in the Qur'an that indicates familiarity with extracanonical Gospels and other Christian writings that were not accepted into the biblical canon.

*Jesus' death is most fully discussed in 4:157-59. The passage's meaning is ambiguous, leading some Muslims to conclude that Jesus did not die on the cross but someone else took his place.*

An expression of Christian faith that the Qur'an mentions several times is monasticism. In the fifth and sixth centuries c.e., monastic communities were well established in the areas surrounding the Arabian peninsula, including Egypt, Abyssinia (Ethiopia), Syria, Palestine, and Mesopotamia. Just prior to the rise of Islam, some members of these communities began to spread into Arabia, and there is evidence of their presence along the southern coast of the peninsula and in cities like Najran. Extraqur'anic Islamic traditions speak of contact Muhammad had with monks, and the Qur'an indicates that monasticism was known to be an important dimension of Christianity.

Monks (*ruhbān*) are mentioned three times in the Qur'an. They are spoken of in positive terms in 5:82, a verse discussed earlier that puts Christians in a more favorable light than Jews. In reference to Christians, the second half of the verse says, "Among them are priests and ascetics, and they are not boastful, and when they listen to what is revealed to the Messenger, you see their eyes overflowing with tears because they recognize the truth. They say, 'Our Lord, we believe, so count us among the witnesses'" (5:82b-83). This is the only time the Qur'an speaks of priests (*qissīsūn*). This verse describes them and monks as pious individuals who are humble and open to God's word.

Less positive is the description of monks in the other two passages that mention them, which are found within three verses of each other: "They take their scholars [*ahbār*] and their monks as lords, as well as the Messiah, the son of Mary. The only thing they were commanded was to serve only the one God—there is no god but He. Praise him above what they associate with Him. . . . Oh believers, many scholars and monks vainly consume people's wealth and hinder them from God's path. Those who store up gold and silver but do not spend it in God's way—give (Muhammad) them notice of a painful punishment" (9:31, 34). The impression here is that monks are self-centered individuals who are elevated above the other members of their community and care little about the needs of those around them. Also included in these critiques are those referred to as the *aḥbār*, which is sometimes considered to be a reference to rabbis. But since the term refers to any learned person, it is better to translate it as "scholars" and read the verses as a condemnation of Jewish and Christian leaders who abuse their authority.

The Qur'an mentions monasticism only in 57:27, which is an ambiguous verse that is open to a number of interpretations: "We sent our messengers in their footsteps, and then We sent Jesus, son of Mary. We gave him the Gospel and put kindness and mercy in the hearts of those who follow him. But they invented monasticism [*rahbānīya*]. We did not prescribe it for them—only that they desire God's pleasure, but they did not do so properly. We rewarded those who believed, but many of them were transgressors." Some commentators argue that the verse is saying that monasticism was originally intended by God but Christians distorted it into something else. The majority of exegetes, however, claim that the text is condemning monasticism as a purely human innovation that was never part of God's plan for humanity. Regardless of how this verse is understood, it is clear that the Qur'an's assessment of monasticism, like that of Christians and Jews in general, is lukewarm in that some texts view it favorably but the majority of passages less so.

## The People of the Book

(Q 3:3-4; 20:4; 26:192; 32:2; 56:80; 76:23; 25:1; 2:185; 8:29; 3:75; 2:105-9; 3:72-74, 110-13; 29:46-47; 98; 3:98-99; 3:70-71; 5:65-66; 5:68; 3:65; 4:153; 4:171; 3:64)

Jews and Christians are also sometimes identified in the Qur'an as "the People of the Book" (*ahl al-kitāb*), a term that appears in approximately thirty verses and is tied to the Islamic understanding of revelation. According to that understanding, God has spoken to various prophets throughout history, and some of those individuals were given a written text for their communities. Examples of these writings are the Torah (*tawrāt*), which was given to Moses, the Psalms (*zabūr*) of David, and the Gospel (*injīl*), received by Jesus. The message of all these books was the same—God is one, and all people must respond in submission (*islām*) to the divine will. The followers of these prior prophets distorted and falsified

*The word* injīl *is an arabization of the Greek word for "gospel,"* euangelion.

that message, and that led to the need for God to send a final prophet, Muhammad, who accurately transmitted God's message in the Qur'an.

This view of the Qur'an's relationship to the prior revelations is seen in texts like 3:3-4: "He has sent down the book with the truth to you (Muhammad), confirming what came before it. He sent down the Torah and the Gospel previously as a guide for people, and then He sent down the book that distinguishes. Those who do not believe God's revelations will surely suffer severe punishment. God is mighty and capable of retribution." Three times in these verses, verbs from the Arabic root n-z-l are used to describe the act of God "sending down" the message in book form. The word *tanzīl* also comes from that root, a word found fifteen times in the text to describe the revelation of the Qur'an and prior scriptures (cf. 20:4; 26:192; 32:2; 56:80; 76:23).

Another important word in 3:3-4 is *furqān*, a term translated here as "the book that distinguishes," which literally means "the distinction" or "the criterion." It is a word the Qur'an sometimes uses to refer to itself. Chapter 25 of the Qur'an is titled *al- furqān*, and the term is found in its first verse: "Blessed be He who has sent down to His servant the book that distinguishes so that it might be a warning to all" (25:1; cf. 2:185; 8:29). The point behind this designation is that the Qur'an is the text that is able to distinguish good from evil and right from wrong. Similarly, the term calls attention to the corrective relationship the Qur'an has to prior scriptures, like the Bible, that do not accurately preserve God's message for humanity.

The Qur'an's view of the People of the Book, like that of Jews and Christians, is ambivalent. Some texts avoid generalizations by distinguishing between good and bad individuals among the People of the Book: "There are those among the People of the Book who, if you entrust them with a large sum of money, will return it to you. But there are others of them who, if you entrust them with the smallest amount, will not return it to you unless you keep standing over them [demanding it back]. That is because they say, 'We have no obligation toward the gentiles.' But they tell a lie against God, and they know it" (3:75; cf. 2:105-9; 3:72-74, 110-13; 29:46-47). Perhaps the Qur'an's clearest statement on the diversity among the People of the Book is in chapter 98, which spells out the rewards the good among them will receive and the punishment the evil will experience.

Other passages speak more generally about the People of the Book without making a distinction among them. The majority of these texts are critical of them, with a primary fault being that they fail to recognize the legitimacy of Muhammad's prophetic status or his message: "Say (Muhammad), 'Oh People of the Book, why do you not believe God's revelations? God is a witness over everything you do.' Say (Muhammad), 'Oh People of the Book, why do you block believers from God's path and try to make it crooked, when you are witnesses [to the truth]? God is not unaware of what you are doing'" (3:98-99; cf. 3:70-71; 5:65-66).

Those passages that speak positively about the People of the Book recognize them for remaining faithful to the revelation they received, but they also mention the need to accept Muhammad and his revelation: "Say (Muhammad), 'Oh People of the Book, you have nothing until you observe the Torah, the Gospel, and what has been revealed to you from your Lord.' But what has been revealed to you (Muhammad) from your Lord will certainly increase the wickedness and unbelief of many of them. Do not concern yourself with the faithless people" (5:68).

Passages like this one that mention the Torah and Gospel clearly indicate that the designation "People of the Book" refers to Jews and Christians (cf. 3:65). The same can be said for texts like 4:153, which mentions Moses and the golden calf episode, and 4:171, where Jesus is specifically named in reference to the People of the Book. But in most cases, such markers are missing, and so the Qur'an usually does not identify which groups constitute the People of the Book. In addition to Jews and Christians, many commentators include Sabians and Magians, who were mentioned earlier, and some in more recent times have also identified Hindus and Buddhists as among the People of the Book.

As is the case with Qur'an texts that are critical of Jews and Christians, the polemical nature of many of the passages that mention the People of the Book must be understood within their proper historical contexts. Muslim/non-Muslim relations were strained at times during the formative period of Islam, and negative views of the Other in the text usually reflect that contentious state of affairs as early Muslims sought to establish their identity and preserve their community.

Despite that tension, however, the very concept of a "People of the Book" who, like Muslims, are recipients of divine revelation holds the potential to bring those groups together and unite them in a shared heritage. This is best seen in 3:64, a passage that led to the formulation of "A Common Word," the basis of an important interfaith initiative. "Say (Muhammad),

*In 2007, a group of 138 Muslim leaders issued a statement titled, "A Common Word between Us and You," which discusses the common ground shared by Islam and Christianity. It has played an important role in helping to improve and enhance relations between Christians and Muslims (www.acommonword.com).*

'Oh People of the Book, come to a common word between us and you—that we worship only God, that we associate nothing with Him, and that we not take others as lords beside God.' If they turn away, say, 'Witness that we are submitters.'"

## Unbelievers

(Q 16:106; 2:108; 4:137; 35:39; 49:7; 4:48; 4:116; 112; 3:67; 2:135; 10:105; 16:123; 39:3, 38; 53:19-20; 5:73; 2:105)

A final category of non-Muslims to consider are the unbelievers. The Qur'an has a number of different ways of speaking about those who lack faith or whose faith is antithetical to Islam.

Words from the Arabic root k-f-r are often used to describe them. The verb *kafara* appears close to three hundred times in the text, and it can describe various forms of unbelief, including denial or rejection of God, disobedience of a divine command, and blasphemy. In some passages, unbelievers are described as putting their faith in idols, and elsewhere they lack faith in God. The term the Qur'an uses for this state of unbelief is *kufr*, and the one who engages in it is a *kāfir*: "Those who become unbelievers [*kafara*] after believing in God—except for those who are forced to do so while their hearts remain faithful—and open themselves up to unbelief [*kufr*] will have God's wrath upon them. A great punishment is theirs" (16:106; cf. 2:108; 4:137; 35:39; 49:7).

As already seen, another root commonly used in the Qur'an to describe unbelief or false belief is *sh-r-k*, which carries the meaning "to associate." It is found more than one hundred times in the text, and when used theologically it describes the act of associating something or someone with God, thereby violating the unity that is the defining trait of the deity's nature. This can take different forms, including idol worship and ascribing divinity to a created object or being. The term that describes this practice is *shirk*, and the one who engages in it is a *mushrik*. It is a serious offense that is categorically condemned in the Qur'an, which describes it as the only sin that God will not forgive: "God does not forgive associating partners with Him. He forgives anything else as He wishes, but anyone who associates something with God has committed a grave offense" (4:48; cf. 4:116). A succinct description of God's nature that implicitly critiques *shirk* is found in chapter 112 of the Qur'an.

The *mushrik* is often depicted as the antithesis of the *ḥanīf*, the radical monotheist mentioned earlier in this chapter. In eleven of the twelve verses containing the word *ḥanīf*, the term *mushrik* is also found. This occurs a number of times in reference to Abraham, the only individual identified as a *ḥanīf* in the Qur'an. Whenever he is described in this way, as in 3:67, it is immediately stated that he was not a *mushrik*. "Abraham was neither a Jew nor a Christian. He was an upright person [*ḥanīf*] who submitted, and he was not one of those who associate [*mushrik*]" (cf. 2:135; 10:105; 16:123). In this way, the faith of the true monotheist is contrasted with the lack of faith of the quintessential sinner.

It is often difficult to know precisely who the Qur'an has in mind when it speaks of unbelievers, and undoubtedly it refers to different groups in different verses. In the most general terms, anyone who rejects Muhammad and the Qur'an—whether that person is a polytheist, a Jew, or a Christian—is guilty of *kufr*, or unbelief. Given the makeup of the population of Arabia in the sixth century, many of the references to unbelievers were allusions to idolaters and/or polytheists.

There is some evidence in the Qur'an to suggest that at least some of the polytheists of Arabia were in fact henotheists, those who believe in a multiplicity of gods over whom one god reigns supreme (39:3, 38).

*The "satanic verses" incident is part of a tradition that claims that Muhammad once mistook a message from Satan as divine revelation. The message was in reference to 53:19-20, which mentions three goddesses sometimes known as the "daughters of Allah." Muhammad came to realize the error he had made and the offending passage was expurgated. Many Muslims throughout history have rejected the "satanic verses" tradition as spurious.*

This is also supported by references in the Qur'an and other sources to belief among the Arabs in lesser deities, including three goddesses who are mentioned by name in 53:19-20: "Have you considered al-Lāt and al-'Uzzā, and the third one, Manāt?" This text played a central role in the controversy during Muhammad's lifetime known as the "satanic verses." Whether they are to be thought of as polytheists, henotheists, or idolaters, most of the passages that condemn unbelief, particularly during the earlier Meccan period, are directed against religious systems that were not monotheistic rather than against Judaism and/or Christianity.

But in some texts, it is clearly Jews or Christians who are being condemned for their lack of belief. For example, Christians are accused of *kufr* in 5:73 because of their belief in the Trinity: "Those who say that God is the third of three are unbelievers [*kafara*]. There is only One God. If they do not desist in what they are saying, the unbelievers among them will experience a painful punishment." Similarly, a reference in 2:105 to certain People of the Book who lack belief comes immediately after a verse that is clearly speaking of Jews: "Those among the People of the Book who do not believe [*kafarū*] and those who associate something with God do not like that anything good should be sent down to you from your Lord. But in His mercy God favors whomever He will. His bounty is endless." Despite such criticisms, however, it is important to keep in mind that the Qur'an never refers to the People of the Book as *mushrikūn*. This is so because they self-identify as monotheists, and the Qur'an respects that claim, even if it sometimes calls into question how their faith is expressed.

By way of conclusion, it can be said that the Qur'an refers frequently to unbelief, which was undoubtedly considered to be a threat to the survival of the early Muslim community, most of whose members were originally among the ranks of those the text labels "unbelievers." The context of a given passage is important to keep in mind since historical factors and theological concerns dictated who deserved the designation. It is difficult to know their identities with certainty in many texts, but throughout the Qur'an various groups are included among the unbelievers, including other monotheists.

This overview has shown that there is a high level of ambiguity within the Qur'an regarding its attitude toward non-Muslims, especially Jews and Christians. Some texts are conciliatory and speak about the members of other faiths in positive terms, while others adopt a more critical tone that can at times be hostile. This raises a host of important questions for those who look to the Qur'an as a guide to help them understand what Islam teaches about the Other. How do we reconcile the conflicting messages? Are some passages more relevant than others? Is it proper to accept some texts as valid while rejecting others? The answers to such questions will have a significant bearing on how one envisions the future of Muslim/non-Muslim relations.

## Pluralism

Recent decades have seen a growing movement in theological circles that is often referred to as "religious pluralism." In the most general terms, pluralism espouses the idea that all religions are equally valid paths to God, or ultimate reality. This is the opposite position of exclusivism, which holds that one particular religion, usually "mine," is correct, while all other faiths are inferior. Among the world's religions, the monotheistic ones are generally considered to be among the most exclusivist because their adherents often make truth claims that privilege their faith and, either explicitly or implicitly, marginalize other religious traditions.

It should come as no surprise that pluralism has been a controversial topic at times. Some have warmly embraced it as a viable alternative to a prevailing mindset that tends to view the world's variegated religious landscape in black-and-white terms. They believe it offers the best hope to move beyond the stereotypes and prejudices that typify how people perceive other religions and those who follow them. Others are adamantly opposed to pluralism. They consider it to be an example of the relativism and doubt that have come to dominate our morally bankrupt world.

A growing number of Muslim scholars are exploring pluralism from the perspective of Islam. In this section, the work of four of them will be considered, with particular attention paid to what they have to say about the Qur'an and pluralism. Their writings represent what is being done in this emerging area, and they give some indication of what the future might have in store for Muslim/non-Muslim relations.

## Mahmut Aydin
(Q 3:85; 3:19; 5:3; 109:6; 3:67; 2:133; 2:127-28; 12:101; 3:52; 22:78; 2:62; 5:69; 33:40; 2:112)

Mahmut Aydin is a Turkish scholar who has written extensively on Muslim/non-Muslim relations, and several of his works have addressed issues related to religious pluralism. According to Aydin, a pluralist believes that people can experience salvation within their own religious traditions, and there is no need for them to convert to the "true" faith. Drawing upon the work of influential figures within the field, like John Hick and Paul Knitter, Aydin has explored the question of whether or not pluralism is a viable position for a Muslim to hold. In some of his writings, he has considered whether the pluralist perspective is compatible with the Qur'an's message.

Aydin believes insufficient attention has been paid to how certain key words in the Qur'an should be understood and defined, with two of the most important being *dīn* and *al-'islām*. As noted earlier, the term *al-'islām* is mentioned only eight times in the Qur'an. Several of these texts speak of it as the way of life God intends for all humanity. "If one seeks a religion [*dīn*] other than *al-'islām* it will not be accepted from them. They will be among the lost ones in the hereafter" (3:85; cf. 3:19; 5:3).

In these passages, *al-'islām* is described as a *dīn*, a term discussed earlier in this chapter. Aydin explains that people often define *dīn* as "religion," in the sense of an organized institution. But this is to ignore the fact that the word sometimes has a more general meaning that describes a mutual relationship between God and a person. God issues ethical orders, while the person responds with belief and obedience. The exact form *dīn* takes can vary, as in 109:6, where Muhammad uses the term to describe both the belief of the non-Muslim Meccans and his own: "To you your religion [*dīn*], and to me my religion [*dīn*]." But this other, non-institutional sense of *dīn* is sometimes overlooked, with the result that some identify *al-'islām* with the religion of Islam.

Aydin calls for a redefinition of *al-'islām* in these passages that is more inclusive, and he understands it to be a mindset or a perspective rather than an organized religion. In keeping with the literal sense of the word, he says it is used in the Qur'an to describe submission or surrender to

God's will by anyone, regardless of whether or not that person is a Muslim and professes the religion of Islam.

This is why the Qur'an describes some people who lived long before the time of Muhammad as "muslims." They submitted themselves to God's will even though they could not formally embrace the religion that would be established by Muhammad centuries later. "Abraham was neither a Jew nor a Christian. He was an upright person [ḥanīf] who submitted [muslim], and he was not one of those who associate [mushrikūn]" (3:67). Others called muslim in the Qur'an include Jacob's sons (2:133), Ishmael (2:127-28), Joseph (12:101), Jesus' disciples (3:52), and the descendants of Abraham (22:78). According to Aydin, al-'islām is the essence of dīn because it is the quality that unites the teachings of all the prophets since the beginning of time.

Aydin concludes that the words al-'islām and muslim are used in the Qur'an not in reference to the institutionalized religion we know today as Islam but as ways of designating the act of submission to God's will and those who practice it. He believes that the traditional view that one particular religion supplants and abrogates all others needs to be rethought in light of the Qur'an's teaching. He argues for a Copernican Revolution in Muslim thought that puts al-'islām, rather than Islam, at the center. This would create a more inclusive attitude toward those of other faiths and put all people who submit to God's will on equal footing, regardless of their different religious affiliations.

This tolerant attitude is reflected in some of the Qur'an passages discussed earlier in this chapter, which Aydin believes express the egalitarian ethos that is central to the Qur'an. "Regarding believers, Jews, Christians, and Sabians—those who believe in God and the Last Day and do good deeds—their reward is with their Lord. No fear will come upon them, nor will they grieve" (2:62; cf. 5:69). He faults the tafsīr writings for downplaying or ignoring texts like these that claim that salvation is open to anyone who believes in God and the last day and does good deeds. With his criticism of the commentators, Aydin makes an argument similar to that of feminists who claim that the Muslim community has tended to rely more on interpretations of the Qur'an rather than the Qur'an itself regarding what it teaches about gender.

In Aydin's opinion, then, when it comes to Muslim/non-Muslim relations, the Qur'an is an inclusive text. To be a Muslim is to be a pluralist. This is a view that not all Muslims would agree with, but Aydin says it is the only intellectually responsible position to hold in a theologically diverse world in which advanced technology and forms of communication put people of different faith traditions in frequent contact with one another.

Aydin believes that more Muslims will respond to this challenge and embrace pluralism only if they develop a new way of thinking about the Qur'an and the Prophet Muhammad. To explain how this might be done, he makes use of American theologian Paul Knitter's ideas about the need for Christians to modify their understanding of Jesus' uniqueness if they are to move beyond exclusivism toward pluralism.

The new model can be summed up in two sentences, one a negation and the other an affirmation. In the first place, Muslims should not consider God's revelation in the Qur'an to be full, definitive, and unsurpassable. Three things are denied in this statement:

1) That the Qur'an is the complete and total record of God's message to humanity.
2) That only the Qur'an is the word of God and no other source reveals the divine will.
3) That it is impossible for God's revelation to be found in other forms and at other times.

At the same time, Muslims should consider God's revelation in the Qur'an to be universal, decisive, and indispensable. Three things are affirmed in this statement:

1) That the Qur'an is a message for all times and places that is relevant for all people.
2) That the Qur'an transforms lives from being self-centered to being God-centered.
3) That the Qur'an is essential because it will continue to enrich humanity.

Aydin is quick to point out that making these six claims in no way negates for Muslims the uniqueness of the Qur'an or the finality of the Prophet Muhammad. It simply enables them to be more tolerant and open to the legitimacy of other faiths. For Muslims, the Qur'an continues to be the normative revelation from God to humanity, and Muhammad remains the seal of the prophets (33:40). But if they take these six principles to heart, Muslims will be better able to acknowledge that those who do not share their faith can still find God through other means. The Qur'an itself says as much: "Truly, those who submit themselves completely to God and do good deeds have their reward with their Lord. They will neither fear nor grieve" (2:112).

## Asma Afsaruddin

(Q 49:13; 5:48b)

As with some of the other topics treated in this book, it can be a challenge to try to discern whether the Qur'an has an attitude toward pluralism, because it is a modern concept. The Qur'an does not use the term *pluralism*, and so one must identify texts that are somehow related to the topic even if it is not specifically mentioned. Interpreters and readers who adopt this approach look for clues that give them a sense of the text's attitude toward or perspective on an issue when the modern term for it is not used. This is not a situation unique to the Qur'an. Scholars of the Bible and other writings from antiquity often find themselves engaged in similar methods in their efforts to determine what ancient texts might have to say about modern concerns.

Asma Afsaruddin is a Muslim scholar who has published widely on Islamic intellectual history and has attempted to uncover the Quran's view of pluralism in this manner. She has argued that the concept of mutual knowledge in the Qur'an indicates that reconciliation and pluralism are central to the text's message and ethos.

Two texts are central to her argument, with the first being 49:13: "Oh humanity, We created you male and female and made you into peoples and tribes so that you might know one another. The most honorable of you before God are the ones who are most pious. Truly, God knows and is aware." This is a verse that acknowledges the diversity that exists within humanity and says that it is part of God's plan. Beyond that, there is a reason for that diversity—it is an opportunity for people to know and learn about one another. Afsaruddin points out that this verse is insisting on something more than simple toleration of those who are different from oneself. It calls for active engagement by interacting with them and seeking to discover who they are.

In its original context, this verse was probably a command to the early Muslim community to transcend the limits imposed by their tribal-based society so that they could form connections with others outside their own groups. Afsaruddin believes that this message can be modified in the modern world to become an appeal for people to engage in constructive dialogue with others from different cultures, countries, and religions. She explains that the text concludes with a caution against stereotyping and labeling others because God rewards piety, not affiliation with a particular group.

The other text calling for mutual knowledge is 5:48b: "We have prescribed a law and a way for each of you. If God had willed, He could have made you one community, but He tests you through what He has given you. So race one another in doing good deeds. All of you will return to God, and He will explain to you what you differed about." This text makes the same point as 49:13, that the pluralism and diversity found in the world are part of God's plan. Afsaruddin notes that, according to this verse, the only competition that should exist among people is in their efforts to outdo one another in goodness. The reminder that all will return to God, who will settle all differences, is meant to discourage people from judging others since that is not their role. Only at the end of time, when all have "returned to God," will the differences among people be resolved and fully understood. Until that time, people should see their diversity as an opportunity to learn from each other and act graciously toward one another.

The passage begins with the comment that each community has its own law and way of life. The first half of the verse makes it clear that the text is speaking about Muslims and the People of the Book. It reminds Muhammad that the Qur'an confirms the Bible, while at the same time acknowledging the differences between Muslims and the People of the Book. The implication is that each group should follow the way that God has revealed to it and leave judgment in the hands of God. Afsaruddin considers this to be representative of the Qur'an's pluralistic perspective.

## Mahmoud Ayoub
### (Q 2:62; 5:69)

One of the leading Muslim voices on interfaith relations, especially between Islam and Christianity, belongs to Mahmoud Ayoub, who taught at Temple University for many years in a long and distinguished career. He maintains that the Qur'an's view of religion is clearly pluralistic and tolerant of all those who engage in good works and believe in God and the last day. Ayoub argues that the frequent criticisms directed toward Jews and Christians in the Qur'an are not attacks on Judaism and/or Christianity as a whole but are aimed at specific beliefs or actions of particular individuals with whom Muhammad came in contact. As such, they should not be used to negate the many passages that are more positive and encourage mutual understanding between Muslims and the People of the Book.

Key texts for Ayoub are 2:62 and 5:69, discussed several times earlier in this chapter, which state that Jews, Christians, and Sabians will be rewarded by God because their beliefs and actions are like those of Muslims. To explain why this call for tolerance is often not followed, Ayoub points his finger in the same direction that Mahmut Aydin and many feminist scholars place the blame—the *tafsīr* writings. He says that many commentators throughout history have chosen to ignore the pluralistic message of the Qur'an by adopting the position that Islam is the only true religion and the only way a non-Muslim can be saved is by converting. Ayoub counters that there is no support for this supersessionist position, which is based on long-standing religious, social, economic, and political rivalries between Muslims and non-Muslims rather than on textual evidence.

Ayoub strongly criticizes commentators who attempt to explain away Qur'an passages that openly call for peaceful and cooperative relations between Muslims and non-Muslims. He is particularly harsh on those who distort the obvious sense of a text in order to justify their preconceived notions of Islam's superiority. Common examples of this kind of interpretive move can be seen in some of the ways commentators have dealt with Qur'an passages that speak positively about Christians. Some exegetes have argued that these are references to Christians who lived only during the period before Muhammad and the emergence of Islam, while others have claimed that such texts have in mind only those Christians who left Christianity in order to convert to Islam. Ayoub says there is absolutely no support in the Qur'an for such interpretations, which negate the text's pluralist message and are the cause of much of the strife that exists between Muslims and non-Muslims today.

According to Ayoub, the Qur'an's main theme is faith, not religion. It speaks about faith in universal terms as submission to God's will, but it does not envision a world of religious uniformity in which all must be Muslims. The many passages that celebrate the diversity of creation and hold up the followers of other religions as good and honorable people testify to this. Ayoub does not deny the fact that other texts in the Qur'an are critical of non-Muslims and do not reflect the tolerance and pluralism that he believes are at its core, but he considers those texts to be context-specific and not meant to be universally relevant for all times and places.

Ayoub unabashedly admits that he prefers to highlight the portions of the Qur'an that present a hopeful image of Muslim/non-Muslim relations. His reading that privileges pluralism stems from his conviction that people must find ways to get along in a diverse world that we can either improve by working together or tear down in isolation from one another. Some might accuse him of ignoring the passages that are most problematic, but Ayoub maintains that the future depends on our ability to be selective in the texts and concepts we highlight by preferring those that facilitate cooperation and dialogue.

## Abdulaziz Sachedina

(Q 2:256; 10:99-100)

A Muslim scholar who has written a great deal on pluralism, human rights, and ethics is Abdulaziz Sachedina, a professor at the University

of Virginia. He maintains that at the heart of the Qur'an's notion of pluralism is its recognition of freedom of conscience in matters related to
faith and belief. This is seen in texts like 2:256, with its prohibition against
forcing religion upon someone, and 10:99-100, which warns the Prophet
Muhammad against trying to do something that only God can do: "Had
your Lord so willed, all the people on earth would believe. So can you
(Muhammad) force people to become believers? No person can believe
except with God's permission, and He brings dishonor on those who do
not exercise reason."

According to Sachedina, the Qur'an's acknowledgment of a person's
right to freely choose to follow one religion or another is evidence of its
endorsement of pluralism. Consequently, attempting to persuade someone
to adopt a particular faith or criticizing someone for following a certain
religion is a violation of this basic principle of the Qur'an and therefore
goes against God's will.

Like Ayoub, Sachedina places much of the blame for the inability to
accept what the Qur'an has to say about other religions on the supersessionism that some Muslims espouse. The idea that Islam has replaced and
supplanted all previous religions is a theological doctrine that he says
hinders the ability to recognize the legitimacy of other faiths. Sachedina
believes the supersessionist perspective is an outgrowth of the concept of
abrogation, the commonly held view that some passages in the Qur'an nullify or invalidate others with which they disagree. Some Muslims extend
abrogation to include the nullification of previous scriptures like the Bible
and therefore the religions that are based on them.

But Sachedina points out that there is no basis in the Qur'an for such
an extension of meaning because the text does not claim that it abrogates
prior revelations from God. The Qur'an itself states that abrogation functions only in legal matters, and it does not say abrogation should have a
role in shaping attitudes toward other religions. In addition to its likely
origin in the concept of abrogation, Sachedina believes external factors
also played a role. In particular, he suggests that Muslim views on supersessionism were probably influenced in part by Christian attitudes about
their own faith superseding Judaism.

The four scholars discussed here, and others like them who are in
favor of a pluralistic view of religion, maintain that it holds the most
promise for addressing the problems of the world and enhancing relationships among people of diverse faiths. The opposite mentality—that
of the exclusivist who clings to the belief that only his or her religion is
true—hardens the lines of division and creates ill will toward the Other.
The journey from exclusivity to inclusivity is difficult to make, but it is

easier to start down that road if it can be demonstrated that tolerance and respect for others is at the heart of one's religion. No other source reveals a community's core like its sacred text, and that is why these scholars base their arguments in support of pluralism on the Qur'an.

## key TERMS

*dīn; milla; aslama; ḥanīf; majūs; sābi'ūn; yahūd; banū isrā'īl; mīthāq; taḥrīf; masīḥ; naṣārā; 'awliyā'; ruhbān; qissīsūn; aḥbār; rahbānīya; ahl al-kitāb; tawrāt; zabūr; injīl; tanzīl; furqān; kufr; mushrik;* supersessionism

## QUESTIONS for discussion

1. Is it possible to reconcile the Qur'an's conflicting messages on how Muslims should relate to non-Muslims?

2. When conflicting messages exist, is it proper to accept some texts as relevant for the modern world while rejecting others?

3. Are there other alternatives for interreligious relations beyond those of exclusivism and pluralism?

4. What are some of the strengths and weaknesses of the positions of the four scholars discussed at the end of the chapter?

## further READING

Ismail Acar, "Theological Foundations of Religious Tolerance in Islam: A Qur'anic Perspective," in *Religious Tolerance in World Religions*, ed. Jacob Neusner and Bruce Chilton (West Conshohocken, Pa.: Templeton Foundation Press, 2008), 297–315.

Asma Afsaruddin, "Celebrating Pluralism and Dialogue: Qur'anic Perspectives," *Journal of Ecumenical Studies* 42, no. 3 (2007): 389–406.

Mahmut Aydin, "Religious Pluralism: A Challenge for Muslims—A Theological Evaluation," *Journal of Ecumenical Studies* 38, no. 2–3 (2001): 330–52.

Mahmoud Ayoub, "Nearest in Amity: Christians in the Qur'ān and Contemporary Exegetical Tradition," *Islam and Christian-Muslim Relations* 8, no. 2 (1997): 145–64.

Basit Bilal Koshul, "The Qur'anic Self, the Biblical Other and the Contemporary Islam–West Encounter," in *Scripture, Reason, and the Contemporary Islam-West Encounter*, ed. Basit Bilal Koshul and Steven Kepnes (New York: Palgrave Macmillan, 2007), 9–38.

Abdulaziz Sachedina, *The Islamic Roots of Democratic Pluralism* (Oxford: Oxford University Press, 2007).

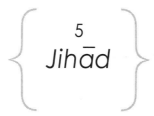

# 5
# *Jihād*

CHAPTER OUTLINE
A Complex Term; *Jihād* in the Qur'an; The Two Forms of *Jihād*;
Usama bin Ladin's *Jihād* and Use of the Qur'an

I s there another Arabic word associated with Islamic practice that has a more central place in the non-Muslim lexicon than *jihād*? Probably not. It is frequently mentioned in forms of discourse as diverse as scholarly analysis, media reports, talk radio, and everyday conversations. You would be hard-pressed to find an educated, well-informed non-Muslim living in the West today who would not be able to offer a definition of *jihād*.

Such familiarity was not always the case, and if one had to choose a moment when the word *jihād* fully entered the vocabulary and conscious-ness of non-Muslims it would have to be September 11, 2001. A quick sur-vey of media sources supports that claim. According to a search of the 1,970 American newspapers listed at the NewsBank website, in the eight years prior to 9/11, just over 20,000 articles were published that contained the word *jihād*. In the eight years after 9/11, that number spiked to more than 90,000.

## A Complex Term

Because of its close connection with the events of 9/11, many non-Muslims, especially in the West, associate *jihād* with violence and bloodshed, but it is a more complex term than the vast majority of them think it is. A common translation of the word, often reinforced by media coverage, is "holy war." In fact, the phrase "holy war" never appears a single time in the Qur'an. When it is equated with *jihād*, the result is a distortion of the true meaning of a term that is central to the Qur'an and is at the very heart of Muslim faith and practice. It is therefore an ironic fact that one of the Arabic words best known by people who do not speak the language is also one of the most misunderstood.

This chapter examines the use of the word *jihād* in the Qur'an to explain why it should not be understood one-dimensionally as referring solely to violent behavior. It comes from the Arabic root *jahada*, which carries the basic meaning of putting forth great effort to achieve a goal. The aim of that effort can be anything at all. It might be something tangible, or it could be something abstract and theoretical. This can be seen in relation to another word that comes from this root and is an important concept in Islamic law. *Ijtihād* refers to the ability to exercise the power of reason to arrive at a legal opinion. In this case a word from the root *jahada* describes the mental effort that one puts forth in order to formulate a rational position on a matter.

## *Jihād* in the Qur'an

(Q 9:24; 22:77-78; 25:48-52; 60:1)

Non-Muslims are often surprised to learn that the word *jihād* appears only four times in the entire text of the Qur'an. Despite that relatively limited usage, however, an analysis of those four occurrences gives a sense of the breadth and range of meanings the

> *The word* jihād *is found only four times in the Qur'an.*

term has while supporting the contention that it should not be too quickly identified with violence.

It is first found in the Qur'an in 9:24: "Say (Muhammad), 'If your parents, children, siblings, spouses, families, the wealth you have accumulated, the business that you fear will falter, and the dwellings that please you are dearer to you than God and His Messenger and the struggle [*jihād*] in His cause, then wait until God brings about His punishment.' God does not guide transgressors." In this verse, *jihād* is something that is expected of all Muslims, and it is a mark of the true believer. In language reminiscent of that used by Jesus in certain Gospel passages in the New Testament, the text says that if one wishes to truly follow God's will one must not be overly attached to the people and things one loves. Such attachment becomes an obstacle to *jihād*, striving or struggling "in God's cause." The verse does not explain how exactly *jihād* is to be undertaken, but there is nothing in it that associates it explicitly with violence.

The second mention is in 22:77-78: "Oh believers, bow down, prostrate, and worship your Lord. Do good deeds so that you might have success. Strive in God's way with a striving [*jihād*] worthy of Him. He chose you and he put no difficulty on you in faith—the faith of your father Abraham. He called you Muslims earlier and in this [the Qur'an] so that the Messenger can be a witness for

*The five pillars of Islam: profession of faith, prayer, almsgiving, fasting, and pilgrimage.*

you and that you can be witnesses for all humanity. So engage in prayer, pay the alms, and take refuge in God. He is your protector—the best protector and helper." This passage contains a series of exhortations meant to encourage Muslims to express their faith outwardly. In the beginning, they are commanded to perform the actions that are associated with their prayer ritual—bowing and prostrating—and at the end, they are reminded to pray and give alms, two of the five pillars of Islam.

The verse also contains two statements of a more general nature urging good deeds and devotion to God. In the midst of this summons to action is another command—strive a striving (*jihād*) worthy of God. The call to *jihād* is found within a section that encourages Muslims to engage in actions that are required of all members of their faith. In other words, the effort they are asked to put forth here is simply meant to ensure that they follow the dictates of their faith. Once again, the verse lacks any explicit reference to violence.

The third occurrence of *jihād* is found in 25:52, which can be properly understood only within its larger literary context: "God is the one who sends the winds announcing the good news of His Mercy. We send down from the heavens pure water to revive a dead land with it. We give it as a drink to the many animals and people We have created. We have explained this to people so that they might be reminded, but most only continue to be ungrateful. If We had desired, We would have sent to every town a warner. Do not listen (Muhammad) to the unbelievers, but strive a great striving [*jihād*] against them with this [Qur'an]" (25:48-52). In this case, too, the word *jihād* does not carry a violent connotation. The verses prior to and after this section speak of the many things God has done for humanity, and yet many people fail to recognize them. Muhammad is told to engage in a *jihād* by being the warner to people that they have never had. The "weapon" or instrument he is to use in his striving is the Qur'an, containing the record of what God has done for humanity. In this way, Muhammad is being asked to engage in what is sometimes referred to as a "*jihād* of the tongue."

The fourth and final reference to *jihād* in the Qur'an is in 60:1: "Oh believers, do not take My enemies and yours as your allies, being their friends when they have denied the truth that has come to you and have driven out the Messenger and you because you believe in God, your Lord. If you go forth with a striving [*jihād*] for My path seeking My pleasure, can you secretly be their friends? I am aware of everything you hide and everything you reveal. Any of you who do this have strayed from the right path." This chapter comes from the Medinan period, and according to tradition the verse was revealed when a Muslim betrayed the Islamic community by telling his friends and family back in Mecca that Muhammad was preparing a return to their city and warned them to take the necessary precautions.

> *Three different types of* jihād *are often distinguished:* jihād *of the heart—striving to combat evil within oneself;* jihād *of the tongue—striving to spread the faith by word;* jihād *of the sword—striving to defend the faith when it is attacked.*

In this context, the term *jihād* describes the commitment necessary to remain faithful to the divine will and win God's approval. As with the first verse mentioned above (9:24), this sometimes entails reorienting one's life so that personal relationships and everyday concerns do not get in the way of one's obligations to God. The word *jihād* is used to describe the intense effort that must be put forth to remain true to the teachings of the faith, referred to here as "the right path."

Not one of the four occurrences of *jihād* in the Qur'an explicitly endorses violence, and it would be difficult to argue that such a sense is implicitly found in these verses. In each case, *jihād* describes the inner resolve a true believer must possess that allows him or her to remain faithful. It is a mindset one must adopt in order to meet and overcome the challenges and temptations one confronts from many quarters. Those potential obstacles are named or alluded to in each passage. They could be family members, wealth, or possessions that compete for one's attention and allegiance (9:24; 60:1), or they might come in the form of unbelievers who cause one to forget that God is the supreme authority throughout creation (25:52). The primary purpose of *jihād* is summed up well in 22:78, where it enables one to express outwardly one's Muslim identity through prayer, almsgiving, and good works.

If all the references to *jihād* in the Qur'an are peaceful, where does its association with violence come from? In the Qur'an, there are other words that come from the root *jahada*, approximately forty in all, and some of them speak of another type of striving that is more aggressive. These passages recognize that, at times, the forces and challenges that confronted the early Muslim community were such serious physical threats that the only recourse was to respond in kind. To not do so would have been to risk annihilation.

Here, as always, is it essential that the historical context be kept in mind. These are passages directed to a growing and expanding community that sometimes met opposition from those who sought to stifle or suffocate it. Sometimes the threat was of a physical type rather than spiritual. In those instances, the concept of *jihād*, in the sense of striving or struggling, was used to describe the appropriate response to attempts to harm or destroy the *umma*. It is a type of effort that threatened minority groups must sometimes exert to guarantee their future survival.

*[margin handwriting: Violence may be called for]*

### Nonviolent *Jihād*
(Q 16:110; 29:69; 49:15; 49:13)

Some of the other texts that use words derived from the Arabic root *jahada* are similar to the ones just mentioned because they do not require that a violent sense be given to them. They are simply calling Muslims to strive to do God's will. An example of this is seen in 16:110: "To those who strive [*jāhadū*] and persevere when they flee their homes after persecution your Lord is forgiving and merciful." This passage advises those who have been persecuted not to launch a counterattack but to relocate to another place that is safer for them. In other words, the verse is implicitly rejecting a violent response in favor of a nonviolent one. This passive reading of the text is supported by the larger literary context as well. The verses prior to this one are critical of those who do not believe in God's revelation as found in the Qur'an, and they say that these people will be punished. But the passage does not ask Muslims to attack the unbelievers or act aggressively toward them. It rather states that their punishment will come from God in the afterlife, when they will be judged and found wanting because they refused to believe the message of the Qur'an.

A similar point is made in 29:69, where a section that levels criticism at unbelievers for their lack of faith is followed by a verse about Muslims. It does not urge them to assail those who reject Islam because they will be judged by God after death. Those who engage in *jihād* are held up as a model to be followed because they will be rewarded in this life and beyond. There is no element of violence in the text at all. "As for those who strive [*jāhadū*] in Our cause, We will guide them on Our paths. Truly, God is with those who do good."

A final example of a nonviolent use of a word related to *jihād* is seen in 49:15. What makes this one noteworthy is that it is found two verses after an important text that is discussed in the chapter on relations with non-Muslims. According to 49:13, the diversity found within creation is a gift from God that is meant to encourage learning and mutual understanding: "Oh humanity, We created you male and female and made you into peoples and tribes so that you might know one another. The most honorable of you before God are the ones who are most pious. Truly, God knows and is aware." This is a remarkable statement that celebrates differences among people and calls them to live in harmony and peace.

The verse right after it speaks of the Arabs of the desert, sometimes called the bedouin, whose faith is not yet mature since they have not submitted to God and the message Muhammad has brought to them. This is followed in 49:15 by a description of the qualities possessed by those with authentic faith: "Believers are those who believe in God and His Messenger, show no doubt, and struggle [*jāhadū*] with their possessions and their lives in God's way. They are the sincere ones." These two groups of people—the desert Arabs and the true believers—personify the different races and tribes mentioned in 49:13 that are meant to recognize and learn from one another. Coming so closely on the heels of a call for coexistence, there is no way that the allusion to *jihād* can be interpreted as an endorsement of violence.

### Violent *Jihād*
(Q 2:218; 2:216-17; 9:14-16; 9:38-41; 9:81-84)

There are other texts in which words etymologically related to *jihād* do describe violent activity. This is usually found in passages that advocate war, including some discussed in the chapter on violence. An example is 2:218, which comes right after a brief section that says fighting is sometimes required of Muslims even though they dislike it and that it is permissible to engage in warfare during the prohibited month if it is a defensive response to an attack (2:216-17). This is followed by a description of those who will be rewarded: "Those who have believed and those who have migrated and striven [*jāhadū*] for God's cause are the ones who can hope for God's mercy. God is forgiving and merciful." As elsewhere, this verse recommends that people strive to do God's will, but this time it is found in a context that makes several references to fighting and killing.

This juxtaposition suggests that, under the right circumstances, like when one acts in self-defense, *jihād* can take a more aggressive form.

This understanding of *jihād* is found a number of times in chapter 9, which has the title "Repentance." Warfare is a theme in several sections of this *sūra*, and striving or struggling is often mentioned in them. Speaking of people who violate their oaths and seek to remove the Prophet Muhammad from their midst, verses 14-16 state, "Fight them, for God will punish them at your hands. He will humiliate them, and give you victory over them. He will heal the breasts of believers and remove the fury from their hearts, for God turns to whomever He wishes. God is knowing and wise. Do you think you will be left alone without God knowing which of you will strive [*jāhadū*] and take no supporters other than God, His Messenger, and fellow believers? God is aware of what you do." Here, too, the plain sense of the text seems to be that *jihād* can be an armed struggle when the community is under attack.

The association with violence and warfare is more explicit a bit later in chapter 9, when the people are chastised for not fighting and are warned of the consequences if they continue to refuse to engage the enemy: "Oh believers, when you are told, 'Go forth and fight in God's way,' why are you weighed down to the ground? Do you prefer the life of the world over the hereafter? The pleasure of the life of the world is little compared to the hereafter. If you do not go forth and fight, God will severely punish you and replace you with others. But you are not able to harm God in any way—God has power over everything. If you do not assist him (Muhammad), remember that God helped him previously when the unbelievers drove him out. Two of them were in the cave and he said to his companion, 'Do not be troubled, God is with us.' Then God sent down His peace upon him, assisted him with armies you did not see, and humbled the word of the unbelievers. God's word is highest, for God is powerful and wise. Go forth, lightly or heavily armed, and struggle [*jāhidū*] in God's way with your possessions and your lives. That is best for you, if only you knew" (9:38-41).

A direct link is established in this text between striving, or *jihād*, and doing battle with the enemy. An interesting feature of this passage is that it cites an episode from Muhammad's life as a way to inspire the

*According to Islamic tradition, Muhammad was able to leave Mecca and make the* hijra *through a clever ruse by having his cousin and son-in-law, Ali, take his place in bed. His enemies among the Meccans assumed Muhammad was still sleeping while he and Abu Bakr fled to Yathrib, later known as Medina.*

community and convince them to fight. Commentators agree that this is a reference to the Prophet's experience during the *hijra*. As he and his companion Abu Bakr were making their journey to Medina from Mecca, they stopped to rest in a cave, where Muhammad expressed his confidence that God would come to their assistance. This historical reference is directed toward Muslims who are hesitant to do battle—whether they are fearful or outnumbered, they must be like Muhammad and trust that God is on their side.

As seen in the passage just discussed, the Qur'an sometimes uses the verb "to go out" as a way of expressing in a literal way what those who answer the call to battle must do. They leave their homes and familiar surroundings in order to respond to the command to meet the enemy and defend the community. Verbs that convey the opposite sense are used in 9:81-83 to describe those who do not heed the call—they are the ones who "remain behind" or "sit at home." These homebodies are viewed pejoratively in the Qur'an because they put themselves before the needs of the community and are the personification of a selfish person: "Those who were left behind were glad to remain back when God's Messenger set out. They despised having to strive [*yujāhidū*] with their possessions and their lives in God's way. They said, 'Do not go forth in this heat.' Say (Muhammd), 'The fire of hell is hotter!' If only they understood. Let them laugh a little bit now; they will weep much in payment for what they have done. Therefore, if God brings you [Muhammad] back to a group of them and they ask permission to go forth [in battle], tell them, 'You will never go out with me to fight an enemy. You preferred to remain back the first time, so continue to remain with those who stay behind.'"

### THE *MUJĀHIDĪN*
(Q 4:95; 47:31; 47:20-30; 47:32, 34)

Another term the Qur'an uses to identify a group of people is worth mentioning because it has appeared frequently in the media since the 1980s. The *mujāhidīn* first achieved notoriety in Afghanistan when they fought against forces from the Soviet Union and the Afghan government. When the Soviets withdrew from the conflict in the late 1980s, the *mujāhidīn* continued to fight among themselves and against government troops, and one of the people who helped to support and finance their efforts was Usama bin Ladin. The term *mujāhidīn*, sometimes spelled *mujāhideen*, came to be applied to other paramilitary groups throughout the world that band together under a militant Islamist ideology. It is the plural form of the word *mujāhid*, which means "one who struggles."

The word appears four times in the Qur'an, and three of those occurrences are in 4:95, where they are favorably compared to those who stay at home: "The believers who remain at home, except for those with an incapacity, are not on the same level as those who commit their possessions and themselves to striving in God's way [mujāhidīn]. God has raised the latter [mujāhidīn] to a degree above those who remain at home. God has promised good things for all, but those who strive [mujāhidīn] are favored with a great reward over those who remain at home." References to those who "stay at home" in the Qur'an are typically found in texts that relate to war, and it is a way of criticizing those who refuse to go out to defend the community. That appears to be the case in this verse, where an exception is made for those who are incapacitated and therefore excused from military service. The triple mention of mujāhidīn here therefore refers to those engaged in armed combat.

This is also the case with the other reference to mujāhidīn in 47:31: "We will test you until We know which of you strive [mujāhidīn] and persevere. We will put to the test your record of accomplishment." When read in isolation, it is impossible to know whether this verse is using mujāhidīn in a violent or a nonviolent sense, but when we take into account the wider literary context, it is clear that the former is meant. The verses prior to it (vv. 20-30) speak disparagingly of those who accept only certain parts of the Qur'an while rejecting others, and the example it gives describes those Muslims who become fainthearted and fearful when they are commanded by God to fight their enemies. The verses immediately after 47:31 outline their offenses and warn of what will happen to them for their lack of faith. Among the things they are guilty of is blocking others from God's path (vv. 32, 34).

GOD'S PATH

(Q 2:218; 9:41, 81; 49:15; 47:32-34)

The Arabic term for "God's path" is sabīl allāh. Following and staying on God's path is a central theme throughout the Qur'an, and it would not be an exaggeration to say that this summarizes very well the essence and goal of Islam. This path is, in a sense, another way of speaking about God's will—if you remain on the path, you are doing what God wants you to do.

In some passages, the way to follow God's path is to accept the teachings and engage in the practices that are required of all Muslims. Elsewhere, the path is realized through more violent means, as when it is stated that one must fight or struggle "in God's path." Examples of this have already been seen in texts mentioned earlier (2:218; 9:41, 81; 49:15).

References to "God's path," therefore, are sometimes found in passages that permit or endorse violent behavior. A further example of this is seen in 47:32-34, discussed above. Those who are "blocking others from God's path" are in all likelihood harming the rest of the community through their unwillingness to make war. The text does not describe the exact circumstances, but a number of scenarios are possible. It might be that a sufficiently large number of people were rejecting the command to fight, which depleted the ranks of the military and made victory difficult or impossible. Or it could be that those refusing to fight were convincing others to do the same, and the number of available warriors was dwindling to a dangerously low level. Whatever the case, the very fact that the Qur'an devotes a significant amount of space to the issue indicates that this was a serious concern that reflects difference of opinion and disagreement within the early community on the matter of going to war.

All four references to *mujāhidīn*, then, are somehow related to warfare. Keeping in mind that rather limited usage, it might be said that the qur'anic evidence supports the association commonly made in the modern day between *mujāhidīn* and violence. But it must be kept in mind that engaging in *jihād* does not always entail physical violence or harm to others. The first set of texts discussed earlier in this chapter describes a form of striving and struggle that is directed inward as people attempt to overcome and control the forces and inclinations that might prevent them from following God's path. Such people might also be called *mujāhidīn*, even if they are not defined as such explicitly in the Qur'an.

> The term "God's path" (sabīl allāh) is found more than seventy times in the Qur'an.

## The Two Forms of *Jihād*

This examination of the term's use in the Qur'an shows that there are different manifestations of *jihād*. The presence of verses that support both a violent and a nonviolent meaning for the word is why Muslims commonly make a distinction between what they refer to as the "greater *jihād*" and the "lesser *jihād*." The greater *jihād* refers to the ongoing struggle one must engage in to remain faithful and avoid the ever-present temptations to go astray that are a part of life. These enticements to sin can take many forms—internal and external, material and spiritual, personal and impersonal—and so a person must be mindful and alert to put forth the required effort to stay on the correct path.

The lesser *jihād* refers to those rare moments when the struggle is a physical one and Muslims are permitted to engage in violent activity. But the Qur'an and the subsequent Islamic law that emerged in part from it make it clear that the conditions for such aggression are carefully pre-scribed. It should only be a defensive response to a direct attack, and it must be carried out in a legal and appropriate manner. Extremists like Usama bin Ladin have sometimes presented a distorted sense of what constitutes a legitimate attack in

 *The four sources of Islamic law: the Qur'an, the ḥadīth, analogy, and consensus of the community.*

order to justify violence done in the name of Islam that has been rejected by the overwhelming majority of Muslims. This is a topic that will be dis-cussed in detail later in this chapter.

The distinction between lesser and greater *jihād* has roots that stretch back to the early period of the Islamic community. An often-cited *ḥadīth* has the Prophet Muhammad coming home from war with his followers when he tells them, "We have now returned from the lesser *jihād* to take up the greater *jihād*." This brief statement gets right at the heart of the multidimensional nature of this important Muslim concept. While it may allow violence under certain conditions, it is the nonviolent form of *jihād* that is "greater." For Muslims, it is the confrontation with oneself in the effort to live a faithful life, and not the confrontation with the enemy, that is the primary battle.

## Terms Related to *Jihād*

(Q 2:61; 3:112; 5:30; 28:19; 60:12; 4:90; 60:9; 4:76; 73:20; 2:217; 4:77; 33:25; 47:20; 8:65; 30:3; 37:116; 54:10; 48:1, 18, 27; 57:10; 61:13; 5:33; 9:107; 2:279; 5:64; 8:57; 47:4)

In addition to *jihād*, a number of other terms are used in the Qur'an to describe military engagement. The most frequent are those that come from the Arabic root *q-t-l*, which is found approximately 170 times in the text. About one-half of those occurrences are in the first form of the verb (*qatala*), which has the meaning "to kill" (2:61; 3:112; 5:30; 28:19; 60:12). Another fifty examples come from the third form of the verb (*qātala*), a form that carries a reciprocal sense and is usually translated "to fight" (4:90; 60:9; 4:76; 73:20). A common word for the act of fighting is the related term *qitāl*, found 13 times in the Qur'an (2:217; 4:77; 33:25; 47:20). Another rather large collection of words related to warfare come from the root *gh-l-b*, "to defeat, subdue, overcome," which is cited approximately 30 times in the text (8:65; 30:3; 37:116; 54:10).

The root *f-t-ḥ* usually means "to open," but in some passages it describes victory or success in battle (48:1, 18, 27; 57:10; 61:13). This usage was continued after Muhammad's death when Islam began to spread throughout the world and words from the root were used to talk about new areas that had been "opened up" to the faith. Words from *ḥ-r-b* are used only twice to describe the act of fighting (5:33; 9:107), but it is an important root because the word *ḥarb* ("war") comes from it. This latter word is found only four times in the entire text of the Qur'an (2:279; 5:64; 8:57; 47:4), further evidence that terms from the root *q-t-l* are the preferred way to discuss and describe warfare.

## Examples of Lesser *Jihād* Mentioned in the Qur'an

It can be difficult to know the exact circumstances a given Qur'an passage was originally addressing because the text usually does not speak about the specific events in Muhammad's life to which it is responding. This is the case in passages that discuss warfare, or lesser *jihād*. For this reason, extraqur'anic sources like the *asbab al-nuzul* ("occasions of revelation") and *tafsīr*, or commentary on the Qur'an, are valuable aids in the attempt to identify a plausible historical context. Another resource that is often used is the *maghāzī* ("campaign") literature, which recounts the various raids, battles, and wars Muhammad and the early community took part in. This is a component of the *sīra*, or biography of the Prophet, that is best represented in the works of Ibn Isḥāq (d. 767), Muhammad's earliest biographer, and al-Wāqidī (d. 823), who gathered together accounts of early Islamic military campaigns.

The *maghāzī* writings associate each important war in the post-*hijra* period with a particular chapter or section of a chapter in the Qur'an. In the majority of cases, the war or battle is not explicitly mentioned in the passage, but the authors of the *maghāzī* appeal to the *asbab al-nuzul* or the content of the text to support the association. In recent times, scholars have become increasingly doubtful about the connections that are drawn between text and context in this literature, and many argue that these works are unreliable because they come from long after Muhammad's time and it is impossible to create an accurate chronology of the military engagements that can be mapped onto the Qur'an.

In all likelihood, the *maghāzī* material is a continuation of a pre-Islamic practice of preserving oral traditions about intertribal battles among Arab groups and the heroes who took part in them. The difference, however, is that the presence of references to the Qur'an in the *maghāzī* (which were probably not in their original compositions) introduces a religious component not found in the earlier forms of the genre. The *maghāzī* stories therefore can be seen as a type of *asbab al-nuzul* that link sections of the Qur'an to specific moments in the

> *The word* maghāzī *comes from an Arabic root that means "to carry out a raid or military expedition."*

Prophet's life. The following are some of the Qur'an texts that are often linked to specific military engagements in the early days of Islam.

### THE BATTLE OF BADR
(Q 3:123; 8:7, 9, 11-12)

Among the important battles, or examples of lesser *jihād*, fought by Muhammad and the early Muslim community, three of the most famous were those at Badr, which took place in 624, Uḥud (625), and al-Khandaq, or "The Trench" (627). Of the three, only Badr is mentioned by name in the Qur'an, and it is found in only one place. "God helped you at Badr when you were weak and vulnerable. Be mindful of God, that you may give thanks" (3:123). This is a reference to an encounter that took place at a small town near the Red Sea about one hundred miles southwest of Medina (see Map, p. 8). A Meccan caravan loaded with goods was returning home when a Muslim group numbering three hundred attacked it. An army from Mecca of more than one thousand was sent to defend the caravan, but despite its numerical advantage it was roundly defeated by the Muslims. This verse interprets the victory theologically as a sign that God was on the side of the outnumbered Muslim forces.

FIGURE 20 *A sixteenth-century depiction of the Battle of Badr.*

The theme of divine aid is further developed in chapter 8, which does not refer to Badr specifically, but it is generally held that portions of it are speaking about the battle. In verse 7, mention is made of a promise by God that the caravan and the army (literally, "the two factions") would be defeated. The people cry out for help, and God sends one thousand angels to help them (vv. 9, 12). God enables them to sleep the night before the encounter and also provides rain for them (v. 11). The message throughout is clear—without God's help the Muslims could not have defeated their enemies.

### THE BATTLE OF UHUD
(Q 3:152-53)

The following year, the Meccans sought vengeance for their embarrassing defeat at Badr by sending an army of three thousand to Medina (see Map 1, p. 8). Rather than enter the city, they chose to draw the Muslims out into the surrounding area. At first, Muhammad resisted this tactic and kept to his original plan of engaging the enemy in the city. But when the Meccans began to destroy Muslim crops, Muhammad relented, left Medina, and set up a base in the area of Mount Uhud, about five miles north of the city. Not all the Muslims agreed with this strategy, and some refused to leave Medina, leaving the Muslim forces shorthanded. A group of about one thousand Muslims did battle against a group three times its size, and it was forced to retreat to the higher ground of Mount Uhud rather than risk annihilation. At that point, the Meccans declared victory after inflicting heavy casualties on the Muslims, including an injury suffered by Muhammad.

These events are not recorded in the Qur'an, but scholars have long held that 3:152-53 is speaking to the situation at Uhud: "God kept His promise to you when you were defeating them with His permission. But then you weakened, questioned the order, and defied it just when He showed you what you most desired—some among you want the world, while others want the hereafter—then He diverted you away from them to test you. God, Who is gracious to believers, has forgiven you. You fled to higher ground without looking around as the Messenger called out to you from behind you. So God rewarded you with sorrow for sorrow in order that you may not be troubled by what you did not get or what happened to you. God is aware of everything you do." Here, too, the outcome of the battle is a result of divine, not human, initiative. Because some of the Muslims refused to follow the Prophet's command and obey the will of God, they were routed by the enemy.

THE BATTLE OF THE TRENCH
(Q 33:9-27)

A third example of lesser *jihād* that is believed to be the context of 33:9-27 is described in great detail in the biographical writings and *maghāzī* material. This is the Battle of the Trench (*al-khandaq*), which took place in 627. According to the sources, a coalition of Arabian tribes (which is the basis for the title of chapter 33) joined forces to invade the Muslims

> *Estimates of the number of males from the Qurayẓa tribe killed at the Battle of the Trench range between four hundred and nine hundred.*

in Medina. The besieged occupants responded by digging a ditch around their entire town that warded off their attackers until they disbanded and went away.

The text begins with the familiar theme that the victory belongs to God alone: "Oh believers, remember how God's grace came upon you when armies were against you. We sent a wind and invisible armies against them. God sees what you do" (33:9). The passage goes on to describe how the initial response of some to the invasion was to doubt God's power and the Prophet's authority (vv. 10-12), causing many to want to flee for their lives (vv. 13-17). This group is contrasted with the believers who remained faithful to God and the Messenger despite the dire circumstances (vv. 22-24). Their fidelity was rewarded when they did not have to fight because the enemy retreated (v. 25). As elsewhere, a passage whose main theme is warfare offers a lesson in what true belief is and a warning to those who fail to heed that lesson.

This battle forms part of the background to a controversial episode in Muhammad's life whose significance has long been debated. Among the several Jewish tribes in Medina who predated Muhammad's arrival, there were the Qurayẓa, who were sometimes at odds with the Muslim community. According to the sources, the Qurayẓa had aided the attacking coalition of tribes in their effort to take over Medina. When the invading forces departed and Muhammad discovered this betrayal, he ordered the execution of all the males of the Qurayẓa tribe, had their women and children sold into slavery, and allowed the Muslims to keep their possessions for themselves.

Estimates of the death toll vary between four hundred and nine hundred. This is usually cited as the occasion of revelation for the final two verses of the passage: "He brought down from their fortresses those People of the Book who supported them and put fear in their hearts. You killed some of them and another group you captured. He bequeathed to you their land, their houses, their possessions, and a land you had not yet visited. God has power over everything" (33:26-27).

This event is sometimes pointed to as an example of early Muslim intolerance and excessive violence that reflects Islam's true attitude toward non-Muslims. But such interpretations often fail to take into account the historical circumstances that led to the mass execution or to recognize that the one Qur'an passage that is associated with it does not endorse similar violence in future encounters with non-Muslims. As noted in the chapter on Muslim/non-Muslim relations, many texts move in the opposite direction and call for peaceful relations with members of other faiths.

### Lesser *Jihād* as a Form of Sacrifice?

(Q 3:123; 8:17; 9:25-26; 3:166-67; 8:65-66; 48:22-23; 9:14-15)

Some of the passages discussed above show that the Qur'an shares with the Bible the notion of God as a divine warrior. In the biblical book of Joshua, for example, it is often stated that God is at the head of the Israelite forces, leading the charge against the Canaanites, who must be removed from the Promised Land. A similar motif is seen in Qur'an passages that speak of God assisting Muslims who are fighting. There is an avoidance of the anthropomorphization of God that is characteristic of some biblical texts, but divine influence in the outcome of a war is sometimes found in the Qur'an.

This is seen in the reference to God's helping the Muslims defeat the enemy in the Battle of Badr and sending angels to ensure the victory (3:123; 8:17). A similar statement is made about the Battle of Hunayn, which took place in 630: "God has come to your aid on many battlefields, like on the day of the Battle of Hunayn. Your large numbers satisfied you, but they did you no good. The land was wide but it felt too constraining, so you turned around and retreated. Then God sent down His tranquility upon His Messenger and the believers, and He sent down invisible armies. He punished the unbelievers—that is what they deserve" (9:25-26; cf. 3:166-67; 8:65-66; 48:22-23).

> The Battle of Hunayn took place a day's journey from Mecca, soon after the city's inhabitants accepted Islam and become Muslims. It was waged against people from the city of al-Ṭā'if.

These and similar texts convey the idea that war is ultimately God's business. Humans engage in the fighting and kill the enemy, but they are simply following orders and doing what God wants of them. In the biblical tradition, the death of the enemy is sometimes referred to as a sacrifice that is meant to satisfy and appease God. Some scholars have argued that this is a way of making the act of killing another person more acceptable and tolerable. It is not easy to take another life, but understanding it as a way of expressing one's obedience to God transforms it into a pious act that reduces the guilt and torment one feels.

The Qur'an does not use the language of sacrifice in an explicit way when it calls for the defeat of the enemy in lesser *jihād*, but the same dynamic may be present. Muslims are to make war because it is God's will, and it is the way they express their commitment and fidelity to the deity. The nonbeliever is considered to be a threat or polluting agent that must be removed in order to guarantee the health and survival of the believing community. Although the word "sacrifice" is not used, the death of the enemy in the Qur'an functions in a way similar to the way it does in the Bible because it pleases God and therefore makes the act of killing more palatable.

An awareness of the psychological dimension of the command to kill may be present in 9:14-15, a text that was discussed earlier. After outlining the offenses of certain non-Muslims who broke their oaths, tried to expel the Prophet Muhammad, and mistreated believers, the text goes on to describe what should be done with them: "Fight them, for God will punish them at your hands. He will humiliate them, and give you victory over them. He will heal the breasts of believers and remove the fury from their hearts, for God turns to whomever He wishes. God is knowing and wise."

An initial command ("Fight them!") directed to the community is followed by a string of three verbs that all have God as their subject. The shift to the divine actor reinforces the key point—the people may be fighting, but it is really God who is punishing, disgracing, and conquering. This has the effect of distancing the people from the effects of their fighting and softening their sense of culpability. The next two divine actions are the most telling and interesting—God will heal the believers and remove the anger they feel. From what do they need to be healed, and why are they so enraged? The text is not explicit about this, but it could be an allusion to the pangs of remorse felt by those who act violently. The text appears to recognize the horrific toll violence can have on those who perpetrate it while suggesting that transferring the responsibility to God is a way to lessen their feelings of guilt.

## Usama bin Ladin's *Jihād* and Use of the Qur'an

(Q 8:24; 9:38-39; 2:193; 9:5)

In the Qur'an, as in the Bible, there is often a theological justification for warfare. It is divinely mandated violence whose purpose is to obey

God's will and ensure the safety and survival of the believing community. Throughout history, wars have been fought and battles have been waged in the name of Islam, and the Qur'an has been the primary text Muslims have cited to legitimate those actions. The great majority of those wars have been fought within the parameters of what Muslim theologians and ethicists have determined are acceptable terms for entering into and engaging in lesser *jihād*.

But there have been exceptions. On occasion, Muslims have failed to meet those standards by disregarding the norms for what constitutes a valid and legitimate use of force. This has been the case in a number of highly publicized attacks in recent times. Among them, none has had a more dramatic and profound impact on the world than the events of September 11, 2001. The seeds of what unfolded on that day were sown years before by Usama bin Ladin, the mastermind of the attacks. In his attempt to lay the groundwork and make his case, he cited the Qur'an, but the way he did so reminds us of the danger of misinterpretation and the tragedy that can result when the meanings of sacred texts are distorted.

In February 1998, bin Ladin and four other Muslim extremists, including the second in command of al-Qaeda, Ayman al-Zawahiri, issued a *fatwa* titled "Statement of the World Islamic Front Urging Jihād against Jews and Crusaders." In this brief document, bin Ladin and his coauthors lay out their case for why it is incumbent upon Muslims to attack Americans, and they reach a chilling conclusion: "The ruling to kill the Americans and their allies—civilians and military—is an individual duty for every Muslim who can do it in any country in which it is possible to do it, in order to liberate the al-Aqsa Mosque and the holy mosque [Mecca] from their grip, and in order for their armies to move out of all the lands of Islam, defeated and unable to threaten any Muslim."

> A fatwa *is a legal opinion that offers a ruling on some matter. The one issuing the ruling is known as a mufti, a title reserved for those with training and expertise in Islamic jurisprudence.*

They based this ruling on three "facts" that they say are known to all: (1) the U.S. occupation of the Arabian Peninsula as a launching pad from which to attack neighboring Muslim countries; (2) the U.S.-Israeli atrocities committed against the Iraqi people; and (3) U.S. support of unfair Israeli policies and practices in the region that have left the Muslim community weak and fragmented. By framing the context in this way, however inaccurate it might be, they sought to paint the United States as an aggressor and therefore a legitimate target for a lesser *jihād*.

In labeling the obligation to kill Americans an "individual duty" for each Muslim, the authors were drawing upon Islamic legal terminology.

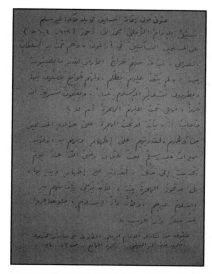

FIGURES 21 AND 22
*Two examples of a
fatwa.*

A distinction is made between a collective duty (*farḍ kifāya*), something
that the community as a whole is
required to do, and an individual
duty (*farḍ `ayn*), which must be done
by each member of the community.
Identifying the murder command
as the latter meant that it is legitimate, even required, that all Muslims
actively seek to kill Americans wher-
ever they can. While the overwhelming majority of Muslims have rejected
bin Ladin's call to arms, the attacks of September 11, 2001, and similar

> *An example of a collective duty (*farḍ
> kifāya) is the obligation to defend
> the faith when it is attacked. The
> requirement to pray five times a day is
> an example of an individual duty (*farḍ
> `ayn).*

events demonstrate that some have heeded the *fatwa.* The analysis of the *fatwa* that follows is based on an article written by Rosalind Gwynne.

The document quotes fewer than ten passages from the Qur'an, and it typically does so through prooftexting that is meant to undergird and legitimate the authors' position and to influence the reader's behavior. For example, 8:24 and 9:38-39 are cited to urge Muslims to respond to God's call to action, and they suggest that there will be unwanted consequences for those who fail to do so. The rhetorical force of these verses is abundantly clear—ignoring the *fatwa*'s ruling to kill Americans will have disastrous results. "Oh believers, answer God and His Messenger when he calls you to what gives you life. Know that God comes between a person and his or her heart and that you will be gathered to Him" (8:24).

In some places, bin Ladin and his coauthors are selective in their quotations from the Qur'an by leaving out sections of verses in order to garner scriptural validation for the violent actions they call for. An example of this is in their use of 2:193, the portion of which they cite says, "Fight them until there is no more persecution, and religion is devoted to God." The second part of the verse is not included, which reads, "If they desist let there be no further hostility, except against transgressors." In its literary context, the tone of the more compassionate and tolerant second half of the verse is reinforced by the verses before and after 2:193, which both stress that warfare should only be defensive and that Muslims should relent when the enemy withdraws. Such a message does not fit bin Ladin's agenda, and so only the half-verse that serves his purpose is lifted out and inserted into the *fatwa.*

This is an egregious error on the authors' part because it distorts the verse's meaning, but it also violates certain principles established in *tajwīd*, which is concerned with proper pronunciation and vocalization of the text of the Qur'an. One element of *tajwīd* has to do with the pauses that are permissible for one to take when reading or reciting the Qur'an, and some works on *tajwīd* determine where it is not allowed for one to stop reading. Sometimes these indications are found in the middle of a given verse and sometimes at its end. According to these works, it is recommended that one not stop reading at precisely the point at which bin Ladin and his coauthors break off the verse. Ironically, these authors who appeal to Islamic tradition to justify their misguided message are guilty of ignoring long-standing principles regarding how to read and interpret their primary source.

In a similar example of a partial citation, the authors begin the document with a reference to the beginning of 9:5, the "sword verse," which will be discussed in more detail in the following chapter: "When the forbidden months have passed kill the idolaters wherever you find them—seize them, besiege them, and ambush them." The rest of this verse and the next one go on to call for leniency if the enemy has a change of heart or seeks protection. Here, too, that section of the text is disregarded because it is in direct opposition to the authors' intent. A curious aspect of bin Ladin's use of the "sword verse" is that he does not appeal to the principle of abrogation to give it a privileged place. It is generally held to be a late verse, and many who support abrogation in the Qur'an consider it to be the text's final word on how to treat non-Muslims. This would fit the authors' purposes very well, but for some reason they do not mention it in their *fatwa*.

The analysis in this chapter indicates that *jihād* is a concept rich in meaning for Muslims and does not have a primarily violent connotation for them. But this fact is easily missed by non-Muslims who often equate it with the limited and distorted understanding espoused by the bin Ladins of the world. When this occurs, a double tragedy results: non-Muslims unfairly malign an entire faith, and they miss the ironic fact that *jihād* is not a term that has to divide people. It can also unite them as fellow *mujāhidīn* who are all struggling to lead good lives.

## key TERMS

*jahada; ijtihād; mujāhidīn; sabīl allah; qatala; maghāzī*; Badr; Uḥud; al-Khandaq; *fatwa; farḍ kifāya; farḍ `ayn; tajwīd*

## QUESTIONS for discussion

1. What are some of the challenges one faces when trying to decide which type of *jihād* a particular passage in the Qur'an is discussing?

2. Can you identify terms or concepts in other religious traditions that, like *jihād*, have more than one meaning?

3. How does the concept of lesser *jihād* compare to the Christian idea of "just war"?

4. Do you think that, as suggested in the chapter, *jihād* can be understood as a form of sacrifice?

## further READING

Richard Bonney, *Jihād: From Qur'ān to bin Laden* (New York: Palgrave Macmillan, 2005).

David Cook, *Understanding Jihad* (Berkeley: University of California Press, 2005).

J. Harold Ellens, "Jihad in the Qur'an, Then and Now," in *The Destructive Power of Religion: Violence in Judaism, Christianity, and Islam*, ed. J. Harold Ellens (Westport: Praeger, 2004), 3:39–52.

Reuven Firestone, "Jihād," in *The Blackwell Companion to the Qur'ān*, ed. Andrew Rippin (Chichester: Blackwell, 2006), 308–20.

Rosalind W. Gwynne, "Usama bin Ladin, the Qur'an and Jihad," *Religion* 36 (2006): 61–90.

Rudolph Peters, *Jihad in Classical and Modern Islam* (Princeton: Markus Wiener, 1996).

# 6
# Violence and War

**CHAPTER OUTLINE**
The Language of Violence; Types of Violence in the Qur'an;
A Range of Responses; Explaining the Violence

ontrary to what some people believe, the Qur'an is not an inherently
violent book. This is not to say that the Qur'an does not mention
or describe violent acts. Murder, infanticide, flogging, crucifixion,
rape, amputation, and other acts of violence are all found in its pages. The
same thing, of course, can be said about the Bible and other sacred texts.
The presence of such topics does not make a book in and of itself violent.
But when speaking of the Qur'an, some would counter that it is a violent
book because it describes violence directed against non-Muslims. Here,
too, many biblical passages could be cited that present outsiders being
treated in a similar way.

It is sometimes further argued that a key difference is that the
Qur'an does not just describe violence, it teaches and encourages modern
Muslims to behave violently toward those who do not share their faith.
The Qur'an is not just a record of past examples of violent behavior. It's
a how-to book for today's world that teaches intolerance and hatred of
the Other. Look at Usama bin Ladin and others like him, so the argument
goes—they base their ideas and actions on the Qur'an, which is a blueprint for terrorism.

Such views are held for any number of different reasons, but the thing many of those reasons have in common is ignorance. Most non-Muslims have very little experience with reading the Qur'an, and those who do usually do not make it too far into the text before reaching for the next book on their shelf. This lack of familiarity with the Qur'an, along with a dependence on biased or uninformed sources for what little information they *do* have, is a main reason why many non-Muslims remain unprepared to understand and discuss the Qur'an's perspective on critical issues of concern, like violence, to the modern world.

This chapter considers qur'anic texts that have been influential in shaping Muslim views regarding violence and war. Throughout the discussion, the important role of context is stressed. Today's world is a very different one from that inhabited by the Prophet Muhammad and his early followers, and that difference is one that all readers, both Muslim and non-Muslim, should always keep in mind.

## The Language of Violence

(Q 2:163; 18:110; 22:25)

The basic message of Islam, undergirding every verse of the Qur'an, centers on the oneness and unity of God. Any group or individual who does not acknowledge that unity is in serious error and is guilty of the one sin the Qur'an says cannot be forgiven. It is the duty and responsibility of the Muslim community to proclaim and protect God's unity, and most of the texts that have a violent component are somehow responding to the circumstances of the small, vulnerable early Islamic community confronted by forces that threatened its beliefs and existence. The Qur'an therefore speaks of violence, both real and potential, that moves in two different directions. One is the violence that comes from the non-Muslim side that

*The term* tawḥīd, *which comes from the same Arabic root as the number one* (wāḥid), *is used to describe the unity of God. One of the ninety-nine names of God is "the One" (2:163; 18:110).*

seeks to suppress and harm the *umma*. The other originates on the Muslim side and describes the measures it must take to survive and flourish in the face of external and internal opposition.

The difference between these types of violence is seen in the two Arabic roots that are most commonly used in the Qur'an to describe violent behavior. Words related to the root ẓ-l-m occur approximately 320 times, making it the most frequently used Arabic root that conveys a sense of violence. When referring to individuals and their actions, it describes injustice, tyranny, oppression, and the like. It can also sometimes be used in reference to those who disbelieve or reject a teaching. In the vast majority of cases in the Qur'an, it describes unbelievers who refuse Muhammad's message, do not follow the straight path, and sometimes seek to harm members of the Muslim community. In other words, it is primarily used to describe the violence, both literal and metaphorical, directed toward Muslims and the faith they follow. The fate awaiting those who behave this way and practice _zulm_, or injustice, is summed up in 22:25: "Regarding disbelievers who prevent others from God's path and from the Sacred Mosque—which We made for all, both resident and visitor—and who desecrate it through injustice [_zulm_], We will make them taste painful punishment."

The other relevant Arabic root is _q-t-l_, which will be treated in detail below. This is the basis for a number of words in the Qur'an that describe the acts of fighting and killing. Such terms are found almost 175 times in the text, and when they are used in reference to the Muslim community, they denote how the believers are to respond to challenges from outsiders who seek to destroy the community or nullify its message.

Put another way, words from _q-t-l_ are used to explain how to counter and overcome the threat posed by words from _z-l-m_. When they were confronted with hostility and injustice, as the early Muslims frequently were, they were allowed to defend themselves within the limits established by the Qur'an. As noted above, this permission to engage in violence can be properly understood only with an awareness of the original context the text was responding to and the theological worldview on which the text is based.

## Types of Violence in the Qur'an

Much of this chapter focuses on what the Qur'an has to say about warfare, one of the most violent of human activities. But other forms of violence are found in the Qur'an, and some of them will be considered first before turning to the battlefield. Violence is defined here as any action that intentionally causes or inflicts physical pain on oneself or another person. This definition is adopted in order to narrow down and limit a very broad topic and is not meant to trivialize or downplay the very real pain caused by nonphysical forms of violence.

## Homicide

(Q 16:57-58; 81:8-9, 14; 17:31; 6:137, 140, 151; 60:12; 4:29; 5:32a; 5:27-32; 17:33; 25:68; 5:45; 2:178; 4:92; 3:4b; 14:47; 39:37; 43:55; 43:25; 7:136; 30:47; 5:95; 32:22; 43:41; 44:16)

The Qur'an values and affirms human life frequently, including in passages that denounce the practice of infanticide. In seven places, the Qur'an speaks out against killing newborn children, and two of them (16:57-58; 81:8-9, 14) refer specifically to the murder of female infants. These texts prohibit a practice that was prevalent among the pre-Islamic Arabs and was sometimes resorted to for economic reasons. "Do not kill your children out of your fear of poverty. We will provide both for them and for you, so killing them is a great sin" (17:31; cf. 6:137, 140, 151; 60:12).

Elsewhere, the Qur'an issues a blanket ban on taking the life of another person: "Do not kill one another, for God is truly merciful to you" (4:29b). The Qur'an's story of Cain and Abel traces the roots of this prohibition to the first pair of siblings. After the account of the first homicide, the text goes on to say, "Because of that, We prescribed for the children of Israel that whenever anyone kills another person—except in cases of murder or corrupting the land—it is as if he or she has killed all humanity. But if anyone saves another life, it is as if he or she has saved all humanity" (5:32a). While this verse refers specifically to the Israelites, most Muslim commentators have understood it to be a universal law against murder that is applicable to all peoples.

*The sons of Adam and Eve, who are identified as Cain and Abel in the Bible, are unnamed in the Qur'an. Their story is found in 5:27-32, which has much in common with the biblical account in Genesis 4.*

As this text indicates, the Qur'an recognizes that not all acts of killing are the same. A distinction is made, for example, between voluntary and involuntary manslaughter. It also recognizes a difference between unjustifiable and justifiable homicide, as mentioned in 17:33: "Do not kill another person, which God has forbidden except for just cause. Regarding the one who is killed unjustly, We have given power to the next of kin. But he should not exceed the limits in killing, for he has already been given assistance" (cf. 25:68). This verse appears to allow for the possibility of vengeance killing by someone else acting on behalf of the deceased. Along these lines, the Qur'an shares with the Bible the practice of *lex talionis*, or the law of retribution, in 5:45: "We prescribed for them in it [the Torah] a life for a life, an eye for an eye, a nose for a nose, an ear for an ear, a tooth for a tooth, and a wound for a wound. The one who abstains from this receives atonement. Those who do not act in accord with what God has revealed are unjust."

While this verse seems to discourage seeking vengeance (*qiṣaṣ*) by taking the life of another person, it is still permissible in other texts. The best example of this is in 2:178a, which begins by saying, "Oh believers, retribution is granted for you regarding murder—the free person for the free person, the slave for the slave, and the female for the female." The text does not differentiate between intentional and accidental killing, but it goes on to say that, if the family of the deceased does not demand blood for blood, a payment may be made as retribution: "But when someone is forgiven by a brother, the latter's wish shall be granted and the guilty party shall pay a reasonable amount."

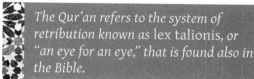

*The Qur'an refers to the system of retribution known as* lex talionis, *or "an eye for an eye," that is found also in the Bible.*

Another text that clearly differentiates between intentional and unintentional killing is 4:92, which refers to payment in the case of accidental death. It is the only verse in the Qur'an that mentions the Arabic term *diya*, which is usually translated "blood money" but perhaps is better understood to be a form of compensation or reparation. This lengthy verse offers a number of different hypothetical scenarios, suggesting that the issue of homicide and its penalties was something that the early *umma* took very seriously. Another interesting aspect of the verse is the attention paid to whether or not the deceased was a "believer," or Muslim: "A believer should not kill another believer, except by mistake. Whoever kills a believer by mistake should free one believing slave and pay compensation [*diya*] to the family of the deceased, unless they decline it. If the deceased was a believer but belonged to an enemy people, then a believing slave should be freed. If the deceased belonged to a people with whom you have a treaty, then compensation should be given the family and a believing slave should be freed. Anyone unable to do this should fast for two consecutive months as a form of penance to God. God is all-knowing, all-wise."

Texts granting permission to exact vengeance in the event of a murder always stipulate that only one person may be killed in retaliation. This was meant to close off the possibility of mass carnage and prevent an escalation in violence. It is also striking that the Qur'an consistently encourages people not to resort to vengeance but to forgive the offending party and accept a peace payment in place of blood. This became the standard view when Islamic law took shape in the centuries after Muhammad—retaliation, payment, and forgiveness were considered to be the three ways to resolve conflicts that arise as a result of death or personal injury.

It is not just humans who exact vengeance on one another in the Qur'an; it is also something God does: "Those who do not believe God's signs will suffer severe punishment. God is powerful and able to seek retribution" (3:4b; cf. 14:47; 39:37; 43:55). In addition to those who refuse to believe (43:25), others who experience divine vengeance in the Qur'an are the Egyptians who are drowned as Moses leads the Israelites to safety (7:136), evildoers (30:47), and people who have been forgiven and then sin again (5:95). It is such an important aspect of the divine nature that "The Avenger" (al-muntaqim) is one of the ninety-nine names that have been assigned to God by Islamic tradition (32:22; 43:41; 44:16). Here, too, we see an interesting juxtaposition between vengeance and forgiveness that is echoed in the Qur'an texts that speak of human interactions. Like humans, God is able to seek retribution, but the dominant quality of the deity—one that all people are called to possess—is mercy. Nowhere is this better seen than in the first two of the ninety-nine names—The Merciful (al-raḥmān) and The Compassionate (al-raḥīm)—which form part of the basmala that opens every chapter of the Qur'an but one.

## Punishment for Crimes

When non-Muslims think of violence in the Qur'an, their thoughts often turn to the punishments (ḥudūd) that are mentioned in the text for various offenses. Among the most well-known are those for adultery and theft.

> The word the Qur'an uses for the punishments (ḥudūd) prescribed by God comes from an Arabic root that describes a border or a limit. These are the boundaries of God that should not be transgressed.

### ADULTERY
(Q 24:2; 4:15; 24:4-5)

Flogging is the punishment for those who are found guilty of adultery: "Flog the adulteress and the adulterer one hundred times. Do not let compassion for them prevent you from carrying out God's demand, if you believe in God and the Last Day. Make sure a group of believers witnesses their punishment" (24:2). The verse makes no distinction between the man and the woman, and it stipulates that the punishment be carried out in public to serve as a deterrent for other members of the community.

Another text that is often understood to be speaking about adultery, even though the precise offense is not identified, is 4:15. But here the punishment is different and entails confining the offending party at home for life: "If any of your women commit an indecent act, call four witnesses from among you. If they testify to their guilt, confine them at home until they die or until God shows them a way." The reference to being shown "a way" and the fact that only women are mentioned in the verse have led some commentators to the conclusion that the verse is actually concerned with homosexuality, not adultery. This interpretation is supported by the next verse, which says a similar thing about men: "If two men commit an indecent act, punish them both. If they repent and change their ways, leave them alone. God is pardoning and merciful." These verses are discussed in more detail in chapter 3, on gender and sexuality.

The reference to witnesses in 4:15 is part of Islamic law, which requires that four people actually see the act of penetration when adultery takes place. Many have observed that this condition makes it virtually impossible to prove an adulterous relationship. To ensure that the rights of the accused are protected, the Qur'an calls for an almost equally harsh punishment for those who falsely accuse someone of adultery: "Regarding those who accuse honorable women of fornication but do not produce four witnesses, you should flog them eighty times and not accept their testimony ever again. They are evildoers, except for those who repent and change their ways later on. God is forgiving and merciful" (24:4-5).

In recent times, media reports occasionally circulate about Muslims, usually women, who have been charged with adultery and are put to death by stoning. Non-Muslims commonly assume that this form of capital punishment has its basis in the Qur'an, but they are mistaken. In fact, the Qur'an does not ever mention stoning as a punishment for committing adultery nor does it consider it to be a capital offense. But it is mentioned in a number of *ḥadīth* where the Prophet Muhammad orders those guilty of fornication to be stoned, and that is how the punishment entered Islamic law. It is important to keep in mind, though, that this and the other punishments being discussed here are very rarely implemented in modern times. It is only in those few places in the world that have a legal system based on a literal reading of the Qur'an and other sources where these penalties are found.

*The Qur'an does not mention stoning as a punishment for adultery.*

THEFT
(Q 5:38; 24:2)
Perhaps the most infamous punishment mentioned in the Qur'an concerns the fate of those who are accused of theft: "Cut off the hands of thieves, both male and female, for what they have done as a punishment from God. Truly, God is almighty and wise" (5:38). As with the first

text examined that treats adultery (24:2), no distinction is made between males and females. Some scholars have argued that this verse is calling for some type of superficial cut or injury to the hand rather than amputation. This is possible because the Arabic verb used here (*qata`a*) can mean, "to cut" rather than "to cut off." Others suggest that the verse should be read metaphorically as an appeal to somehow reincorporate the thief back into the community.

The verse that immediately follows it seems to point in this direction because it accepts remorse from the accused party as a clear sign of rehabilitation: "But as for those who repent after doing wrong and change their ways, God forgives them. God is forgiving and merciful." Even if the verse is referring to amputation, this is not the way thieves are treated in the great majority of Muslim countries. Most recognize that the context of seventh-century Arabia was markedly different from our own and that ancient notions of justice do not always apply today. In other words, Muslims tend to view some of the laws and punishments in the Qur'an in much the same way that Jews and Christians understand much of the legal material in the book of Leviticus and elsewhere in the Bible.

## Suicide

(Q 2:195; 4:29)

A final area to consider is suicide. This has become a particularly important topic in recent times as suicide bombings and attacks that lead to the destruction of oneself and others have become an all-too-frequent fact of life in some parts of the world. While the Qur'an does not contain an unambiguous prohibition against the act, two verses strongly suggest that taking one's own life is morally wrong. The first is found in 2:195: "Spend in accord with God's way. Do not bring about your destruction by your own hands, but do good. Truly, God loves those who do good." A literal translation of what is to be avoided would read, "Do not throw yourselves with your own hands to destruction." This could be interpreted in a number of different ways, but the sense of the verse is broad enough to suggest that a ban on suicide can be included.

*The term* sunna, *meaning "way" or "path," refers to how the Prophet Muhammad lived his life. It includes the things he said, did, and observed, and it provides an example for later Muslims to emulate. Sources of the* sunna *include the Qur'an, the* hadīth, *and biographical writings about the Prophet.*

The other verse relates more directly to the topic because it contains an admonition against killing: "Believers, do not vainly eat up each other's wealth but engage in mutual trade fairly. Do not kill each other, for God is merciful to you" (4:29). The object of the verb "to kill" is open to two meanings. The Arabic *anfusakum* can be translated as either "each other" or "yourselves." If we opt for the latter meaning, the verse can be interpreted as forbidding suicide. The evidence from these two verses, along with the Qur'an's general ethos to avoid murder and respect life, strongly suggests that the Islamic scripture forbids suicide. This is in agreement with the evidence from the *sunna*, where several *ḥadīth* have the Prophet Muhammad prohibiting the act.

The modern Arabic term for suicide (*intiḥār*) is not found in the Qur'an, and neither are the words that are commonly used today for violence (*ʿunf*) and terrorism (*irhāb*). Despite this lack of explicit use of key terminology related to present-day manifestations of religiously motivated aggression, the Qur'an remains the central source for those seeking to justify or denounce violent acts done in the name of Islam. The primary texts cited in this regard are those having to do with warfare, which is an important topic in the Qur'an. How the war passages are interpreted and applied has been an issue of vital importance throughout history and remains so today.

## A Range of Responses

The text of the Qur'an outlines various ways of responding to those who could pose a threat to the Muslim community. It holds up peaceful coexistence as the ideal, but it recognizes that at times this is not possible and allows for the use of force under certain conditions.

### The Preference for Pacifism

(Q 6:106; 15:94-96; 2:109; 45:14-15; 64:14; 5:13; 7:180; 42:15; 50:39-41; 76:29-31; 2:256; 50:45; 10:99; 88:21-24; 60:8)

The Qur'an acknowledges that tensions sometimes exist between Muslims and those who do not follow Islam, and in some passages it urges a nonviolent response toward those who might be perceived as enemies. At times it instructs Muhammad and Muslims simply to ignore those who do not accept the teachings of Islam: "Comply with what you have been commanded, and reject unbelievers. We are sufficient for you in the face of the scorners. Those who set up another god in addition to God will come to know" (15:94-96; cf. 6:106). These texts sometimes suggest that paying no heed to non-Muslims is the best response since interaction with them might lead to a return to false worship.

Elsewhere, the Qur'an encourages the Prophet and the community to forgive and pardon those who disagree with them: "Tell the believers to forgive those who do not hope for God's days. God will recompense a people for what they have done. Whoever does good benefits oneself and whoever does wrong harms oneself, for you will all return to your Lord" (45:14-15; cf. 2:109). "Oh believers, you have enemies even among your spouses and your children. Beware of them, but if you excuse them, pardon them, and forgive them, then God is forgiving and merciful" (64:14; cf. 5:13; 7:180; 42:15; 50:39-41). These texts call for a more compassionate response that seeks to improve or repair the relationship that exists between Muslims and non-Muslims.

Most of the passages cited above mention God and recognize the power and authority of the deity. They imply that one's ultimate fate rests with God alone, and this is the main reason why Muslims should avoid confrontation with those who disagree with them. Their most appropriate response is to forgive their opponents and leave everything else to God. This notion of divine control and authority is one that is central to the Qur'an. According to Muslim belief, nothing happens without God's involvement or permission, and the Qur'an reinforces this point wherever it can.

This is not to say that humans do not have free will and that every aspect of a person's life is predestined. That issue was debated long and hard in the early centuries of Islam, and it was eventually rejected in favor of the view that humans make their own choices and exercise free will while still not undermining God's authority. This idea is best captured in those Qur'an verses that criticize coercion in matters of religious belief and prohibit forcing any form of religion on a person.

*The Qur'an does not always agree with itself on the matter of free will. Certain passages stress the importance of human choice, while others suggest that things are predetermined. The text's ambiguity is captured well in 76:29-31, which begins by endorsing free will but ends by saying all is predestined by God.*

One of the passages most commonly cited to illustrate the Qur'an's message of tolerance is the beginning of 2:256, which states, "There is no compulsion in religion." Muslims sometimes quote this verse in response to non-Muslim claims that the goal of Islam is to make everyone in the world Muslim. This idea, which goes against the notion of free will, is challenged by the Qur'an in several places, and it is another example of the text's tolerant attitude toward non-Muslims as seen, for example, in the passages discussed earlier. Accordingly, the Qur'an's message is a warning that people are free to accept or reject, rather than a rule that is imposed upon them. "We know best what they [the unbelievers] are saying, but you (Muhammad) are not to coerce them. With the Qur'an, remind those who fear punishment" (50:45; cf. 10:99; 88:21-24).

In light of such texts, it can be said that, in places, the Qur'an discourages direct confrontation and violence between Muslims and non-Muslims. Rather, it teaches people to tolerate differences among themselves, at times even urging them to forgive and pardon one another. This is quite different from the view many non-Muslims have of the Qur'an as a violent, oppressive text. At the root of its message is a belief that God has the capacity to bring together people who are at odds and to heal the divisions that have kept them apart. "God does not prohibit you from acting kindly and justly toward those who have not fought you on account of your faith or driven you from your homes. Truly, God loves those who act justly" (60:8).

## The Permission for Violence
(Q 16:125-26; 29:46)

The verse just cited suggests that under certain conditions it is appropriate for Muslims to respond aggressively against those who oppose them. They are to be peaceful toward all, except those who have "fought you on account of your faith" or "driven you from your homes." Here and elsewhere, the Qur'an recognizes that at times the situation may require that Muslims stand up to and confront the forces against them. According to some passages, this should be only a last resort after all peaceful means have been exhausted: "Call [people] to your Lord's way with wisdom and good instruction, and argue with them in the best manner. Your Lord knows best both those who have strayed from His way and those who follow it. If you must retaliate, do so in a way proportionate to how you were attacked. But if you show restraint it is better" (16:125-26; cf. 29:46).

The aggressive response such passages permit is most fully expressed in texts where matters of warfare and the defeat of the enemy are discussed in detail. Such passages tend to be the ones that non-Muslims draw upon to form their understanding of how the Qur'an tells Muslims to relate to members of other faiths. But to do this is to downplay or ignore the passages discussed earlier, and others like them that adopt a conciliatory and passive tone. The Qur'an, like the Bible, is a text that reflects human life and experience in all its richness and diversity. Both books contain sections that are peaceful and harmonious, while elsewhere violence is permitted and legitimated. It is important to acknowledge the presence of both types of texts within the Qur'an (and the Bible) in order to have an accurate understanding of its message and its meaning.

## Explaining the Violence

Before turning to some of the controversial passages, it will be helpful to consider how scholars and other readers have attempted to understand and interpret the presence of different viewpoints in the Qur'an regarding how Muslims should interact with non-Muslims. How can one explain the fact that violent and peaceful messages exist side-by-side in Islam's sacred text?

### The Evolutionary Model

One of the most common ways of understanding how the Qur'an's various perspectives on war and peace interrelate has been to adopt what is often referred to as an "evolutionary" approach. It maintains that there was a more or less orderly progression of viewpoints and attitudes toward relations with non-Muslims in the early decades of Islam, with each new one replacing or nullifying the ones that existed prior to it. This model recognizes the influential role of the sociocultural context in shaping the form and content of the Qur'an's message. As the circumstances of the community developed over time, Muslims found themselves interacting with non-Muslims in new and ever-changing ways. Because the context was always shifting, what was appropriate and necessary at one point in time would not necessarily be suitable later on.

In its standard formulation, the evolutionary model proposes four different stages in the development of the Qur'an's attitude toward non-Muslims, with each one permitting more violence than its predecessor. This general framework can already be seen in the early centuries of Islam as scholars drew upon the *asbab al-nuzul* ("occasions of revelation" literature) and other sources to explain the development of the Qur'an's view of relations with non-Muslims. Specific examples of each stage will be considered below, after a general overview of the evolutionary model.

The first stage is reflected in some of the passages already discussed that are nonconfrontational in nature and call for peaceful relations with non-Muslims. The second stage is represented by passages that permit only defensive fighting. According to these texts, if Muslims were attacked, they were allowed, even required, to defend themselves and their community. In the third phase, Muslims could be the aggressors and initiate fighting but only within the bounds of the rules and limitations that constituted legitimate warfare during the time period. In the final stage, the Qur'an permitted unconditional fighting against non-Muslims that had no limitations placed upon it.

The movement from relative peace to unrestrained war should be apparent from the descriptions of the four stages. The evolutionary dimension of this fourfold process is its primary feature. According to many interpretations of this model, each phase replaces the previous ones, rendering them null and void. In this way, the Qur'an and the Islamic community became increasingly more violent over time. As discussed below, in recent times some have proposed other ways of interpreting the evidence that lead to different conclusions. Nonetheless, the evolutionary understanding of the Qur'an's message has played an influential role throughout history, including in the modern day when radicals and extremists have sometimes appealed to it to justify violence and acts of terrorism.

The concept of abrogation, explained in the introductory chapter, is at the core of how the evolutionary model works. Abrogation is a way of trying to address the fact that the Qur'an is not always consistent in its teaching on certain matters. Simply put, abrogation makes the claim that some passages in the Qur'an replace others with which they disagree. There is a chronological component to the concept in that later passages abrogate earlier ones and never vice versa. Abrogation is based on the principle that, as the community developed and confronted new circumstances, the divine revelation sometimes had to be reframed in ways that would adequately respond to the later context.

> The four stages of the evolutionary model: (1) peaceful texts, (2) passages that permit defensive fighting, (3) texts that allow fighting to be initiated within limits, and (4) passages that permit unconditional fighting.

## Problems with the Evolutionary Model

As noted above, the evolutionary model has not been endorsed by all, and its critics often take issue with certain aspects of abrogation. For one thing, they claim that it can create a hierarchy of texts in which some verses are more highly regarded than others. If only the texts revealed later accurately reflect the divine will, what happens to those that were revealed earlier? Are they somehow rendered inferior or obsolete? Abrogation can hinder the effort to adopt a holistic reading of the Qur'an in which each verse and passage is given equal weight and contributes to the overall message.

The implications of this criticism are significant when it is considered in connection with the theme of this chapter, war and violence. An evolutionary understanding of how the Qur'an treats the topic means that, as time went on, the Muslim community became increasingly more violent until, when the fourth stage was reached, they could engage in warfare against anyone at any time for any reason. Verses from earlier periods that called for peaceful relations with non-Muslims were no longer to be followed because they had been abrogated and superseded by others endorsing violence.

If the evolutionary model is strictly followed, it becomes virtually impossible for Muslims to interact with non-Muslims in a positive and peaceful manner. This is reflected in the views of modern-day extremists like Usama bin Ladin and others like him. In their reading of the Qur'an, the principle of abrogation requires that Muslims be in a constant state of war against all who do not share their faith. Other texts that encourage Muslims to avoid violence are downplayed or ignored, and a significant portion of the Qur'an's message on the topic is silenced.

Alternatively, one can accept the validity of abrogation and still recognize the value and authority of texts that have been abrogated. In that case, it might be said that the peaceful verses and the violent verses are responding to two different contexts, and the latter ones are abrogating in the sense that they are now making permissible a response—violence—that was not allowed previously. Peace with others remains an option, and it is the context at a given time that determines what the appropriate response should be. This allows for a more holistic approach to the Qur'an, but it still leaves open the possibility that one could choose to engage in violence.

A further problem with abrogation, or *naskh*, is that the Qur'an never explains exactly where or how it is to be applied. As already seen, there are a few general references to revelation being abrogated, erased, or substituted, but they do not provide any details on which verses are being referred to or the method by which abrogation is to be identified. The verses that discuss it state that it is something God does for God's own reasons, but they give no information on how humans can recognize it. The Muslim community came to understand these verses as referring to those places where the Qur'an's message is inconsistent, but this is not explicitly stated in the verses themselves. In fact, some have suggested that it is possible these are not references to the text of the Qur'an as we have it. They could be speaking about other messages that were initially revealed to Muhammad that were abrogated and not included in the final version of the text.

A final difficulty regarding the evolutionary model that is sometimes mentioned concerns the extraqur'anic sources on which it is based. Two main types of works are consulted to help determine the chronology of the Qur'an. The first are those that treat the *asbab al-nuzul*, or occasions of revelation. These works attempt to connect verses and passages in the Qur'an with a particular time in Muhammad's life. Depending on the text in question, it might be fixed to a general period or phase, or it might be identified with a specific episode or moment in the Prophet's life. The oldest example of such a work dates to the eleventh century c.e., but prior to that time, commentators on the Qur'an regularly proposed specific contexts for particular verses and passages in their writings.

The other source is the *naskh* literature, which identifies the abrogated and abrogating verses in the Qur'an. This, too, is available in works dedicated specifically to abrogation as well as in the more general category of exegesis of the Qur'an known as *tafsīr*. Using both these resources, which can be of assistance in establishing the chronology of the content of the Qur'an, one could theoretically lay out how the text evolved into its final form.

Unfortunately, however, the process is not as simple and straightforward as it might appear, because there are some significant problems with these sources. There is a great deal of disagreement in the *naskh* literature over which verses abrogate and which ones are abrogated, so the analysis can vary depending on which commentators one consults. The situation is similar with the *asbab al-nuzul* material since the dating of the occasions of revelation is often inconsistent and various contexts are proposed for the same verse or passage by different scholars.

The ambiguous and confusing nature of these sources means that any attempt to establish a chronology for the Qur'an's content is bound to be tentative and speculative. Because of this, some have suggested that the notion of evolutionary development in the Qur'an's teaching on war should be rejected and replaced by a model that more accurately reflects the state of the sources. Reuven Firestone of Hebrew Union College has been one of the main voices calling for such a shift, and he has put forward an alternative that many have found attractive.

> Most of the Qur'an's treatment of war is found in chapters 2, 3, 8, and 9.

## A Nonevolutionary Alternative Model

(Q 15:94-95; 16:125; 22:39-40; 2:190; 2:217; 2:191; 2:216; 9:5; 9:29)

Firestone believes it is often not as easy to establish the dating and context of a given Qur'an passage as the evolutionary model suggests. Part of the reason for this is the unreliable nature of the sources like the *asbab an-nuzul* and *naskh* literature. In addition, he believes that when the Qur'an was given its final form, passages from different time periods were sometimes joined together because they shared common themes. He thinks this is especially the case with material that discusses warfare, which is found in some dozen or so chapters and tends to be concentrated in chapters 2, 3, 8, and 9. In the process of the Qur'an's final editing and compilation, verses that were originally independent and unattached to one another were brought together due to their shared topic in order to form a more detailed and systematic treatment of the theme. This created a sense of cohesion and connectedness among the verses that obscured their separate origins and contexts.

*Scholars Trying to work thru this problem*

Firestone carefully analyzes nine passages that have been cited by scholars throughout history in support of an evolutionary model that says the early prohibition against fighting gradually gave way to unlimited warfare. That proposed development can be traced by reading the following texts in order: 15:94-95; 16:125; 22:39-40; 2:190; 2:217; 2:191; 2:216; 9:5; 9:29. In his analysis, however, Firestone points out many inconsistencies among scholars regarding the chronological ordering of these verses, the occasions of revelation (*asbab al-nuzul*) with which they are associated, and why they are connected with particular events in Muhammad's life. He therefore concludes that an alternative model is required that does not presuppose a neat chronological development.

A major innovation of Firestone's schema is his claim that the conflicting messages within the Qur'an regarding war are not due to changing attitudes over time. Rather, they reflect the views of different factions within the community that were contemporaneous. The more militant stream eventually won out and this became the dominant voice in the text as it has come down to us, but there remains in the Qur'an evidence of the perspectives of more peaceful and passive groups. Consequently, his four categories, whose names overlap somewhat with those of the evolutionary model, are more fluid and flexible to the point that in some cases a verse might be categorized in more than one way.

> Firestone's nonevolutionary model: (1) nonmilitant verses, (2) verses with restrictions on fighting, (3) verses that evidence conflict between God's command and the people's response, and (4) verses that advocate war for God's religion.

## THE PEACE OPTION

(Q 6:106; 15:94; 16:125; 50:39; 2:109; 42:15; 5:13; 29:46)

Firestone labels his first category "Nonmilitant Verses," and it presents a serious challenge to the evolutionary model. He cites eight verses in this category, half of which come from the Meccan period while the other four originate in the Medinan context, after the *hijra*. Some examples from the Meccan group have already been discussed, including 15:94: "Comply with what you have been commanded, and reject the unbelievers." Also included among the Meccan nonmilitant verses are 6:106, 16:125, and 50:39.

A characteristic of the Medinan passages Firestone cites is that they refer directly to the People of the Book or in some other way indicate that Muslims are now living among members of other faiths that have a revealed text. They are explicitly mentioned in 2:109, another text mentioned earlier: "Even after the truth has been shown to them, many of the People of the Book, out of selfish envy, wish to return you back to disbelief after you have believed. But forgive and pardon until God gives the command. God is powerful over everything." Their presence is implied in 42:15, where Muslims are instructed to live with others in peace: "So [Muhammad] call [people to faith], stand firm as you have been commanded, and do not follow their desires. Say, 'I believe in whatever book God has sent down, and I am commanded to act justly among you. God is our Lord and your Lord. Our deeds are for us and your deeds are for you, so there should be no dispute between us. God will gather us together, and we will all return to Him.'" Other examples of Medinan nonmilitant verses given by Firestone are 5:13 and 29:46.

This first category of passages directly challenges the evolutionary model because it shows that the call for peace toward non-Muslims extended over a long period of time and was not limited to the earliest phase. It was present in Mecca, when Muslims were in a minority and had to avoid conflict in order to guarantee their future. But it was also present in Medina, where Muhammad had achieved a certain level of respect and did not need to be as concerned about his community's survival. The nonmilitant verses therefore effectively refute the idea that later violent passages replaced earlier peaceful ones.

 FIGHTING WITHIN LIMITS
(Q 2:190; 9:36; 22:39-40)

Firestone's second category is labeled "Restrictions on Fighting." Most, if not all, cultures throughout history have followed a code of conduct in warfare, and ancient Arabia was no different. Some verses in the Qur'an reflect an awareness of and respect for such a code that Muslims should not violate. A general prohibition is mandated in 2:190: "Fight in God's way against those who fight you, but do not transgress the limits. Truly, God does not love those who transgress the limits." The precise limits one is not to transgress are not identified, but commentators have suggested it could be a reference to avoiding attacks on innocent people like women or children, or perhaps a prohibition against fighting in the holy area of Mecca. Firestone notes that the command in this verse to "fight in God's way" is an important element that signals a shift from the pre-Islamic period, when one fought for the honor of one's tribe or kin, to a new ideology in which fighting is motivated by faith and religious commitment.

A further restriction can be seen in those verses that mention the "sacred months" as times when people were expected to refrain from fighting. "There are twelve months by God's decree, written in God's Book on the day He created the heavens and earth. The correct reckoning is that four of them are sacred. Do not behave unjustly during those months, but it is permissible to fight the unbelievers if they attack you first. Know that God is with the pious ones" (9:36). This passage shows respect for the ancient custom while still allowing for the possibility of engaging in warfare during the sacred months if one is acting in self-defense. The multiple references to God in the verse serve to place time under the authority and power of the deity in a way that downplays the pre-Islamic origin of the observance of the sacred months.

A final example of a text that places a restriction on fighting is 22:39-40, a passage that many exegetes believe was the first one revealed to Muhammad that allowed Muslims to engage in violence: "Permission is granted to those who are fighting because they have been wronged—God has the power to bring them victory. [They are] those who have been forced unjustly from their homes only because they say, 'Our Lord is God.' If God had not held off some people by means of others, monasteries, places of worship, house of prayer, and mosques in which God's name is often invoked would have been destroyed. God helps those who help Him—God is strong and powerful."

Here, too, the restriction against fighting can be lifted only in the case of self-defense. An interesting aspect of this passage is that it offers a detailed justification for why violence is permitted. Those who have been attacked and forcibly removed from their homes on account of their faith have every right to defend themselves. But the theological perspective noted in some of the other passages is operative here as well, perhaps to a greater degree. It is God, not just the persecuted individuals, who is responding to and warding off the attacks of those who seek to do harm. If this were indeed the first time Muslims were given permission to fight, that would explain why the justification and theological dimension are spelled out in such detail. A community that had refrained from violence up to that point was now moving into uncharted waters.

RELUCTANCE TO FIGHT

(Q 2:216; 4:77; 9:38-39; 4:72; 4:95; 5:24; 9:46, 86; 4:137-38; 3:167; 47:20-21; 33:9-27)

Firestone's third category is identified as "Conflict between God's Command and the Response of the People." These are passages that indicate that there was sometimes ambivalence or complete unwillingness on the part of some Muslims to engage in warfare. This is the largest of the four categories, and the frequent occurrence of such passages suggests that fighting was a controversial topic that was being debated within the community. The reluctance to fight is bluntly stated in 2:216, where it is considered to be a position that goes against the divine will: "Fighting is prescribed for you, although you do not like it. It may be that you dislike something that is good for you, or that you like something that is bad for you. God knows but you do not know." Elsewhere, the Qur'an typically presents those who refuse to fight in a negative light, and it frames their position as a rejection of what God wants for the community.

The Arabic word used here for fighting is qitāl, which is found thirteen times in the Qur'an. It comes from the third form (qātala) of the root qatala, which means "to kill." In their treatments of this verse, Muslim commentators frequently discuss the nature of the requirement to fight. Is it personal or communal? As discussed in the chapter on jihād, in legal and theological discourse a distinction is commonly made between something that is required of every Muslim, known as a fard 'ayn, and an obligation that is required of the community as a whole, or a fard kifāya. The verse does not specify which of the two is more appropriate in this case, and scholars have differed on the matter. This is an issue that has a significant bearing on the use of the Qur'an to justify violence in the modern world.

In other passages, the desire to avoid fighting is so strong that the text describes Muslims who pray to God asking that the command be lifted: "Have you (Muhammad) not seen those who were told, 'Avoid fighting, pray, and give alms'? When fighting was prescribed for them, a group of them feared other people as much as—even more than—they feared God. They said, 'Lord, why have You prescribed fighting for us? Please give us a little more time.' Say, 'The pleasure of this world is nothing, while the hereafter is better for the pious. You will not be treated unjustly in the least bit'" (4:77). This verse acknowledges a shift from a time when fighting was not allowed, most likely in Mecca, when the community was small and vulnerable, to the later Medinan context, when fighting was commanded. But it should not be interpreted as supporting the evolutionary model because, as seen, there is clear evidence that the message to refrain from violence is also found in Medinan verses.

The temptation to ignore the command to fight must have been so great on the part of some that certain texts threaten the community with punishment should they refuse to take up the call. In 9:38-39, Muslims are warned that they will be replaced with others if they choose to disobey the order to fight: "Oh believers, when you are told, 'Go forth and fight in God's way,' why are you weighed down to the ground? Do you prefer the life of the world over the hereafter? The pleasure of the life of the world is little compared to the hereafter. If you do not go forth and fight, God will severely punish you and replace you with others. But you are not able to harm God in any way—God has power over everything." Such texts are undoubtedly addressed to situations in which Muhammad was having a hard time convincing Muslims of the necessity of warfare.

Those who are reluctant to fight are described in a number of different ways in the Qur'an. In 4:72 they are the ones who "lag behind" and breathe a sigh of relief when they avoid the action of the battlefield: "Among you there are those who lag behind. When a disaster occurs he says, 'God has been gracious to me that I was not present among them.'" Elsewhere, they are "those who sit [at home]" and do not go out with their fellow Muslims to respond to the call to arms. They are mentioned three times in 4:95, where they are judged to be inferior to those who go out on behalf of the community: "The believers who remain at home, except for those with an incapacity, are not on the same level as those who commit their possessions and themselves to striving in God's way. God has raised the latter to a degree above those who remain at home. God has promised good things for all, but those who strive are favored with a great reward over those who remain at home" (cf. 5:24; 9:46, 86). Here, they are compared unfavorably to "those who strive," a term that comes from the same Arabic root as the word *jihād*.

Another word used to describe those who avoid warfare is "hypocrite," or as Firestone prefers to translate the term, "dissenter" (*munāfiq*). This word is found more than thirty times in the Qur'an, and it generally refers to someone whose commitment vacillates or who says one thing but does another. Their shortcoming is summed up well in 4:137-38: "Regarding those who believe, then disbelieve, then believe again, then disbelieve again and increase their disbelief, God will not forgive them or give them guidance. Let the hypocrites know that they will have a painful punishment." In 3:167, they are presented as being lukewarm about fighting: "When the hypocrites were told, 'Come, fight in the way of God, or defend yourselves,' they said, 'We would follow you if we knew how to fight.' They were closer to disbelief than belief on that day. They say with their lips what is not in their hearts, but God knows best what they hide."

A final way of describing those who prefer not to fight is found in 47:20-21, where they are cowards who are, literally, according to the Arabic, sick in their hearts: "Those who believe ask why no revelation has been sent down. But when a clear revelation is sent down that mentions fighting, the sick at heart look at you (Muhammad) as they are about to pass out at the prospect of death. Obedience and appropriate words would be better for them, as would be trusting in God when the matter is resolved."

A rather lengthy section that mentions the various responses to the command to fight is found in 33:9-27. The historical context with which it is usually identified is the Battle of the Trench in 627 c.e., which some Muslims entered into willingly while others hesitated or refused. That battle is discussed in some detail in the chapter on *jihād*.

The large number of verses in the Qur'an describing reluctance to follow God's command to fight indicates that there were differences of opinion in the early community on the issue of warfare. As Firestone points out, the textual evidence suggests an environment in which various factions were competing to have their voices heard. The prowarfare party won out, as seen in the negative way those who held another view are consistently portrayed. This is in keeping with the old axiom that history is written by the winners. What is interesting in the case of the Qur'an is the amount of attention devoted to the perspective of those who lost, which suggests that this was a contentious issue in the early decades of Islam.

## THE WAR VERSES

(Q 2:191; 2:190-95; 2:217; 8:39; 9:73; 66:9; 9:123)

Firestone's final category is "Verses Strongly Advocating War for God's Religion." These are among the most controversial sections of the Qur'an since they are the passages that non-Muslims typically cite in support of the idea that the Qur'an is a violent book and Islam is an intolerant faith. Many Muslim exegetes throughout history have considered these texts to be among the Qur'an's most authoritative on the subject of war because they have been identified as abrogating verses that render previous revelations null and void.

Because of the important role they have played in shaping perceptions about Muslim attitudes toward war and violence, it is essential to have a proper understanding of the original contexts of these passages in order to correctly evaluate their significance for the modern day. "Contexts" means not just the sociohistorical situation from which a given text emerged or to which it responded. Also included is the wider literary context of a passage since it can be properly understood only when it is interpreted in light of the verses that surround it.

The importance of literary context is seen with regard to 2:191, a verse that contains six references to fighting or killing. Speaking of the opponents, it commands, "Kill them where you find them and drive them out from where they drove you out, for persecution is worse than killing. Do not fight them at the Sacred Mosque unless they fight you in it. If they fight you, then kill them—thus is the reward for unbelievers." In no uncertain terms, Muslims are ordered to annihilate the enemy wherever they are. The latter part of the verse might strike the reader as a disproportionate expression of force—the enemy fights, but Muslims are to kill. Some commentators and translations try to soften this imbalance by translating both verbs as "kill" or "fight," but this is not supported by the Arabic text. As noted earlier, the meaning "to fight" is indicated by a long first vowel (*qātala*), while with the meaning "to kill" it is short (*qatala*). Both are found in this part of the verse, so it is clearly calling for a disproportionate response to being attacked.

The literary context of this verse is 2:190-95, and in this section there is an inconsistency in the message that makes it difficult to know precisely what the community is being instructed to do and why they are to do it. Verse 190 has already been treated under the second category of verses that place restrictions on fighting. "Fight in God's way against those who fight you, but do not transgress the limits. Truly, God does not love those who transgress the limits." Here warfare should be only defensive in nature, and that same limitation appears to be operative in verse 191, with its reference to avoiding fighting at the sacred mosque in Mecca unless the enemy initiates the conflict. If they do make the first move, then Muslims are to kill them. So what appears at first to be a call to unchecked bloodshed is, when seen from another perspective, very much in line with texts in the second category that permit violence only within prescribed parameters.

The ambiguous nature of the passage is further amplified in verse 193: "Fight them until there is no more persecution, and religion is devoted to God. If they desist let there be no further hostility, except against transgressors." Here, too, the reader gets mixed signals. On the one hand, Muslims are to vanquish the enemy so that proper faith reigns supreme. This appears to echo the command given at the beginning of verse 191 to defeat the enemy and drive them out so that their "persecution" will cease. It is a call to arms that can be read as a permission to engage in any form of violence one wishes. At the same time, though, the second sentence of the verse recalls the presence of limits and restraints. If the enemy no longer attacks, the community is to refrain as well. What starts out as a verse that gives free rein to unlimited violence shifts modes and carefully delineates when hostility is permitted.

This is a good illustration of how the meaning of a Qur'an passage is not always as cut-and-dried as one might assume. The references to engaging in defensive fighting only and refraining from warfare if the enemy relents suggest that these verses are not calling for unrestrained bloodshed, as is sometimes claimed. The commands to kill the opponents are not to be ignored or downplayed by any means, but the sections that are more compassionate and humane add a nuance that changes the overall tone of the passage. Firestone attributes this multivocal message to his belief, mentioned earlier, that when the Qur'an was given its final shape, originally independent traditions from a variety of contexts and settings were joined together because they shared a common theme, in this case warfare. Whether or not that is the case, analysis suggests that the text of the Qur'an is more complex and nuanced than is sometimes assumed.

The Arabic term translated "persecution" in the verses just discussed is *fitna*, an important concept in the Qur'an that is found thirty-four times in the text. It can have a variety of meanings, including "temptation," "trial," "sedition," "apostasy," and "dissension." In these verses, it carries a theological sense that is closer to false worship or idolatry, which is semantically related to the meanings "temptation" and "apostasy." This is particularly clear in verse 193, where the removal of *fitna* will lead to worship of God alone. It is a word that continues to be used frequently in modern times, often in reference to those, including Muslims, who act in ways that try to sow strife and undermine the Muslim community.

The theological meaning of *fitna* is more fully stated in 2:217: "They ask you (Muhammad) about fighting in the prohibited month. Say, 'Fighting in that month is a serious transgression, but obstructing access to God's path, not believing in God, denying entry to the Sacred Mosque, and expelling people from it are even greater offenses before God. Persecution [*fitna*] is worse than killing.' They will not cease fighting you until they make you renounce your faith, if they are able. The deeds of

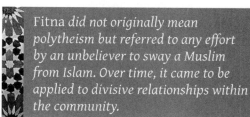

Fitna *did not originally mean polytheism but referred to any effort by an unbeliever to sway a Muslim from Islam. Over time, it came to be applied to divisive relationships within the community.*

those who renounce their faith and die as unbelievers will come to nothing in this world and the hereafter. They will be inhabitants of the fire for eternity" (cf. 8:39). In this verse, *fitna*, again translated as "persecution," is found within a religious context and can take several forms—lack of belief in God, causing others to stray from their faith, and denying access to holy places. The hierarchy of evil mentioned in 2:191 is also operative here, with *fitna* being worse than killing. An interesting aspect of this passage is that it permits fighting the enemy in the sacred month, and many scholars say it abrogates the earlier prohibition. While frowned upon as a "great offense," granting this permission is a good indication of the threat to the community that *fitna* was perceived to be. Other passages that advocate war include 9:73, which is repeated verbatim in 66:9 and 9:123.

### THE "SWORD VERSE"
(Q 9:5; 2:217; 2:190-95; 9:6; 9:29)

The most well-known, some might say notorious, verse in this last category is 9:5, which is commonly referred to as the "sword verse" because it calls for the death of all unbelievers wherever they are found: "When the forbidden months have passed, kill the idolaters wherever you find them—seize them, besiege them, and ambush them. If they repent, maintain the prayer, and pay the required alms, allow them to go on their way. Truly, God is forgiving and merciful." This is considered by some exegetes to be the definitive abrogating verse that expresses the Qur'an's final word on war and the treatment of enemies.

The months mentioned in this text should not be identified with the sacred months of the pre-Islamic period that Muslims are told to respect in other passages of the Qur'an, like 2:217. In all likelihood, the months described here are the same ones mentioned at the beginning of chapter 9 that functioned as a kind of grace period during which unbelievers were free to come and go as they wished. After the months ended, all previous treaties and covenants were declared invalid and, according to 9:5, Muslims were then free to attack and make war against them.

When this verse is cited, sometimes only its first half is quoted and the second half is left off. This is occasionally done by non-Muslims to justify their claim that Islam is a vile religion that mistreats those who do not follow it. But it is also done at times by Muslims who seek qur'anic support for their belief that non-Muslims are enemies of Islam and are therefore legitimate targets of their attacks. As discussed in the chapter on *jihād*, Usama bin Ladin is one who has resorted to this type of selective citation of the passage. The reason why this is done is obvious. The second half of the verse is less violent than the first since it presents a live-and-let-live scenario in which the enemy is left alone and not attacked.

The identity of the enemy is an important question to consider. In 2:190-95, they are "those who fight against you," while in 9:5 they are "idolaters." The Arabic term used in the latter passage is *mushrikūn*, a plural noun that appears more than forty times in the Qur'an. It derives from the Arabic root *sh-r-k*, which means "to associate, or ascribe partners to something." A *mushrik* is someone who engages in the sin of *shirk*, associating something with God and thereby violating the essential oneness and unity of God that is at the heart of Islam's understanding of the deity. As already noted, according to the Qur'an, *shirk* is the most serious offense an individual can be guilty of, and it is the one sin that God will not forgive. It often takes the form of worshiping more than one God or putting something else, like an image or a statue, in God's place. Consequently, the term *mushrik* is sometimes translated as "polytheist," in addition to "idolater" and "unbeliever."

This is important background for understanding the second half of the verse—the *mushrik* who changes his or her ways, turns to God, and engages in proper worship is forgiven and is no longer considered to be an enemy. The verse immediately following the "sword verse" adopts a sympathetic view of the *mushrik* as one who is misguided through no fault of his or her own, and it imagines a situation in which they might actively seek to learn about Islam: "If one of the idolaters asks for your (Muhammad) protection, give it to him so that he might hear God's word. Then take him to his safe place, for they are a people who do not know" (9:6).

The Qur'an never considers other monotheists, like Jews and Christians, to be *mushrikūn*. They believe in one God and they have already heard God's word through their own scriptures, so they are a separate category unto themselves. Therefore, since the *mushrikūn* in 9:5 who should be besieged, seized, and killed do not include Christians or Jews, it is wrong to suggest that the verse describes how Muslims should treat other monotheists, whether in antiquity or in the modern world. That is not to deny the fact that some people, both Muslim and non-Muslim, have read the text that way throughout history and some continue to do so today. But such readings are actually misreadings that are not supported by the text of the Qur'an or Islamic views on other monotheistic faiths.

A common designation in the Qur'an for Jews and Christians is "People of the Book," a term that highlights the fact that these communities, like Muslims, are the recipients of revealed texts referred to in the Qur'an as the *tawrāt* (Torah) and the *injīl* (gospel). The People of the Book are discussed in greater detail above in the chapter on relations with non-Muslims. That Jews and Christians are not to be included among the "idolaters" mentioned in 9:5 is further supported by a reference to them as the People of the Book a bit later in the chapter, where instructions are given about how to treat them: "Fight those of the People of the Book who do not believe in God and the Last Day, who do not forbid what God and His Messenger have forbidden, and who do not obey the rule of justice, until they pay the tax and have been humbled" (9:29).

This passage describes a different set of circumstances and desired outcomes than what is found in 9:5, again indicating that the People of the Book and the *mushrikūn* are two distinct groups. Here it is only a portion of the People of the Book who are to be fought—those who lack faith in God and the day of judgment, who choose not to follow the regulations God has established, and who do not live justly. These are all requirements that any Jew or Christian can easily assent to because they conform to the teachings and expectations of their religions.

The text is therefore not making unreasonable demands on the People of the Book, nor is it asking them to act in violation of their core beliefs and principles. In effect, it is urging Muslims to live peacefully with Jews and Christians who follow the precepts of their faiths. The only extra requirement it places on them is that they pay the *jizya*, a special tax imposed on non-Muslims that exempted them from military service and paying other taxes while guaranteeing them they would be protected by the Muslim authorities in the

> When Islam spread after the death of Muhammad, a non-Muslim who paid the *jizya* became a dhimmī, or protected person. The latter Arabic term is not found in the Qur'an.

event of war or attack. This brief comment in 9:29 is the only reference to the *jizya* tax in the Qur'an, and the above description of how it functioned is taken from later extraqur'anic sources that explain it in more detail. It was commonly imposed on non-Muslims as Islam spread, and the sources indicate that it was a relatively modest payment that was required only of those who could afford it.

Firestone's four-part classification is an interesting alternative to the evolutionary model amd deserves careful consideration for a number of reasons. It suggests that, while the early Muslim community's use of violence may have become more common over time, the peace option with non-Muslims was never rejected or abandoned. The call to live amicably with others, particularly Jews, Christians, and other People of the Book, is found consistently in the Qur'an in material from both the Meccan and Medinan periods. Even those passages that are considered to be the most violent, like the sword verse of 9:5, often remind the reader that aggression is a last resort permitted only in self-defense that should never become a permanent state of affairs. Therefore, any claim that the Qur'an is a text whose sole message is the destruction and annihilation of non-Muslims has distorted its true meaning.

Firestone reminds us that the root cause of the violence the Qur'an permits is another factor to keep in mind. Throughout the text, the enemies are typically identified and criticized with reference to their rejection of Islam and/or their objectionable religious beliefs and practices. It is their faith, or lack of faith—not their family lineage, political affiliation, or any other aspect of their identity—that sets them apart and marks them as the adversary. Violence in the Qur'an is always theologically motivated and directed toward the religious "other." It is called for and justified by a desire to protect and preserve true faith. In other words, the Qur'an's ideology of war, as that of the Bible, has a theological foundation.

Another issue that Firestone's alternative model calls our attention to is the critical role that various factions played in determining the ethos and practice of the early Islamic community as found in its sacred text. The differing perspectives on war and violence in the Qur'an reflect the attitudes of competing groups that were all wrestling with questions of interaction, identity, and survival. The viewpoints of these groups can be traced in the text, which is a patchwork of discussion and debate that gives evidence of the diversity present among the first Muslims. Like all other religious systems, Islam is the product of much interaction and argument.

As Firestone points out, the text of the Qur'an as it has come down to us indicates that the factions favoring violence won out over the peace-promoting ones. If expressed in the proper way and done with the right motivation, aggression is permitted and in some cases required. But the reasons for that permission must be kept in mind, or one runs the risk of distorting the Qur'an and the faith whose basis it is. The text's endorsement of violence must be read and interpreted in light of the fragile and trying circumstances experienced by Muhammad and his followers. That context was fraught with uncertainty and instability as the community encountered significant resistance from those opposed to it. The extra-qur'anic sources contain many traditions that describe the challenges and obstacles the first Muslims endured in the early years. In such an environment, they sometimes had to respond in kind and fight fire with fire, or run the risk of annihilation. Muslims therefore had to resort to violence and warfare at times in order to guarantee their own survival. This is said not to diminish or whitewash the violence found in the Qur'an but to explain it.

This type of contextualized reading is the best way to approach difficult or controversial passages, whether they are found in the Qur'an, the Bible, or any other sacred text. Throughout history, people have read these books to inform their behavior and to give their lives meaning, but it should not be forgotten that their original audiences lived many centuries ago under conditions very different from those of the modern world.

Some of the material in the Bible and the Qur'an had relevance for its first readers but is less applicable to later times. That is the case with much of what the Qur'an (and the Bible) has to say about war. The context of modern Muslims is unlike that of their earliest ancestors since Islam is now one of the great religions of the world and its followers are not in danger of extinction. In light of that changed set of circumstances what the Qur'an teaches about why and how Muslims may engage in warfare has less relevance today.

## key TERMS

*zulm*; *lex talionis*; *qiṣaṣ*; *diya*; *ḥudūd*; *sunna*; *naskh*; *qitāl*; *farḍ kifāya*; *farḍ 'ayn*; *fitna*; *munāfiq*; *jizya*

## QUESTIONS for discussion

1. Does the presence of violent passages in the Qur'an make it a violent text?

2. Is Firestone's model a viable alternative to the evolutionary approach for understanding the relationship between peaceful and violent passages in the Qur'an?

3. Are there any other ways to explain the presence of peaceful and violent passages in the Qur'an?

4. Can you identify elements or issues in other faith traditions that should be understood or interpreted contextually?

## further READING

Clinton Bennett and Geros Kunkel, "The Concept of Violence, War and *Jihad* in Islam," *Dialogue & Alliance* 18, no. 1 (2004): 31–51.

John L. Esposito, *Unholy War: Terror in the Name of Islam* (Oxford: Oxford University Press, 2002).

Reuven Firestone, *Jihad: The Origin of Holy War in Islam* (Oxford: Oxford University Press, 1999).

John Kelsay, *Arguing the Just War in Islam* (Cambridge: Harvard University Press, 2007).

Abduljalil Sajid, "Qur'anic Text and Violence," *Dialogue & Alliance* 20, no. 2 (2006): 33–49.

Seif I. Tag El-Din, "War, Peace and the Islamic State from the Qur'ānic Perspective: Some Critical Observations," *Encounters* 9, no. 2 (2003): 153–70.

# 7
## Death and the Afterlife

Reward and Punishment; Repentance; Death; Eschatology;
Hell; Heaven

(Q 40:28-45; 3:185; 2:86; 6:32; 13:26; 14:3; 28:60; 29:64)

In 40:28-45, within the context of a discussion of Moses, the Qur'an mentions someone in Pharaoh's household who is described simply as "the man who believed." In the passage he tries to save Moses, from a plot to have him killed, and the members of Pharaoh's family, who refuse to accept God's signs and reject false worship: "The man who believed said, 'Oh my people, follow me! I will guide you to the proper path. Oh my people, the life of the world is a temporary pleasure; the Hereafter is the permanent home. Whoever does evil will be repaid the same in return. But whoever does good and believes, whether male or female, will enter the garden and be provided for beyond measure" (40:38-40).

In these three verses, the unnamed man who believes articulates some of the central teachings the Qur'an conveys regarding life, death, and life after death. He first calls attention to the transitory and temporary nature of human existence. We are here for a short period of time, and then we are gone. He goes on to state that after this life we go somewhere else that is permanent and enduring, a place he refers to as "the Hereafter." But, he

215

is quick to point out, people will not all have the same experience in the Hereafter. Depending on how one lives one's life, the Hereafter will be a place filled with either pain or pleasure.

In other words, short-term actions have long-term consequences. This is the Qur'an's view of the human condition in a nutshell, and the text goes to great lengths to remind its readers of their mortality and the need to prepare for what awaits them at death. They can best do this by avoiding the temptation to think of the here-and-now as the forever-and-always. "Every soul will taste death, and you will be paid your full compensation on the day of resurrection. The one who is preserved from the fire and admitted to the garden is victorious. The present world is nothing but the pleasure of an illusion" (3:185; cf. 2:86; 6:32; 13:26; 14:3; 28:60; 29:64). Despite the difference between this world and the next, however, the Qur'an leaves no doubt that there is a direct relationship between the present life and the life to come. This chapter explores the contours of that relationship by presenting an overview of key qur'anic passages and concepts related to death and the afterlife, including reward and punishment, heaven, hell, and the end times.

## Reward and Punishment

(Q 99:7-8; 4:134; 3:148; 46:19; 33:30-31; 28:54; 57:10; 34:37; 6:160; 11:19-20; 16:88; 25:69; 53:31; 34:17; 2:7; 3:77; 4:138; 5:36; 9:61; 14:22; 8:13, 25, 48, 52; 2:211; 3:11; 5:2; 59:4, 7; 5:48; 6:165; 7:167; 32:22; 5:95; 15:79; 30:47; 44:16; 14:47; 3:4; 5:95; 39:37; 70:22-35; 23:1-9; 25:63-76; 42:16; 45:9-10; 85:10; 2:262; 61:11-2; 47:4-6; 58:16; 3:21; 5:73; 2:284; 3:129; 5:40; 29:21: 48:14)

Before turning to how death and the afterlife are conceived of in the Qur'an, it is important first to consider how the text understands divine justice is measured out through reward and punishment. This theme is found throughout the Qur'an, and it is seen in chapters from both Mecca and, as in 99:7-8, Medina: "Whoever does the tiniest bit of good will see it, and whoever does the tiniest bit of evil will see it." In its simplest formulation, God rewards believers and punishes unbelievers. Some texts envision this taking place at the end of time, when God will separate the good from the evil and each person will be assigned to either heaven or hell. But other texts acknowledge that justice is also attained in the present world: "Whoever wants the rewards of this world—the rewards of this world and the next are both with God, Who hears and sees" (4:134; cf. 3:148).

Various degrees of reward and punishment are mentioned in the Qur'an (46:19). Muhammad's wives will be doubly rewarded or punished for their actions (33:30-31). Others who will be doubly rewarded include people to whom prior scriptures were given, like Jews and Christians (28:54), those who have fought for the faith (57:10), and those who do good deeds (34:37). One text states that the value of a good deed will be increased tenfold, but the same will not be the case with an evil deed (6:160). Among those mentioned whose punishment will be increased are those who prevent others from following God (11:19-20), unbelievers (16:88), and murderers and adulterers (25:69).

Much of the vocabulary that is used in the Qur'an to describe the reward a person receives from God comes from Arabic roots that have meanings related to payment or compensation. This use of language from the world of business transactions highlights an important aspect of the Qur'an's understanding of divine reward and punishment—they are a form of "payback" that is due to the person because of what he or she has already done. In other words, divine justice is always deserved and it says something important about the person to whom it is directed.

The most commonly used words in this area are derived from the root j-z-y, which describes both reward and punishment in the Qur'an. In the 105 places in the text that use words from this root to describe what God gives to a person, 60 are some type of punishment while 45 are a reward. The double-duty the root can perform is nicely portrayed in 53:31, where the same verb is found twice, once with the sense of punishment and the other time with the sense of reward: "All in the heavens and earth belongs to God. He repays [yujzīa] those who do evil according to their deeds, and rewards [yujzīa] with goodness those who do good."

The most commonly used Arabic root to describe divine punishment is '-dh-b. It is found in verbal forms approximately fifty times, and the noun 'adhāb ("punishment," "torment," "torture") appears more than three hundred times in the Qur'an. Many of these are found in formulaic phrases like "a painful punishment awaits them," and among those who will suffer the wrath of God are unbelievers, those who break covenants, hypocrites, those who insult Muhammad, and evildoers (2:7; 3:77; 4:138; 5:36; 9:61; 14:22).

Another word often used to describe God's punishment is 'iqāb, with the majority of its twenty uses in the Qur'an found in an expression that warns God's retribution is "mighty" or "strong" (shadīd al-'iqāb). Its heaviest concentration is in chapter 8, where it is found four times and functions as a type of refrain throughout the chapter (8:13, 25, 48, 52). This expression is usually the part of a passage that identifies those who will experience God's anger (2:211; 3:11; 5:2; 59:4, 7), and in a few cases, it is quickly followed by the reminder that God is also merciful (5:48; 6:165; 7:167).

Another set of words commonly used to speak of God's retribution centers on the concept of vengeance present in the Arabic root n-q-m: "Who does more wrong than the one who, when revelations from his Lord are recited, turns away from them? We will take revenge on the guilty ones" (32:22; cf. 5:95; 15:79; 30:47; 44:16). One of the ninety-nine names of God is "The Vengeful" (al-muntaqim), a word not found in the Qur'an but taken from passages that describe the deity with this trait. "Do not suppose that God would go back on His promise to His messengers. Truly, God is mighty, and vengeful [intiqām]" (14:47; cf. 3:4; 5:95; 39:37). Here, too, human culpability is to the fore since revenge, by its very definition, is an action in response to something else. In this case, it is a person's transgression that leads to God's retribution, and so God does not initiate the punishment for no reason.

It has already been noted that references to reward and punishment are found in texts from both the Meccan and Medinan periods. The earlier Meccan material sometimes contains lists of the qualities that will lead to one's reward. "Not so those who pray constantly, who devote a portion of their wealth to those in need and the disadvantaged; those who trust in the Day of Judgment, and are anxious about the punishment of their Lord—for the punishment of their Lord is nothing they can feel secure about; those who guard their private parts from all except their spouses and their slave-girls—there is no guilt associated with them, but those who go beyond this are transgressors; those who follow through on their trusts and their pledges; those who stand by their testimony, and pray attentively. All of these will be honored in gardens" (70:22-35; cf. 23:1-9; 25:63-76). Those who will be punished in the Meccan chapters include those who argue about God (42:16), those who make fun of revelation (45:9-10), and those who persecute believers (85:10).

In the Medinan chapters, many of the same things will lead to reward or punishment, but some others are added in light of the new context. For example, the introduction of armed struggle led to other ways of experiencing God's blessing, including financial support for military operations (2:262), engaging in battle (61:11-12), and dying in combat (47:4-6). Similarly, the move to Medina and the subsequent tensions with other monotheists that developed there led to other offenses for which one could be punished. These included making alliances with God's enemies (58:16), murdering prophets (3:21), and believing in the divinity of Jesus (5:73).

As stated above, texts that describe God's anger and punishment are sometimes accompanied by references to divine mercy and forgiveness.
This is an important point to keep in mind because it acknowledges a central quality of the deity in the Qur'an—compassion—and it highlights God's freedom to respond in any way to human sin and weakness. God may choose to punish a person or to exonerate a person—the choice

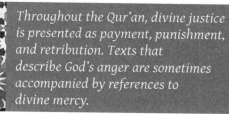

*Throughout the Qur'an, divine justice is presented as payment, punishment, and retribution. Texts that describe God's anger are sometimes accompanied by references to divine mercy.*

is God's alone. But the possibility of forgiveness has important ramifications for how people should conduct themselves because good behavior in the present might mean divine favor in the future. "All in the heavens and on the earth belongs to God. Whether you disclose your inner thoughts or conceal them, God will hold you accountable for them. God forgives whom He will and punishes whom He will. God has power over everything" (2:284; cf. 3:129; 5:40; 29:21; 48:14).

## Repentance

(Q 5:39; 2:160; 4:26-27; 9:117-18; 2:37, 54, 128, 160, 222; 4:16, 64; 9:104, 118; 24:10; 49:12; 110:3; 32:12; 6:27; 7:53; 23:99; 35:37; 39:58; 42:44; 5:31; 7:143; 38:24; 38:35; 7:148-54)

Because of the possibility of forgiveness, repentance is an important concept in Islam and the Qur'an. The Arabic root that expresses the idea of repentance is *t-w-b*, which in its most basic sense means "to return" and is used in the Qur'an to describe both the act of repentance on the part of the believer and God's turning to the person to accept that repentance. Words from the root are found approximately eighty-five times in the Qur'an, and there is an almost even split among them, with about half having God as the subject who does the turning and the remainder referring to human repentance. Sometimes the verb is used twice in the same verse, once to refer to a person's action and again to describe what God does. "Whoever repents [*tāba*] after an injustice and makes things right, God turns toward [*yatūbu*]. Truly, God is forgiving and merciful" (5:39; cf. 2:160).

When God responds favorably to a person's repentance, the normal response is forgiveness, without the individual's having to do any penance or other act as compensation. Chapter 9 of the Qur'an is titled "Repentance" (*al-tawba*), and according to verse 104 of that chapter, God is always eager to receive back a penitent person: "Do they not know that God accepts repentance from His servants and receives what is given? He is the One who returns, the merciful One." In some cases, it even appears that God takes the initiative by turning to a wayward person so that he or she may return back to God (4:26-27; 9:117-18). It is perhaps for this reason that one of the ninety-nine names of God is "The One Who Returns" (*al-tawwāb*), a title that describes the deity twelve times in the Qur'an (2:37, 54, 128, 160, 222; 4:16, 64; 9:104, 118; 24:10; 49:12; 110:3).

> The term tawba *refers both to humans' turning to God in repentance and God's turning to humanity in mercy.*

Although forgiveness is possible, it is not guaranteed. Sometimes repentance comes at the last moment, but it is too late for the person to be spared. The Qur'an describes in several places the tragic scene of the damned begging for a second chance to no avail: "If you (Muhammad) could see the guilty ones hanging their heads before their Lord [saying], 'Our Lord, we have seen and we have heard—send us back and we will do good deeds. We are convinced!'" (32:12; cf. 6:27; 7:53; 23:99; 35:37; 39:58; 42:44).

Among those who repent of their mistakes in the Qur'an are a number of biblical figures. After he kills his brother, the Cain of the Qur'an expresses a level of remorse that is not present in his biblical counterpart (5:31). Moses also turns to God in repentance when he foolishly asks to see God's face (7:143). Like his biblical self, David asks forgiveness for his sin when he hears the Qur'an's version of the parable of the man who steals another's ewe (38:24; cf. 2 Sam 12:1-7). Solomon, too, admits to his shortcomings and begs God to pardon him (38:35). Perhaps the most interesting example of turning to God in the Qur'an is done by the Israelites after the golden calf episode, when they are the complete opposite of the way they are depicted in Exodus 32, where they do not acknowledge their mistake.

> Unlike in the Bible, in the Qur'an's *golden calf story, the Israelites express regret and beg forgiveness for their lack of belief (7:148-54).*

## Death

(Q 35:19-22; 45:24-26; 29:57; 3:145, 185; 4:78; 21:34-35; 31:34; 25:58; 50:15-19; 6:29; 23:37; 6:93; 56:83-94; 8:50; 2:55-56; 3:49; 5:110; 9:84)

The Qur'an states explicitly that the living and the dead are different from one another: "The blind and those with sight are not alike, nor are darkness and light; nor are shade and heat; the living and the dead are not alike. God makes anyone He will hear, but you cannot make those in their graves hear" (35:19-22). Although they are different as night and day, the living and the dead share something important in that they both witness to the power and authority of God.

In the pre-Islamic period, it was believed that one's future was in the hands of time or fate, a concept defined by the Arabs of that era as *dahr*. But the message of the Qur'an introduced the notion of a single God who controls the destiny of each person: "They say, 'There is nothing but our earthly life. We die, we live, and nothing destroys us but time [*dahr*].' They know nothing about it—they are only conjecturing. When Our clear revelations are recited to them, their only response is to say, 'Bring back our ancestors if you are truthful.' Say (Muhammad), 'God gives you life, causes you to die, and then gathers all of you for the day of resurrection. There is no doubt about it, but most people do not know it'" (45:24-26).

To die, then, is to follow the will of God, who designates the moment of death (*mawt*) for each person. No one knows where, when, or how his or her death will come, and no one has ever been able to avoid death: "Every soul will taste death, and then you all will be returned to Us" (29:57; cf. 3:145, 185; 4:78; 21:34-35; 31:34). The Qur'an's theocentric understanding of death means that people are radically dependent upon God at every moment of their lives because God is the only one who does not die. According to 25:58, God is the Living One (*al-hayy*), another of the ninety-nine names Muslims use to refer to the deity. "Place your trust in the Living One who does not die, and sing out His praise. He is sufficiently aware of the sins of his servants."

Their total dependence on a supreme being who keeps human beings alive during every moment of their lives means God is present throughout the course of one's existence. No passage in the Qur'an better captures this aspect of the divine-human relationship than 50:15-9, which refers to two angels who record everything a person says and does: "Were We incapable of the first creation? Of course not! Yet they are in doubt about a new creation. We created humanity, and We know what his soul whispers to him. We are nearer to him than his jugular vein. When the two greeters sit down, one on the right side and one on the left, he does not say a word without an observer ready at hand. The death throes have truly come—this is what you tried to avoid." The image of God being closer than one's jugular vein is a vivid one that expresses a level of

*According to Islamic tradition, Nakir and Munkar are the names of the two angels who question the dead in their graves to determine how faithful they were in life.*

intimacy that is the antithesis of the impersonal notion of fate that dominated the earlier worldview and understood time (*dahr*) to be in charge of humanity's fate (6:29; 23:37).

Those who reject the Qur'an's message are incapable of acknowledging God's closeness, and the text describes the end of their lives in graphic terms that highlight their anguish and punishment. Angels will reach out to them, taunting them to give up their souls because of their lack of belief (6:93). At the moment of the death rattle in their throats, God continues to be near, but they will be rejected and suffer eternal punishment because they refused to listen (56:83-94). Elsewhere, the unfaithful dead will be subjected to physical abuse by the angels of death: "If only you [Muhammad] could see how, when the unbelievers die, the angels strike their faces and backs [saying], 'Taste the punishment of the Fire!'" (8:50).

Judgment day and the final resurrection will be discussed below, but for now it should be noted that in a couple of places the Qur'an mentions that on occasion dead people have been brought back to life. One such reference is in 2:55-56, where it is stated that some of the Israelites were struck down by thunderbolts after they demanded to see God face-to-face but then were brought back to life by the deity. Some translations attempt to make the scene less miraculous by saying the Israelites had fainted, but the Arabic noun (*mawt*) used in the verse is the most common word for physical death.

In two other places, it is stated that God gave Jesus the power to raise the dead back to life. "[God] will send him [Jesus] as a messenger to the Children of Israel [saying], 'I come to you with a sign from your Lord. Out of clay I will make the shape of a bird for you. Then I will breathe into it and, by God's leave, it will become a real bird. I will also heal the blind and the leprous, and bring the dead back to life, all by God's leave. I will tell you what you are permitted to eat and what should be stored in your houses.' Truly, there is a sign for you in this, if you are believers" (3:49; cf. 5:110).

> *The Qur'an mentions some of the miracles Jesus performed during his lifetime, but it does not contain any miracle stories like those found in the Gospels.*

The Qur'an sometimes uses the words "living" and "dead" metaphorically to refer to believers and unbelievers. One who believes in God is in touch with the source of life because God is "the Living One." Those who do not believe, on the other hand, have rejected the possibility of eternal life and so, even though they are still alive, they are experiencing a kind of death that holds out no promise for future reward. In this way, one's openness to or rejection of the Qur'an's message determines whether one is on the side of life or the side of death.

Death is an important theme in the Qur'an, but the text has very little to say about practical matters associated with it like how to care for and bury the dead. The only explicit reference to anything related to this topic is found in 9:84, which prohibits honoring the deceased among unbelievers and hypocrites: "Do not ever pray for any of them when they die, and do not stand by their graves. They did not believe in God and His Messenger, and died transgressors." The verse suggests that prayers for the dead and showing respect for their graves are appropriate only when the deceased are believers and members of the Muslim community. There are no details regarding these graveside activities, but this verse might provide some general insight into the practices and rituals associated with death in early Islam.

Extraqur'anic sources refer to other beliefs and ideas associated with death and burial that are not present in the Qur'an. One of the more well-known describes the suffering experienced by the dead in their graves, a topic discussed in the ḥadīth. Soon after death, the deceased are interrogated by one or more angels about the details of their life and their commitment to Islam. Until the final judgment, they remain in their graves in a type of existence that allows them to feel pain or pleasure, depending on their responses to their angelic questioners. The Qur'an does not refer to such a belief, but the exegetical *tafsīr* writings attempt to associate it with certain texts.

## The Soul

(Q 33:6a; 2:110, 235; 4:111; 5:205; 17:7; 5:45; 2:286; 5:32; 6:151; 11:21; 31:34; 13:42; 2:48, 281; 3:25, 30, 145, 161; 14:51; 63:11; 39:42; 50:16; 9:55; 21:102; 91:7-10)

It is clear that the Qur'an does not consider death to be the end of life. It signals the culmination of one's physical existence on earth, but it is at the same time a threshold experience that leads to continued existence elsewhere. But what part of the individual endures once the person's last breath initiates the physical decay of the body? Like Judaism and Christianity, Islam teaches that each person has a soul that leaves the body at death and will eventually be reunited with it on resurrection day at the end of time. A study of the Qur'an indicates that it supports certain aspects of this teaching, but for the most part these ideas are the result of theological and philosophical reflection that drew on other sources—including Greek, Jewish, and Christian ones—beyond the text of the Qur'an.

Rather than reflect an inherently dualistic system that maintains a sharp distinction between the body and the soul, the Qur'an adopts a more integrated or holistic view that can make it difficult to determine with precision the relationship between the physical and spiritual dimensions of a human being. In other words, it is not always clear in the Qur'an where the body ends and the soul begins, or vice versa. A consideration of the terminology associated with the soul illustrates this point.

The most common word used for the soul in the Qur'an is the term *nafs*, which comes from an Arabic root (*n-f-s*) whose primary meaning has to do with the act of breathing, although words with this sense are absent from the Qur'an. *Nafs* is found frequently in the text, occurring almost three hundred times, and a study of its usage indicates that it typically refers to a person, or some aspect of a person, but its exact connotation can vary. Among the various meanings it can have are "self," "life," "person," and "soul." The semantic connections among these senses are obvious, and that is what makes identifying the precise meaning of *nafs* in the Qur'an so challenging, especially when the context does not resolve the ambiguity. This is similar to what is found in the English language, where the word "soul" can refer to, among other things, a person, a life, or the nonphysical part of a person that many believe lives on after death.

In quite a few cases in the Qur'an, the word carries a reflexive sense that is best rendered as simply "self/selves," or "himself," "herself," "themselves," and the like. This usage is normally very obvious and easy to identify. "The Prophet has a greater claim on the believers than they have on themselves, and his wives are their mothers." (33:6a; cf. 2:110, 235; 4:111; 5:205; 17:7). In a passage like this, there is no reason to consider that a reference to the nonphysical part of a person is being implied. The same is true in those cases where the text uses *nafs* as a general term to speak about an individual human life. This is seen in the Qur'an's citation of the biblical law of *lex talionis*, or vengeance, found in Exodus 21:22-25: "We prescribed for them in it [the Torah] a life for a life [*al-nafs bil-nafs*], an eye for an eye, a nose for a nose, an ear for an ear, a tooth for a tooth, and a wound for a wound. The one who abstains from this receives atonement. Those who do not act in accord with what God has revealed are unjust" (5:45; cf. 2:286; 5:32; 6:151; 11:21).

More difficult to interpret are those places where it is not always completely clear if the verse is referring in a general way to a person or to the non-physical dimension of a person. Sometimes it appears that the former is the case, as in the reference to the *nafs* dying in 31:34: "Truly, God has knowledge of the Hour. He sends down rain, and He knows what is in wombs. No person [*nafs*] knows what he or she will gain tomorrow, and no person [*nafs*] knows where he or she will die. Truly, God knows and is aware." But sometimes it is less clear, as in 13:42a. Is this passage speaking about a person or about the soul of a person? Either reading is plausible: "Those who came before them plotted, but to God belongs all plotting. He knows what every *nafs* will do" (cf. 2:48, 281; 3:25, 30, 145, 161; 14:51; 63:11).

There are, finally, some passages in which the meaning "soul" makes the most sense. This is the case because the text singles out some part of a person through the use of the term *nafs* and clearly is not referring to the individual as a whole: "God takes the souls of the dead at their death, and the souls of the living while they sleep. He keeps those whose death He has decreed and sends back the others until the determined time. Truly, in this are signs for a people who reflect" (39:42). Another good example of this is 50:16, cited above in reference to God's intimate closeness to human beings: "We created humanity, and We know what his soul whispers to him. We are nearer to him than his jugular vein" (cf. 9:55; 21:102; 91:7-10).

Such passages support the idea that the Qur'an understands there to be some portion of a person known as the soul. In those places where the soul is alluded to, it is often found in the context of judgment and reward/punishment, which suggests that the soul is the part of a person that will be held accountable before God. But it is important to keep in mind that unambiguous references to the soul are quite rare in the Qur'an since most texts might be referring to either the soul or the individual as a whole.

> The word nafs *is the Qur'an's most commonly used term to describe the soul, but it can also mean "self," "life," and "person."*

## Eschatology

(Q 56:1-56; 69:13-36; 75:7-15; 80:33-42; 81:1-14; 82–84; 89:21-30; 99; 101; 44:10-12; 27:82; 18:94; 21:96; 42:45; 6:12; 10:93; 20:101; 75:6; 1:4; 37:20; 51:12; 74:46; 83:11; 5:69; 2:126; 3:114; 4:38; 9:18; 33:63; 7:187; 31:34; 41:47; 43:85; 42:17; 54:1; 70:6-7; 6:31; 12:107; 22:55; 43:66; 39:60-75; 27:87; 18:99; 20:102; 36:51; 78:18; 6:38; 42:29; 18:48; 23:100; 69:18-37; 17:13; 81:10; 21:47; 7:8-9; 23:102-3; 101:6-9; 20:109; 2:254; 7:53; 10:3; 74:48; 47:19; 53:26)

One of the most important and frequently discussed topics in the Qur'an concerns what will take place at the final judgment during the end times. It is especially prominent in the early Meccan sections of the Qur'an, but it is a theme Muhammad continued to address throughout the entirety of his prophetic career. Nearly seventy of the Qur'an's chapters comment on some aspect of the last days. Among the earliest passages that speak about the end of the world are the following: 56:1-56; 69:13-36; 75:7-15; 80:33-42; 81:1-14; 82–84; 89:21-30; 99; 101.

The Qur'an is often graphic and vivid in its depiction of what will happen at the end of time, but it does not provide a comprehensive account of the events. Many other works—including the *tafsīr* exegetical writings, *ḥadīth*, stories of the prophets, and works devoted to eschatology—develop and expand the Qur'an passages into an ordered and cohesive framework of what will happen at the last judgment. According to the tradition based on those sources, the end of the world will be accompanied by ten signs: smoke; the deceiver; the beast; sunrise in the west; Jesus' return; the coming of Gog and Magog; earthquakes in the east, the west, and Arabia; and fire. The Qur'an specifically mentions three of these: the smoke (44:10-2), the beast (27:82), and Gog and Magog (18:94; 21:96).

In the early chapters, the most common way of identifying the end times is by the expressions "the day of resurrection" (*yawm al-qiyāma*), which appears seventy times in the Qur'an, and "the day of judgment" (*yawm al-dīn*), which is found thirteen times. "You will see them brought before it [the fire], completely humiliated and glancing about timidly, while the believers say, 'The losers are the ones who lost themselves and their people on the day of resurrection.' Truly, the evildoers will remain in eternal punishment" (42:45; cf. 6:12; 10:93; 20:101; 75:6; for "the day of judgment," see 1:4; 37:20; 51:12; 74:46; 83:11).

In later chapters the expression "the last day" (*al-yawm al-ākhir*) is used approximately twenty-five times. "Regarding believers, Jews, Sabians, and Christians—those who believe in God and the Last Day and do good deeds—they will have no fear, and they will not grieve" (5:69; cf. 2:126; 3:114; 4:38; 9:18). A related term that is found more than one hundred times is "the Hereafter" (*al-ākhira*). There are many other ways the Qur'an refers to the end times, and among the most common are "the hour" (*al-sā`a*), "the day of decision" (*yawm al-faṣl*), and "the day of reckoning" (*yawm al-ḥisāb*). One of the ninety-nine names of God is related to this last phrase—"the One who Reckons" (*al-ḥasīb*).

According to the Qur'an, only God knows when the last judgment will occur: "People ask you about the Hour. Say (Muhammad), 'Knowledge of it resides with God alone.' What will make you understand that perhaps the Hour is near?" (33:63; cf. 7:187; 31:34; 41:47; 43:85). This verse suggests the time could soon be approaching, and other passages indicate that it is closer than people realize (42:17; 54:1; 70:6-7). Whenever it arrives, the Qur'an says it will happen suddenly and catch some people unprepared: "Truly lost are those who deny their meeting with God until, when the

*Although it is not mentioned in the Qur'an, Islam teaches that Jesus will return at the end time to defeat the Antichrist and usher in the final days.*

Hour comes unexpectedly, they will say, 'Woe to us that we ignored it!' They will carry their burdens on their backs. How awful those burdens will be!" (6:31; cf. 12:107; 22:55; 43:66). Just as it does not identify when the last judgment will occur, the Qur'an does not reveal where it will take place.

There is a description of the day of resurrection in 39:60-75 that can be supplemented by other passages to give an overall sense of what the Qur'an says will happen at that time. The blowing of a trumpet will announce the beginning of the end. The trumpet's sounding is mentioned ten times in the Qur'an, with one passage describing the dead coming out of their graves: "The day the trumpet sounds, everyone in heaven and on earth will be terrified, except for those God wills, and all will come to Him in complete humility" (27:87; cf. 18:99; 20:102; 36:51; 78:18). As the end of the verse indicates, this will lead to a gathering of all creatures, including animals and *jinn* (6:38; 42:29), to be presented before God (18:48).

At this point, each person will be judged according to his or her deeds. Books will be opened that contain a record of each person's life, and those who are given the book in their right hand will go to heaven while those who have it placed in their left hand will be consigned to hell (69:18-37; cf. 17:13; 81:10). The Qur'an also mentions that scales of justice will be used to guarantee each person is judged fairly: "We will set up scales of justice for the day of resurrection, and no one will be treated unjustly for anything. Even if something is the weight of a mustard seed, We will bring it forth. We are all that is needed for an accounting!" (21:47; cf. 7:8-9; 23:102-3; 101:6-9).

*A barrier or partition (barzakh) that stands behind the deceased until the day of resurrection is mentioned in 23:100. Various proposals have been put forward for what the barzakh is. Some interpret it temporally as the period of time between physical death and the final resurrection, while others understand it to be a reference to the grave. Whatever its precise meaning, it is some type of barricade meant to prevent the deceased from returning to the world.*

The Qur'an makes it clear that the judgment will be final and irrevocable, but several passages suggest that it might be possible that someone else could intercede on behalf of another: "On that day intercession will do no good, except from those to whom the merciful One has given permission and with whose words He is pleased" (20:109; cf. 2:254; 7:53; 10:3; 74:48). These texts highlight the compassion and authority of God, for whom nothing is impossible. The Qur'an does not specify who might be given permission to intercede at the end time, but among the likely candidates are angels and Muhammad because other texts speak of them as having this capacity when God grants it (47:19; 53:26).

The Qur'an does not speak of an Antichrist, but there are references to such a figure in the *hadīth* and other extraqur'anic sources, where he is referred to as "the liar" (*al-dajjāl*) or "the false Messiah" (*al-masīḥ al-dajjāl*). He is depicted as someone who will lead people into sin and whose arrival signals that the end time is near.

## Hell

(Q 37:50-57)

Hell is mentioned frequently in the Qur'an, and its horrors are described in graphic terms. It is a place containing inhabitants who undergo excruciating pain and punishment because of how they lived their lives. A view of hell is gained from above, so to speak, in a passage at 37:50-57 that describes a conversation among those in heaven. One individual recalls a friend on earth who was skeptical about the final judgment and is spotted among those being tortured: "They approach each other with questions, and one says, 'I had a close friend on earth who used to ask me, "Are you one of those who believe that after we die and become dust and bone, we will be brought to judgment?"' Then he continues to say, 'Would you like to look for him?' He looks down and sees him in the midst of hell, and says to him, 'By God, you nearly destroyed me! Were it not for the grace of my Lord, I would have been one of those taken [to hell].'"

The Qur'an uses a number of different terms and phrases to refer to hell, with the most common being *al-nār* (about 125 times), *jahannam* (77 times), and *jaḥīm* (26 times). The first and third are descriptive of hell's most distinguishing trait, with *al-nār* meaning "fire" and *jaḥīm* describing blazing flames. The origin of *jahannam* has been debated. It does not appear to be Arabic, and in the Qur'an it is the name of hell rather than a description of it. Some have argued that it is etymologically related to the Hebrew Gehenna, a valley near Jerusalem mentioned in the Bible that was notorious as a place of child sacrifice. The references to hell are found throughout the text of the Qur'an, and they come from all periods of Muhammad's prophetic career. It was therefore a prominent and significant theme of his message.

### The Layout of Hell
(Q 4:168-69; 37:23; 15:43-44; 4:145; 50:30; 39:15b-16; 77:32; 2:24; 21:98-100; 3:10; 72:15; 56:42-43, 93; 77:31; 66:6; 74:30-31; 96:18)

The text quoted above suggests that hell was believed to be somewhere below heaven, but its location is never precisely defined. There are, however, detailed descriptions of the environment, with many of them calling attention to the fire and heat that are ever-present. According to 4:168-69 and 37:23, there is a road that leads to hell, but later traditions reconfigured this to be a bridge across which the damned had to traverse before arriving at their destination. The Qur'an also refers to seven doors or gates that give access to hell: "Hell is the appointed place for all of them. It has seven gates, and each one has its allotted share of them" (15:43-44).

The reference to each gate having its own group has led to some speculation. It could simply be a way of stating that each gate is open and functions as an entrance into hell, but some scholars have suggested that it might be that each gate is used by a different type of sinner. Some have also connected this with the belief that hell has seven levels, each one reserved for a different sin. This arrangement is not mentioned in the Qur'an, but it became popular in later Muslim representations of hell. The only text that could be used to argue that there are different levels is the reference in 4:145 to hypocrites being at the very bottom of hell, but even this text does not state explicitly that there are levels or, if so, how many.

It might be that the reference to seven functioning gates is meant to convey the idea that hell is a busy place. If so, this can have a powerful rhetorical effect on the reader—many people fall victim to the sins and temptations that lead to hell, so you must be ever on your guard. That it is a crowded place but still able to accommodate more is memorably expressed in 50:30, where hell actually speaks: "On that day We will ask hell, 'Are you full?' and it will reply, 'Are there any more?'"

The belief that there are levels to hell may have been influenced by a reference in the Qur'an to the fire there being arranged in layers: "Say, 'The losers are those who lose themselves and their people on the day of resurrection. That is the clearest loss! They will be surrounded by fire above them and below them.' This is how God makes His servants fearful. Oh My servants, be mindful of Me" (39:15b-16). The latter part of this passage is noteworthy as a good example of the rhetorical dimension of the Qur'an mentioned above because it is clearly meant to instill fear in the reader. The flames of hell flash and dart out at its inhabitants, and the sparks are as large as tree branches (77:32). The word in this verse that is translated "tree branches" can also mean "palaces," and if that is the sense intended then the size of the sparks is truly overwhelming.

The fuel source that feeds and maintains such a gigantic fire is perhaps the most terrifying aspect of this inferno—it is human beings who keep the flames raging. Some texts mention humans and stones as the fuel source (2:24; 66:6). Elsewhere, they are specified to be particular types of people, including those who have not acted justly, unbelievers, and polytheists and their idols: "You and what you worship besides God will be fuel for Hell, where you will surely go. If these had been actual gods they would not go there, but each will abide in it forever. They [the unbelievers] will wail there, but they [the idols] will not hear" (21:98-100; cf. 3:10; 72:15). Completing the picture of hell's environment, and

*There are many Muslim artistic renderings of hell from the medieval period, and in some of them each level of the underworld is reserved for a particular type of sin. It is possible Dante was influenced by Islamic views of the afterlife in his depiction of it in* The Divine Comedy.

contributing to its image as a very unpleasant place, the Qur'an makes mention of an oppressively hot wind, boiling water, dark smoke, and a lack of shade (56:42-43, 93; 77:31).

In several places, the Qur'an mentions the guardians of hell, who are described as angels in one text. Their job is to make sure God's will is obeyed and to carry out the divine charge: "Oh believers, protect yourselves and your families against a fire that is fueled by people and stones. Stern and strong angels stand over it who do not refuse what God orders them, but obey as they are commanded" (66:6; cf. 74:30-31; 96:18).

## The Inhabitants of Hell

(Q 56:9, 41; 90:18-20; 69:25; 4:29-30; 2:275-76; 8:15-16; 9:46-49; 4:10, 29-30; 2:83-85; 4:12-14; 104; 3:21; 18:106; 21:29; 2:39; 3:21; 7:36; 74:16-26; 10:7-8; 17:18; 25:11-15; 85:10; 9:17; 3:86-90; 2:24; 4:140; 14:30; 40:43; 6:70; 9:63; 4:140; 14:22; 17:62-63; 38:85)

Hell is the abode of a wide range of people who are described in several different ways in the Qur'an. In a couple of passages, they are identified in general terms as the "people of the left" (56:9, 41), reflecting ancient beliefs that the right hand was the side of blessing and reward while the left hand was its opposite. Those on the left will suffer untold pain and punishment: "Those [who believe] will be on the right-hand side. But those who reject Our revelations will be on the left-hand side, and the fire will surround them" (90:18-20; cf. 69:25).

Other texts are more specific about the offenses that have been committed by those who are assigned to hell. Some of these can be considered violations of the social order that harm other individuals or society at large. Included here are murderers (4:29-30), usurers (2:275-76), soldiers who desert or avoid war (8:15-16; 9:46-49), those who misuse the property of orphans or others (4:10, 29-30), those who violate covenants (2:83-85), those who disregard inheritance laws (4:12-14), and people who hoard wealth (104).

In other texts, the actions that lead to hell relate to the area of religion and often single out offenses that would be harmful to the Muslim community. Among these are murdering a prophet (3:21), belittling God's messengers (18:106), claiming oneself to be divine (21:29), denying God's signs and/or revelation (2:39; 3:21; 7:36; 74:16-26), believing this world is all there is (10:7-8; 17:18), denying the reality of judgment day (25:11-15), persecuting believers (85:10), and attending a mosque while professing to be an idolater (9:17).

Elsewhere, the person is guilty not due to a specific act but because of his or her way of life or attitudes. These, too, tend to be offenses that are religious in nature because they undermine the beliefs and integrity of Islam. Included here are apostates who leave the Muslim community (3:86-90), unbelievers (2:24; 4:140), idolaters (14:30), the wasteful (40:43), those who do not obey God and Muhammad (6:70; 9:63), and hypocrites (4:140). It is generally understood that a community does not legislate against behavior unless some people are already engaged in it. If that is correct, then many of the offenses found in these lists were taking place within the early Muslim community, and the warnings to their perpetrators that they would be consigned to hell for them was a way of trying to curtail these actions and attitudes. Considered from this perspective, these texts provide considerable insight into the context and circumstances of early Islam.

A final issue to consider regarding hell's inhabitants is that Satan is rarely mentioned in connection with hell in the Qur'an. In one text, he goads those who have been cast into hell, and in the course of his comments he acknowledges that he is not the master of that fiery domain: "When all has been decided, Satan will say, 'God made a truthful promise to you. I also made promises to you, but I failed to keep them. I had no authority over you except to call you, and you responded to me. So do not blame me, blame yourselves. I cannot help you, and you cannot rescue me. I reject your earlier association of me with God.' The unjust will have a painful punishment" (14:22). The only other association the Qur'an makes between Satan and hell is when, identified as Iblīs, he is sent there as punishment for the sin of refusing to bow down to Adam (17:62-63; 38:85).

> *Satan is rarely associated with hell in the Qur'an.*

In later times, the connection between Satan/the devil and hell became more developed as he came to play a greater role there.

*[handwritten margin note: Acts that lead / to Hell]*

## The Punishments of Hell

(Q 6:70; 10:4; 37:67; 47:15; 56:54, 93; 22:19; 40:72; 44:48; 14:16-17; 18:29; 22:19-
20; 47:15; 56:42, 55, 93; 73:13; 88:6-7; 39:36; 37:62-67; 44:43-46; 56:52-54; 21:39;
2:174; 11:106; 18:29, 53; 32:20; 102:6-7; 4:56; 22:20; 23:104; 6:70; 18:29; 22:19;
40:72; 33:66; 54:48; 22:19; 9:34-35; 14:49; 40:71; 22:19-22; 7:50; 37:50-57; 6:94;
20:74; 14:17; 35:36; 41:19-23; 14:22; 45:33; 7:38-39; 38:59-64; 26:96-102; 41:24;
10:52; 32:14; 41:28; 33:64-65; 3:88; 4:14; 9:17; 16:29; 23:103; 43:74; 59:17; 98:6;
78:23; 6:128; 11:106-7)

The punishment in hell described in the Qur'an is both physical and
mental, with the former being treated at greater length. Pain and humiliation are the results of this chastisement, and each is a form of torture
that can be overwhelming and crushing for the one undergoing it. In texts
that are meant to convey the debilitating effects of such an experience
and to intensify the reader's anxiety level, the Qur'an sometimes has the
occupants of hell verbally respond to the punishment while expressing
remorse or pleading for mercy.

Part of the physical torture stems from the disgusting diet the
damned are forced to survive on in hell. The most common liquid of hell
mentioned in the Qur'an is boiling water, which its inhabitants sometimes drink (6:70; 10:4; 37:67; 47:15; 56:54, 93) and other times is poured
over them (22:19; 40:72; 44:48). On two occasions, it is mentioned in con-
junction with ghassāq, a vile drink that is dark and bitter. It is sometimes
described as "pus," but perhaps a better candidate for that designation is
mā' sadīd, a liquid so putrid it causes one to retch: "Hell is before him. He
will be given pus to drink, and he will force it down but hardly be able to
swallow it. Death will come for him from every side but he will not die,
for a severe punishment awaits him" (14:16-17). Drinking or being doused
with these fluids leads to unspeakable pain because it causes one's bowels
to burn and one's skin to blister (18:29; 22:19-20; 47:15; 56:42, 55, 93).

The solid food in hell is no better. Three different items are mentioned
in the Qur'an, and in one place they are described as food that "causes one
to gag" (73:13). One is darī`, a dry desert plant that is full of thorns and,
according to the Qur'an, fails to relieve hunger or sustain a person (88:6-
7). Another food mentioned only once is ghislīn, which is most commonly
translated as "pus," and 39:36 states it is the only nourishment available in
hell. The third item is the fruit of the zaqqūm, which is a tree that is found
in South Arabia and mentioned three times in the Qur'an. It is no better
than the other fare in hell because it has a bitter fruit shaped like devils'
heads that leads to digestive problems (37:62-67; 44:43-46; 56:52-54).

The painful effects of fire are described frequently in the Qur'an:
"If the unbelievers only knew [the time] when they will not be able to

keep the fire from their faces and their backs, and they will receive no assistance" (21:39; cf. 2:174; 11:106; 18:29, 53; 32:20; 102:6-7). The torture inflicted on the damned includes several things already mentioned, like burned and blistered skin (4:56; 22:20; 23:104) and boiling water poured over or into the body (6:70; 18:29; 22:19; 40:72). Other physical torments described in the Qur'an include having one's face turned about in the fire (33:66), being dragged on one's face through the fire (54:48), clothing made of fire (22:19), being branded on the forehead or body with the gold and silver one stole while alive (9:34-5), and being bound in iron restraints (14:49; 40:71). "Clothing of fire will be made for the unbelievers. Boiling water will be poured over their heads, melting their insides and scorching their skin. There will also be iron instruments of torture. Every time they try in anguish to escape they will be forced back in and [told], 'Taste the punishment of the fire!' (22:19b-22).

The mental torture of hell is as severe as the physical but of a different sort. It was noted earlier that there is communication between the two groups, but those in heaven cannot help those in hell: "The people of the fire will call out to the people of the garden, 'Give us some water, or some of the provisions God has given you!' They will reply, 'God has forbidden them both to the unbelievers'" (7:50; cf. 37:50-57). The inhabitants of hell are all alone, and even the gods they called upon in life are of no use to them now (6:94). The Qur'an describes them as being in a state that is neither life nor death, a vampirelike existence: "Hell is for the one who comes to his Lord as a sinner. There he neither dies nor lives" (20:74; cf. 14:17; 35:36).

*cf Abe / Lazarus*

Those in hell have no one to blame but themselves, and one text has their own skin and other body parts testify against them for the evil they have done (41:19-23; cf. 14:22; 45:33). In some passages, the inhabitants of hell bicker among themselves and try to blame each other for the pathetic situation they find themselves in (7:38-39; 38:59-64), but even those who accept responsibility for their current state do so to no avail. Among the most tragic scenes depicting hell are those that describe remorseful people who admit their wrongs, but their pleas for pardon go unanswered: "They will say as they argue back and forth, 'By God, we made a clear mistake when we made you [our gods] equal with the Lord of the worlds. It was the wicked ones who led us astray, and now we are left without an intercessor or close friend. If we had another chance, we would be believers!'" (26:96-102; cf. 41:24). According to the Qur'an, hell is a lonely and terrifying place whose forlorn denizens are alienated from themselves and one another.

How long will the punishment of hell last? The Qur'an is not consistent on the answer to that question. Words related to the Arabic root *kh-l-d*, which conveys meanings associated with eternity, are often used to describe how long the pain of hell will endure. The word *khuld* ("eternity") is used three times, twice (10:52; 32:14) to tell the damned to taste the "punishment of eternity" and once (41:28) to refer to hell as their "home of eternity." More common is the participial form *khālid* ("forever," "eternally"), used more than thirty-five times to define how long the doomed will remain in hell. "Truly, God has rejected unbelievers and has prepared a blazing fire for them. They will remain there forever [*khālidīn*], with no friend or helper" (33:64-65; cf. 3:88; 4:14; 9:17; 16:29; 23:103; 43:74; 59:17; 98:6).

However, there is some evidence in the Qur'an to suggest that one's stay in hell need not necessarily be eternal. For example, it is stated in 78:23 that the damned will be in hell for many years. Likewise, in 6:128 it is stated that confinement to the fire will be forever unless God wills something else. A similar thing is said in 11:106-7, where there is a double challenge to the idea of eternal punishment since it stipulates that it will endure only as long as the earth lasts or until God wishes it to be a different length of time: "The miserable ones will be wailing and groaning in the fire, remaining there as long as the heavens and earth endure, unless your Lord should wish otherwise. Truly, your Lord accomplishes whatever He wills." It might be that such texts are more interested in highlighting the power and mercy of God than in defining the length of stay in hell. Nonetheless, they present an alternative that is quite different from the more numerous passages that claim hell is a permanent abode.

> The Qur'an is ambiguous regarding how long people will remain in hell.

The image of hell that emerges from the Qur'an is one that reflects and speaks to people's own lives and experiences. Its inhabitants have bodies, eat, drink, speak, and interact with one another just as they did before death. There is continuity between life on earth and existence in hell. At the same time, there are some key differences. Notably absent are references to those things that make life pleasurable, like family, friends, rest, or a good meal. Hell is a place where life goes on, in a sense, but it does not really go on. It is familiar but unfamiliar enough to be disturbing and unsettling. And that is the precise point of presenting it in these terms. Who would want to endure an existence that features the very worst life has to offer, including loneliness, pain, punishment, regret, and lousy food on top of it all? These are things all people have experienced to one degree or another, usually for brief periods of time, and the prospect of having this as one's permanent condition would be frightening. People's ability to relate to the picture of hell presented in the Qur'an is what guarantees that it is a place they would rather avoid at all costs.

# Heaven

The same might be said about how heaven is described in the Qur'an, but it has the opposite effect. This is a place people have had glimpses and tastes of, but they would like more. Like those about hell, references to heaven are found throughout the Qur'an and come from all periods of Muhammad's prophetic career. Consequently, as with hell, the text does not present a single description or account of heaven, so a composite must be compiled from various passages and chapters. This section adopts the same three-part division of the previous one and discusses the layout, inhabitants, and rewards of heaven.

## The Layout of Heaven

(Q 18:107; 23:11; 9:72; 13:23; 18:21; 20:76; 38:50; 61:12; 47:15; 3:136; 9:72; 16:31; 48:5; 57:12; 66:8; 2:25; 4:57; 13:35; 39:20; 29:58; 61:12; 53:14-16)

The most common name for heaven in the Qur'an is "the garden" (al-janna), which is found approximately eighty times in the text and often in its plural form. The word can also refer to any garden, so it is not a technical term used exclusively for heaven. Heaven also goes by several other names, which are used only a few times each. Among them is firdaws, mentioned twice (18:107; 23:11), whose origin is uncertain—it might be from Syrian, Greek, or Hebrew—and is related to the English "paradise." Another is 'adn, which is an Arabic cognate of the Hebrew word that "Eden" is derived from. It is found eleven times in the Qur'an, always describing the word "gardens" (jannāt). It is not present in the versions of the garden story involving Adam and Eve, and it does not function as a proper name in the Qur'an. It is commonly understood to be a reference to the eternal nature of the place and is therefore often translated as "eternal gardens" or "perpetual gardens" (9:72; 13:23; 18:21; 20:76; 38:50; 61:12).

A description of the garden is provided in 47:15, where its dominant topographical features are the rivers flowing through it with various liquids: "Here is what the garden promised to the pious is like—it has rivers of unpolluted water, rivers of milk that never spoils, rivers of wine that is delicious for those who drink it, and rivers of pure honey. They will have every kind of fruit and forgiveness from their Lord." Variations of the expression "gardens with rivers flowing beneath them" are found more than thirty-five times in the Qur'an (3:136; 9:72; 16:31; 48:5; 57:12; 66:8).

In some cases, other elements are added to it, increasing the attractiveness of the location. The fruits (2:25) and shade (4:57; 13:35) provided by the trees are mentioned, as is the abundant food (13:35). Several texts call attention to the luxurious housing available in paradise. "Those who are mindful of their Lord will have lofty dwellings, built one above the other with rivers flowing beneath them. This is God's promise—God does not break His promise" (39:20; cf. 29:58; 61:12).

It was explained in an earlier chapter how the beginning of chapter 53 in the Qur'an is often understood to be speaking about the Prophet Muhammad's miraculous heavenly journey. In verses 14 and 16 of that chapter, a tree that designates a boundary of some sort is mentioned as being near the "garden of repose." This is the only time it is mentioned in the Qur'an, and it has sometimes been identified as a tree of paradise that is meant to indicate its furthest extent.

## The Inhabitants of Heaven

(Q 11:23; 25:24; 36:55; 47:14, 16; 59:20; 57:12; 66:8; 90:18-20; 56:8, 27, 38, 90-91; 74:39; 23:57-61; 35:32; 56:10; 56:11; 4:172; 3:45; 83:22-28; 50:31; 15:45; 26:90; 47:15; 51:15; 68:34; 22:14; 5:9; 22:23; 31:8; 32:19; 42:22; 47:12; 13:19-24; 70:22-35; 4:13; 3:144; 16:96; 3:134; 4:162; 58:22; 76:10; 61:11-12; 3:195; 76:7-12)

A generic term for those in heaven is "the people of the garden" (aṣḥāb al-janna), found thirteen times in the Qur'an. "The people of the fire are not like the people of the garden—the people of the garden have been victorious" (59:20; cf. 11:23; 25:24; 36:55; 47:14, 16). This title does not tell us anything about the occupants of heaven or why they are there, although the last part of this verse indicates that they have achieved a victory. In a couple of places, the Qur'an mentions that light emanates from those destined for heaven, shining before them and to their right: "On the day when you (Muhammad) see the believers, both male and female, with their light shining before them and to their right [it will be said to them], 'Good news for you today! You will stay forever in gardens with rivers flowing beneath them. That is the great victory!'" (57:12; cf. 66:8). The phenomenon of light issuing forth from a person appears elsewhere in Islamic sources, and it always indicates a person of special merit.

*According to Muslim tradition, when Muhammad's mother was pregnant with him, a light shone from her that could be seen in faraway lands.*

Just as the inhabitants of hell are referred to as "the people of the left," those in heaven are known as "the people of the right." As already noted, this is tied to the belief in the ancient world that the right side was the side of blessing and reward: "Those [who believe] will be on the right-hand side. But those who reject Our revelations will be on the left-hand side, and the fire will surround them" (90:18-20; cf. 56:8[2x], 27[2x], 38, 90-91; 74:39). Almost all of these references are found in chapter 56 of the Qur'an, whose topic is the judgment day and offers much information on who will be rewarded in heaven.

In addition to "the people of the right," chapter 56 mentions two other groups. One is called the *sābiqūn* in Arabic, which translates as "those who precede, go before," in the sense that they outdo others in good works and piety. There is a good description of them in 23:57-61, which lists the qualities that set them apart: "Those who stand in awe and fear of their Lord, who believe in the revelations of their Lord, who do not associate anything with their Lord, who give with fearful hearts because they will return to their Lord, those are the ones who race toward good things, and they will be the first to achieve them [*sābiqūn*]" (cf. 35:32). According to 56:10, people like this will get to enjoy paradise.

In the next verse, the *sābiqūn* are identified as members of the other group mentioned, the *muqarrabūn*, or "those brought near [to God]" (56:11). These people will be rewarded with close proximity to God because of how they lived their lives. Elsewhere, the Qur'an mentions that others among the *muqarrabūn* include angels (4:172) and Jesus (3:45). They are therefore in a category that gives them special status, as seen in the description of the joys that await them in heaven: "The righteous will live in happiness, gazing about on couches. You will recognize the glow of happiness in their faces. They will be served a wine that is sealed with musk—let those who aspire, strive for it—mixed with water from *tasnīm*, a spring from which those brought near [*muqarrabūn*] will drink" (83:22-28). Most likely, a cause-and-effect relationship exists between these two categories of people—those who have preceded and outdone others (*sābiqūn*) through their piety and works have been rewarded by being brought near to God (*muqarrabūn*).

*When the angels announce to Mary in the Qur'an that she will give birth to Jesus, she is told that he will be one of those who will be brought near to God (3:45).*

Those in heaven are often described in two other ways in reference to their attitudes and their actions, with each appearing more than fifty times in the Qur'an. The first comes from words related to a form of the Arabic root *w-q-y* that describes those who are pious or fear God. The noun *taqwā* comes from this root and is often translated as "piety" or "fear of God." The Qur'an sometimes describes those in heaven as possessing this quality: "The garden will be brought close to the pious, no longer distant" (50:31; cf. 15:45; 26:90; 47:15; 51:15; 68:34). These texts underscore the mindset or attitude it is essential to have if one wishes to reach heaven.

The other set of texts focuses more on the actions one must accomplish and centers on the phrase, "those who believe and perform good deeds," a very common phrase in the Qur'an. The word for those deeds is *salihāt*, used in various forms in the Qur'an approximately ninety times to describe the way God expects people to behave. The word comes from an Arabic root that means, "to be righteous, good." Those who do *salihāt* are living righteously and are following God's will, and so it is not surprising that they are among those given a heavenly reward. "Truly, God brings those who believe and do good deeds into gardens under which rivers flow. God does whatever He wishes" (22:14; cf. 5:9; 22:23; 31:8; 32:19; 42:22; 47:12).

Some texts identify what these good deeds are in somewhat general terms, and others offer specific examples of particular deeds that will lead to entrance into heaven. Examples of the first type can be seen in 13:19-24 and 70:22-35, which make reference to the following actions among others: keepings one's pledges, loving God and fearing judgment, returning evil with good, giving generously of one's wealth, being chaste, and giving honest testimony in legal cases. Both texts conclude with the statement that those who do these things will experience paradise. Among the personal qualities that will lead to eternal reward are obedience (4:13), thankfulness (3:144), patience (16:96), and forgiveness (3:134).

The Qur'an also identifies particular actions that will be rewarded, and most of them reflect the practices and beliefs that express membership in the Muslim community. Among these deeds are the following: giving alms (3:134), praying (4:162), having faith in the last day (58:22; 76:10), believing in God and the Prophet Muhammad (61:11-12), and fighting and dying for the faith (3:195). Sometimes there is no explicit reference to entry to heaven in these texts, but the language and context suggest that this is what is meant. One text that does refer to paradise is a list of commendable acts and beliefs in 76:7-12: "They fulfill their vows, and they fear a day when evil will be widespread. Out of love for Him they feed the poor, the orphan, and the prisoner [saying,] 'We feed you for the sake of God alone. We do not want payment or thanks from you. We fear from our Lord a dreadful, dreary day.' So God will save them from the woes of that day, and give them brightness and happiness. He will reward them for their perseverance with a garden and silk."

## The Rewards of Heaven

(Q 61:12; 4:13; 5:119; 9:72; 45:30; 85:11; 3:136; 48:5; 10:9-10; 56:25-26; 52:21; 76:11-12; 15:48; 43:71; 50:35; 9:72; 3:15; 55:68; 2:25; 36:57; 37:42; 38:51; 43:73; 44:55; 52:22; 55:52; 56:20, 32; 77:42; 76:13-14; 4:57; 36:56; 56:30; 77:41; 18:31; 22:23; 56:10-26; 76:11-22; 15:47; 18:31; 36:56; 37:44; 52:20; 55:54, 76; 56:15; 76:13; 83:23, 35; 88:13; 18:31; 22:23; 35:33; 44:53; 76:21; 43:71; 76:15; 2:25; 37:41; 52:22; 56:21; 47:15; 37:45-47; 76:17; 52:24; 56:17; 76:19; 4:57; 2:25; 3:15; 44:54; 52:20; 56:22; 37:48-49; 38:52; 55:56; 78:33; 56:36-37; 78:33; 55:56; 38:22)

Those silken robes are just one of the many rewards the blessed will enjoy in paradise. In a number of places, the Qur'an describes the heavenly environment as "the great triumph," indicating that those who achieve it should see themselves as victorious in the contest between good and evil throughout their lives: "He will forgive your sins and bring you into gardens under which rivers flow, with lovely dwellings in the eternal gardens. That is the great victory!" (61:12; cf. 4:13; 5:119; 9:72; 45:30; 85:11).

As with those who lost the battle and were assigned to hell, one's presence in heaven will have both physical and intangible results. As the verse just cited states, among the latter will be the forgiveness of sins (cf. 3:136). Similarly, any bad deeds those in heaven committed during their lifetimes will be blotted out (48:5). Their existence will be a peaceful one, unlike hell, in which no harsh words or gossip will be exchanged (10:9-10; 56:25-26), and they will be united with their loved ones (52:21). They will not be punished on judgment day (76:11-12), they will never grow weary (15:48), and all their desires will be met (43:71; 50:35). A couple of texts say the greatest reward is that they will receive God's *riḍwān*, or pleasure—an important concept in Islam, which describes God's satisfaction and approval of a person: "God has promised the believers—both male and female—gardens under which rivers flow where they will remain forever, and lovely dwellings in the eternal gardens. But the greatest thing of all will be God's approval [*riḍwān*]—that is the supreme victory!" (9:72; cf. 3:15).

> The term riḍwān, referring to God's pleasure or approval, is found thirteen times in the Qur'an, and most of them refer to the heavenly reward of the afterlife.

The most frequently cited physical reward of heaven in the Qur'an is the abundant water and other liquids in the rivers flowing through the gardens of paradise. This allows for lush vegetation that produces fruit, with dates and pomegranates being the only two mentioned specifically in the Qur'an (55:68; cf. 2:25; 36:57; 37:42; 38:51; 43:73; 44:55; 52:22; 55:52; 56:20, 32; 77:42). It is a place of shade and comfortable weather: "They will recline on couches, feeling neither heat nor cold, with shade above them and clusters of fruit hanging nearby" (76:13-14; cf. 4:57; 36:56; 56:30; 77:41). With its endless supply of water, leafy trees, and succulent fruits, paradise is everything seventh-century Arabia was not, and this undoubtedly added to its attractiveness and desirability.

Fairly detailed accounts of the other physical reward of heaven are given in 18:31; 22:23; 56:10-26; and 76:11-22. These passages and others stress the opulence and abundance of the environment, and they frequently remind the inhabitants that they have received these things as compensation for their faithful and committed lives. They will recline and sit upon comfortable sofas that are sometimes described as facing each other and other times as arranged in rows (15:47; 18:31; 36:56; 37:44; 52:20; 55:54, 76; 56:15; 76:13; 83:23, 35; 88:13). They will wear the finest garments fashioned from silk and brocade, and they will be adorned with pearls and bracelets made of gold and silver (18:31; 22:23; 35:33; 44:53; 76:21). Their eating and drinking items will be equally ornate, with their plates, trays, cups, and goblets also made from silver and gold (43:71; 76:15).

They will be amply provided for, and the food they eat will be like that they ate while they were alive: "When they are nourished from the fruits of the gardens, they will say, 'This has been provided to us before,' because they were given something like it. They will have pure spouses and they will stay there forever" (2:25b; cf. 37:41). The food in heaven is rarely specified in the Qur'an, but meat, including that of fowl, will be available (52:22; 56:21). As noted previously, there will also be milk, wine, and honey in heaven, all coming from its rivers (47:15). The Qur'an also mentions another drink that will be shared by the inhabitants of heaven, which is described in 37:45-47: "A drink will be passed among them from a gushing spring. White, and delicious to those who taste it, it will cause neither light-headedness nor intoxication." In another text, reference is made to a drink that is made from ginger (76:17). Young boys who act as servers are mentioned a few times in the context of the drinks that will be available in paradise (52:24; 56:17; 76:19).

The reference to heavenly attendants leads to one of the most commented upon and, especially for non-Muslims, controversial aspects of the Qur'an's depiction of heaven—that men are promised that they will be given women, usually understood to be virgins. The issue is a complex one to unpack because a number of different texts from different periods are relevant, and they do not all use the same terminology. In addition, several different groups are mentioned in the Qur'an, and it is not easy to know if they are meant to be taken as the same or who constitutes those groups. In some cases, texts that have traditionally been understood to be speaking about women are more likely referring to both men and women.

That is the case with the first set of three passages that speak of "pure spouses" being given to those in heaven: "As for those who believe and do good deeds, We will bring them into gardens under which rivers flow, and they will remain there forever. They will have pure spouses there, and We will bring them into comfortable shady places" (4:57; cf. 2:25; 3:15). Although these texts have been commonly interpreted as referring to women who will be given to men as spouses in heaven—perhaps due to influence from other texts that do mention this—these are likely more inclusive texts that speak of those in heaven having spouses, regardless of their gender. It could be that it is a reminder to people that if they live good lives ("as for those who believe and do good deeds"), they will be reunited with their earthly spouses after death.

Two other texts that might be related to the previous ones use the verb "to marry" to describe heavenly unions: "Thus We shall wed them to women with large, dark eyes" (44:54; cf. 52:20). A complication arises here because this second set of texts uses a phrase to describe these spouses that is not used in the first set. They refer to them as ḥūr ʿīn, an expression also found in 56:22. The word ḥūr is a plural form that has been variously understood as referring to some quality of the eyes of the women—they are dark, white, or wide, depending on the translation—or to the whiteness of their skin. The fact that the word ʿīn in the expression means "eye" is a point in favor of the former explanation. What is not disputed is that these women, sometimes referred to as "houris" in English, are meant to be paired with men in paradise.

It should be noted that all these references to ḥūr ʿīn come from the Meccan period and are therefore early, while the other texts that speak of spouses come from the later Medinan period. These passages need to be understood in light of their different contexts, which undoubtedly required different ways of speaking about heaven and its appeal. Some scholars have suggested that there was a shift over time in how the Qur'an presents paradise, with an initial emphasis on the male experience giving way to a vision that is more inclusive of women. The textual evidence suggests this may very well have been the case.

Another phrase used to describe some of the women in paradise is "modest of gaze," probably a reference to their tendency to restrain their eyes out of modesty. It is found three times in the Qur'an, and each time it is used a bit differently. In 37:48-49, it is said that they have beautiful eyes and are as delicate as eggs. That they are compatible in age with the men is stressed in 38:52. In 55:56, it is stated that they have not been touched by men or *jinn*. It is difficult to know if these passages are describing the houris or if they refer to a completely different set of women.

To complete the picture, there are two other passages to consider. One is 78:33, which refers to the presence in heaven of physically mature women. (The Arabic word describes a female whose breasts are developed.) The other is 56:36-37, where the women are described as loving virgins. This, along with 55:56 mentioned above, is the Qur'an's clearest reference to virgins in heaven. Both 78:33 and 55:56, like 38:52, state that the women are compatible in age with the men.

This survey of the houris and other women the Qur'an says are found in heaven results in an understanding of the topic that differs considerably from what many consider to be the "facts." While it is true that the text says there will be unions between men and women in paradise, the picture that emerges from the Qur'an is less salacious and controversial than it is often believed to be. While there is evidence that some of these women are virgins, this is not the case across the board. It might be that the several references to the men and women being the same age is a way of saying the women are not virgins. Similarly, there is nothing in the text to suggest that these are very young or prepubescent girls. The number of women each man will have is not addressed in the Qur'an, and there are no references to martyrs and others who die for Islam being rewarded with virgins in paradise. These and other expansions of the Qur'an's presentation come from elsewhere, with some found in other Islamic sources and others the figments of fertile imaginations.

> *The Qur'an teaches that there will be unions in heaven, but the details regarding the spouses are less controversial and salacious than is often assumed.*

The Qur'an's treatment of heaven and hell highlights the theme mentioned at the outset of this chapter, that one's actions in life have consequences in the afterlife. This notion is central to Islamic ethics and eschatology, leading to a situation in which one's behavior is influenced by a simultaneous fear of hell and desire for heaven. The fact that the Qur'an presents these two places as antitheses of each other reinforces this polarity. Given a choice, who would not prefer the comfort, companionship, and provisions of paradise to the pain, isolation, and emptiness of its opposite? A question remains regarding whether or not these descriptions are meant to be taken literally. It is impossible to know for sure how people of antiquity would have understood the Qur'an's depictions of heaven and hell. Undoubtedly, the graphic images would have made a lasting impression on their minds. In all likelihood, though, they would have been keenly aware of and motivated by what the pleasure of heaven and the punishment of hell represent on a deeper level—union with or alienation from God.

## key TERMS

`adhāb; `iqāb; intiqām; tawba; dahr; mawt; nafs; yawm al-qiyāma; yawm al-dīn; al-yawm al-ākhir; al-ākhira; al-nār; jahannam; jaḥīm; ghassāq; mā' ṣadīd; ḍarī`; ghislīn; zaqqūm; khālid; al-janna; sābiqūn; muqarrabūn; taqwā; ṣaliḥāt; riḍwān; houris

## QUESTIONS for discussion

1.  What do the Qur'an's teachings on reward, punishment, and repentance suggest about its understanding of God?

2.  What are some of the similarities and differences between Islamic thought as reflected in the Qur'an and Jewish and Christian beliefs related to death, the soul, and eschatology?

3.  What is your overall impression of the Qur'an's presentation of the layout, inhabitants, and punishments of hell?

4.  What is your overall impression of the Qur'an's presentation of the layout, inhabitants, and rewards of heaven?

## further READING

Jonathan Brockopp, "Islam," in Death and the Afterlife, ed. Jacob Neusner (Cleveland: Pilgrim, 2000), 60–78.

David Cook, Martyrdom in Islam (Cambridge: Cambridge University Press, 2007).

Muhammad Abdel Haleem, "Life and Beyond in the Qur'an," in Beyond Death: Theological and Philosophical Reflections on Life after Death, ed. Dan Cohn-Sherbok and Christopher Lewis (New York: Palgrave Macmillan, 1995), 66–79.

Nerina Mustomji, The Garden and the Fire: Heaven and Hell in Islamic Culture (New York: Columbia University Press, 2008).

Jane Idleman Smith and Yvonne Yazbeck Haddad, The Islamic Understanding of Death and Resurrection (Oxford: Oxford University Press, 2002).

# Glossary

abrogation – the replacement of one passage of the Qur'an by another with which it disagrees

'adhā – a hardship or ailment

'adhāb – punishment

aḥbār – scholars

ahl al-kitāb – People of the Book

`Aisha – wife of Muhammad who played a key role in the transmission of ḥadīth

al-ākhira – the hereafter

allāh – God

asbāb al-nuzūl – writings that identify when particular sections of the Qur'an were revealed

aslama – verb that describes the act of submission

astrolabe – device invented by Muslims to determine the location of heavenly bodies in the sky

'awliyā' – allies

āya – a verse in the Qur'an; a sign

Badr – a battle that occurred in 624 C.E.

bānū isrā'īl – the Children of Israel

basmala – the phrase that begins every chapter of the Qur'an except the ninth one

dahr – fate, time

ḍaraba – to beat, set an example, or go on a journey

daraja – level, degree, or step

ḍarī` - a dry desert plant found in hell

dīn – religion

diya – compensation, reparation

faḍḍala – to prefer or favor

fāḥisha – an indecent or immoral act

farḍ `ayn – an obligation incumbent upon each individual Muslim

farḍ kifāya – an obligation incumbent upon the Muslim community as a whole

al-fātiḥa – the opening chapter of the Qur'an

fatwa – a legal ruling

fitna – persecution

fiṭra – the natural condition of humanity

furqān – distinction, criterion

furūj – euphemism for the sexual organs

ghassāq – a dark and bitter drink of hell

ghislīn – an unappetizing food of hell

*ḥadīth* – reports that describe what Muhammad said or did during his lifetime

*ḥanīf* – a morally upright person who is a strict monotheist

*ḥijāb* – a screen or separation; often used to describe the veil some Muslim women wear

Hijaz – western area of the Arabian Peninsula where Mecca and Medina are located

*hijra* – the journey Muhammad made with a small group of followers from Mecca to Medina in 632 C.E.

houris – female companions found in heaven

*hudūd* – punishments

Iblīs – the angel who refused to bow down to Adam in the garden

*i'jāz* – the inimitability of the Qur'an

*ijtihād* – to exercise the power of reason in order to arrive at a legal opinion

*injīl* – gospel

*intiqām* – vengeance

*'iqāb* – punishment

*al-islām* – submission

*jahada* – to strive, put forth effort to achieve some goal

*jahannam* – hell

*jaḥīm* – blazing flames

*al-janna* – the garden; a word that describes heaven

*jilbāb* – a loose-fitting article of clothing that covers the upper part of the body

*jinn* – supernatural beings who interact with humanity in both negative and positive ways

*jizya* – a special tax imposed on non-Muslims

Ka'ba – the black cube in the center of the Grand Mosque in Mecca

Khadija – Muhammad's first wife who was one of the first people to convert to Islam

*khālid* – forever, eternally

al-Khandaq – a battle that occurred in 627 C.E.

*khimār* – a head scarf or shawl

*khuṭba* – the sermon delivered on Friday during the noon prayer service

*kufr* – unbelief

*lex talionis* – the law of retribution, sometimes known as "an eye for an eye"

*mā' ṣadīd* - pus

*maghāzī* – literature that recounts raids, battles, and wars in early Islamic history

*maḥīḍ* - menstruation

*majūs* - Magians

*masīḥ* - messiah

*mathal* - a parable

*mawt* - death

*miḥrāb* - the niche in the wall of a mosque that gives the prayer orientation toward Mecca

*milla* - creed

*mi'rāj* - Muhammad's nighttime journey through the seven heavens

*mīthāq* – covenant
*muḥīṭ* – something that is all-encompassing
*mujāhidīn* – those who struggle
*munāfiq* – hypocrite
*muqarrabūn* – those who are brought near (to God)
*muṣḥaf* – the written text of the Qur'an
*mushrik* – one who associates someone or something with God
*muslim* – one who submits

*nafs* – Arabic term with many meanings, including "self," "mind," "heart," "person," and "soul"
*al-nār* – the fire; a word that describes hell
*naṣārā* – Christians
*naskh* – abrogation
Night of Power – the night in the month of Ramadan when the Qur'an was first revealed
*nushūz* – antagonism

patrilineal – a system in which family lineage is traced through the father's side
People of the House – term sometimes used to designate Muhammad's family
polygyny – marriage to more than one woman at the same time

*qānitāt* – devout
*qatala* – to kill
*qawwāmūna* – to be a provider
*qiṣaṣ* – vengeance
*qissīsūn* – priests
*qitāl* – fighting

*al-qur'ān* – term for the Qur'an; literally, "the recitation"
Quraysh – the Arabian tribe Muhammad belonged to

*rafath* – sexual intercourse
*rahbānīya* – monasticism
*riḍwān* – pleasure, approval
*ruhbān* – monks

*sabīl allah* – the way of Allah
*sābiqūn* – those who precede, go before
*sābi'ūn* – Sabians
*sakana* – to find comfort in or to rely upon
*ṣaliḥāt* – good deeds
*shayṭān* - Satan
*shirk* – the sin of associating something or someone with God
*sīra* – biographical writings about Muhammad's life
*sunna* – how the Prophet Muhammad lived his life; literally, "way" or "path"
supersessionism – the idea that one religion replaces or supplants all previous faiths
*sūra* – a chapter in the Qur'an

*tafsīr* – commentary on the Qur'an
*taḥrīf* – falsifying or tampering with divine revelation
*tajwīd* – the set of rules that determine proper recitation of the Qur'an
*ṭalāq* – divorce
*tanzīl* – the act of revelation; literally, "sending down"
*taqwā* – piety
*tawba* – repentance, turning

*tawḥīd* – the unity of God

*ta'wīl* – an interpretation that chooses one among several possible meanings of a text

*tawrāt* – Torah

Uḥud – a battle that occurred in 625 C.E.

*umm al-kitāb* – the source of all scriptures; literally, "the mother of the book"

*umma* – the worldwide community of Muslims

*waḥdat al-wujūd* – the unity of creation

*yahūd* – Jews

*al-yawm al-ākhir* – the last day

*yawm al-dīn* – the day of judgment

*yawm al-qiyāma* – the day of resurrection

*zabūr* – Psalms

*zaqqūm* – a tree found in hell

*zawj* – a spouse or a couple

*zīna* – adornment or decoration

*zinā* – adultery

*ẓulm* - injustice

# Index

## Photo Credits